D0820962

EXPANDING YOUR CONSULTING PRACTICE WITH SEMINARS

MORE BOOKS FOR CONSULTANTS

MARKETING YOUR CONSULTING AND PROFESSIONAL SERVICES,
Richard A. Connor, Jr. & Jeffrey P. Davidson
THE DIRECT MARKETER'S WORKBOOK, Herman Holtz
HOW TO SUCCEED AS AN INDEPENDENT CONSULTANT, Herman Holtz
HOW TO MAKE MONEY WITH YOUR MICRO, Herman Holtz
THE BUSINESS OF PUBLIC SPEAKING, Herman Holtz
THE CONSULTANT'S GUIDE TO PROPOSAL WRITING, Herman Holtz
INSIDE THE TECHNICAL CONSULTING BUSINESS: LAUNCHING AND
BUILDING YOUR INDEPENDENT PRACTICE, Harvey Kaye
BECOME A TOP CONSULTANT, Ron Tepper

Available at your local bookstore or direct from John Wiley & Sons,
605 Third Avenue, New York, New York, 10158 (212)850-6000

EXPANDING YOUR CONSULTING PRACTICE WITH SEMINARS

Herman Holtz

John Wiley & Sons, Inc.
New York ▪ Chichester ▪ Brisbane ▪ Toronto ▪ Singapore

Publisher: Stephen Kippur
Editor: Katherine Bolster
Managing Editor: Ruth Greif
Editing, Design, and Production: Publication Services

TRADEMARK ACKNOWLEDGEMENTS

IBM, IBM PC, IBM AT, IBM XT, and PC-DOS are registered trademarks of International Business Machines Corporation. Word-
Star and MicroPro are registered trademarks of Micropro
International Corporation. Webster's New World is a registered
trademark of Simon and Schuster, Inc. SmartKey is a trademark of Software Research Technologies, Inc. Word Perfect is
a trademark of Satellite Software International.

This publication is designed to provide accurate and authoritative information in regard to the subject matter covered. It is sold with the understanding that the publisher is not engaged in rendering legal, accounting, or other
professional service. If legal advice or other expert assistance is required,
the services of a competent professional person should be sought. FROM A
DECLARATION OF PRINCIPLES JOINTLY ADOPTED BY A COMMIT-
TEE OF THE AMERICAN BAR ASSOCIATION AND A COMMITTEE OF
PUBLISHERS.

Library of Congress Cataloging-in-Publication Data
Holtz, Herman.
  Expanding your consulting practice with seminars.

  1. Consultants. 2. Seminars. I. Title.
HD69.C6H625 1987   658.4'6   87-14231
ISBN 0-471-85899-4
Printed in the United States of America
  10 9 8 7 6 5 4 3

PREFACE

Survival as an independent consultant is not easy; the casualty rate, especially in the first year, is quite high. That is one reason, the most compelling reason, for this book: Producing and presenting professional seminars has been and is an effective answer to the problem of survival and ultimate success for a great many independent consultants. But there are many more benefits than the obvious one, and many of these are unmined even by the experienced and successful producers of seminars who miss the real veins of gold in the seminar business.

There was probably a time—quite long ago—when consulting consisted entirely and exclusively of giving counsel on a direct basis—consultant to client, the consultant conveying a considered judgment and recommendation to the client face to face and/or in writing. But consulting has evolved, as have most things, and it is a rare consultant who can practice successfully on that basis today. Those few modern consultants who can support their practices entirely and exclusively on the basis of fees for rendering their expert opinions are, indeed, rare exceptions. That is simply not the nature of consulting in these times; most of today's clients require more than counsel alone. As an independent consultant today you must deal with clients who expect full-service consulting—not only your expert advice in all matters relevant, but also whatever services are required to implement your advice. This is the modern mode of consulting as practiced by most major consulting firms, and you can offer your own clients no less, within the frame of your specialties.

This is not to say that you won't occasionally find a client who wants counsel only, but that is the exception, and you must recognize it as such. You are not likely to survive for long if you try to restrict your practice to this mode of operation. It is simply too narrow a base to support a consulting practice today for a rather wide variety of reasons.

Readers of my earlier book, *How to Succeed as an Independent Consultant*, may recall the emphasis I placed therein on two factors that I considered most essential to success as an independent consultant. Those are marketing effectively and diversifying the base of services to include more than one profit center. Even with reasonably effective marketing the peaks and valleys of activity in the typical independent consulting practice make it almost mandatory that the independent practitioner develop several sources of income.

In the several years since that book was published I have had many letters and telephone calls from readers and I have met with many independent consultants, some of whom were preparing to launch their practices, while others were struggling to put their practices on a paying basis. Many of those I met face to face were attendees of seminars and lectures I presented; others sought me out individually for advice on how to launch their own practices. Without exception all agreed with the basic premises of that book, and confirmed my belief that their most basic and urgent needs were guidance both in marketing their services and in building other, related sources of income in the early years. Again and again the question asked was "How do I get started?" But the real question was, "How do I start getting paying clients?"

Offering seminars was one key suggestion featured in *How to Succeed as an Independent Consultant*. That was because it is one of the most effective measures you can turn to, not only as a profit center producing substantial income, but also as a means for marketing both your basic consulting services and other income-producing products and services. That is, it is not only a source of income itself, but it is an access route to other sources of income, including that most basic one of direct services to clients on your regular fee basis.

Having said that, it is now necessary to put it all into proper perspective, for seminar presentation is not a "side business" or even an adjunct to your consulting practice; it is itself an elemental consulting service and should be made an integral part of your practice. Properly handled—and I will certainly discuss that matter at great length in the pages to come—it is a kind of group consultation, analogous to group therapy or group insurance. It puts your services within reach of many who might not otherwise be able to avail themselves of consulting services: Attendees at your seminars are clients. Although they are usually clients who would not otherwise be accessible to you, you will find that some do become individual clients. (I would guess that almost nine out of ten times that I have made presentations, whether at my own seminars or as a guest speaker, a consulting assignment of some kind has resulted, sometimes almost immediately, sometimes many months later.)

On a more general basis, seminars have become big business, and are the sole business or at least the principal business of a number of organizations. My morning mail brings me frequent brochures from Shawnee Mission, Kansas, announcing yet another Fred Pryor seminar, and Federal Publications of Washington, DC continues to produce seminars as its principal activity, with grosses in the millions of dollars annually. In fact, the latter organization did not start out to be a producer/presenter of seminars, but a specialty publishing firm, as their name suggests. However, they discovered that seminar production was a more interesting and faster-growing business (as well as one with greater potential) that the production and sale of specialty publications about contracting and related legal matters. There are also many others who have turned seminar production to profit, and it is a rare week that does not produce a few seminar solicitations in my mail. Recently I have found that Human Dynamics is offering sessions in "Advanced Supervision Skills." Padgett-Thompson is currently presenting a "Basic Supervision Seminar" and another called "How to Work with Customers." The Sagamore Institute offers a "Training & Computers Seminar." Softward Institute of American has invited me to attend one session on "Strategic Planning for Data Base" and another on IBM computers and their compatibles. The Performance Seminar Group wants me to learn "How to Buy Printing" in one session and "Designing & Preparing Camera-Ready Artwork" in another, while the Center for Direct Marketing solicits my attendance for a day to hear what they have to say about "Analyzing and Improving Direct Mail." And today's mail brought two more, one in "writing effective advertising & sales literature," at $245 for a one-day session, and one in "desktop publishing," for $795 for a two-day presentation.

Most of these seminar presenters also offer to present their programs as private in-house seminars for client organizations, and usually offer to customize their programs for the clients. This is a particularly interesting aspect of the seminar business that overcomes many of the managerial, logistical, and administrative problems of seminar production.

The hospitality industry has an intense interest in seminars. There are at least three thick trade journals of the hotel business that make quite clear the reliance of hoteliers on conventions, seminars and other meetings for a substantial portion of their gross incomes. So many seminars are now being offered that they have become big business for the hotels, as well as for the many kinds of business organizations, associations, and nonprofit organizations who sponsor, produce, and present them. Hoteliers see to it that I am reminded regularly—almost daily—that they have meeting rooms and many other features to help attract attendance at seminars and other such events.

Of course, seminar production and marketing has its own problems, but they are far less severe than those of many other businesses, and you will find in these pages any ideas and tips, based primarily on my own experience in presenting seminars and influenced only slightly by the conventional wisdom. In fact, I deliberately chose to violate the "rules" of seminar production that so many others accept because I thought that there were better ways. And there were. The methods I employ were tailored to the independent consultant. Large organizations can use these methods profitably, but they do not do so because "that's not the way it's always been done.")

All of these matters are covered in detail in the pages that follow. The methods advocated are my own, developed through independent thinking and trial and error. But just as I refuse to follow others' methods and "rules" slavishly, don't do it my way merely because I did it successfully that way. Think *independently* and creatively about everything you do, and don't be reluctant to try out your own ideas. They may very well prove to be far better than my own. I hope they are.

I have the good fortune to be acquainted with a number of active leaders in the consulting field who have each made substantial contributions to the field. Each has been interested in this effort to pass on hopeful guidance to others in our profession, and each has been kind enough to permit me to quote directly his or her thoughts and counsel on the subject of seminars and the independent consultant. I acknowledge a debt of gratitude and appreciation for their unselfish help. There is, incidentally, no significance in the order of their appearance here.

∎ ∎ ∎

(From the chapter "How to Get Clients," of *How to Become a Successful Consultant in Your Own Field*, Second Edition, by Hubert

Bermont, author and publisher, The Consultant's Library, Glenelg, Maryland, 1985.)

A major stock brokerage of national repute hired a staff of tax shelter experts. Equipped with this new body of expertise, they were now ready to market it. But who comprised the market? And how were they to be reached? Income level is no indicator, because a family could have $250,000 a year and still not have a nickel to shelter. Savings is no indicator because a family could have $250,000 in savings but either not earn enough to shelter and/or have so many tax deductions that the income doesn't require shelter. Yet, the stock brokerage knows that there are at least 50,000 families in any decent sized community that require tax shelters and don't know how to go about getting them. So they asked those families to identify themselves; they advertised a free seminar in the daily newspaper. It was given at a famous hotel on a weekday evening. I attended that seminar to research the brokerage's marketing technique. Three hundred middle-class and upper-middle-class couples showed up. An impressive array of written material was distributed free of charge at the registration desk. But I had to register to get the material and gain entrance to the seminar—name, address, and phone number.

The seminar was excellent. It consisted of four experts, each lecturing for thirty minutes on his particular aspect of tax-sheltering; oil drilling, limited partnerships, real estate, etc. No hard sales pitch was made. Attendees were invited to stay and speak further with any of the lecturers privately. The following Tuesday morning I received a phone call at my office from the brokerage; and then the sales pitch commenced. They were not calling cold! I had expressed prior interest by attending their seminar. I had identified myself. I had even psychologically obligated myself by attending their free seminar. I could not hang up on them. I had to listen to what they had to say.

Pay careful attention and you will notice that this brand of modern two-step marketing is being practiced everywhere by successful professionals. There are a number of means of accomplishing this two-step process. We shall discuss all of them in turn, starting with the effective one just described.

As a consultant, you usually address an executive with authority fairly high up on the corporate ladder; in many cases the C.E.O. himself. So the longer your seminar, the less likely his time constraints permit him to attend. Your free seminar should never take longer than two hours. It should be held during the working week and the working day. The invitation should be in the form of a robo-typed letter which has the appearance of a personal invitation; most word processors are equipped to do this well. You can expect a 5% response (attendance) if you address yourself to a particularly vital current problem of your industry or profession.

In most cases, your attendance should not exceed thirty people (600 letters). The attendees must register. Your lecture must be highly informative so that the prospective clients understand how expert you are in your field. All questions must be answered in a forthright manner without holding back.

A number of attendees will approach you after your lecture to exchange calling cards, ask about your fees, attempt to get you to answer problems, attempt to discuss matters outside the parameters of your lecture, and even set up private appointments with you. And these, of course, are part of the pay-offs. Be certain that everyone leaves with your brochure and any other printed material you have which gives testimony to your expertise.

Within two weeks call the attendees personally on the telephone. Now they are not strangers. Now they will take the call. Now you have their attention. Ask whether they found the seminar helpful and whether you may be of further service to them via a no-obligation exploratory personal meeting.

Should you wish to offset your seminar costs or even make a profit on it by charging a goodly fee, OK. But bear in mind that you will cut your attendance considerably and that your original purpose was to have as many people as possible identify themselves as those in need of your consultative service.

(Remarks by J. Stephen Lanning, Executive Director of Consultants National Resource Center and publisher of *Consulting Opportunities Journal*.)

I have found, in publishing the *Consulting Opportunities Journal* and providing services through the Consultants National Resource Center, that a great many of my subscribers and clients take advantage of the opportunities offered them by seminars and workshops. Seminars are a key marketing tool, as well as a source of income, for many consulting professionals. In fact, one subscriber has reduced the process to a formula. He uses three speaking tools:

1. The one-hour luncheon talk. He uses this is a marketing tool for his full-day seminar, which he outlines in this talk.

2. The two-to-four-hour workshop. Here, this consultant develops one or two topics at some length. He uses this tool at national conventions and conferences, customizing it in each case.

3. The full-day seminar. This is a presentation up to seven hours (or for more than one day, in some cases).

This consultant uses seminars purely to market his direct consulting services—to get clients. He reports that out of every 20 people he addresses he manages to turn 10 of them into prospects, and that this typically results, finally, in two sales within 90 days worth $25,000 to $35,000 each.

But he doesn't stop there. His staff follows up with further appeals to those who attended one of his seminars promoting the following:

1. An advanced seminar.
2. His $195/year newsletter.
3. A weekly publication offering on-going training.
4. In-house/on-site training or the client's staff.
5. Future consulting assignments.

Many consultants write and publish newsletters, manuals, books, and/or other information products, such as audio and video cassettes, in addition to speaking publicly and presenting seminars. They sell these by direct mail and in other ways, but those who make seminars and other public speaking a major activity also make "back-of-the-room sales" a major part of their sales activity. There, they sell a variety of ancillary information products such as books, audio cassettes, video cassettes, newsletters, and manuals. In fact, many professionals report that back-of-the-room sales produce as much revenue as does the lecture or seminar presentation itself, and they consider that sales volume a minimum requirement, but one that is often exceeded in practice by a factor of two or more.

In my opinion, the consultant who ignores all these ancillary avenues to success as a consultant is missing out on several of the greatest opportunities, but even more significant, he or she is neglecting to use these readily available means for reaching the greatest number of people with what he or she has to offer.

(Remarks by Dottie Walters, publisher of *Sharing Ideas* and many books by and for public speakers, President of Walters International

Speakers Bureau, Executive Director of the International Group of Agents and Bureaus, author, and member of the National Speakers Association, among other honors, achievements, and activities.)

While seminars are highly profitable in themselves, they are a superhighway to many other profit centers and higher fees. Each seminar can develop additional business in other fields, a giant wheel of business that constantly gains momentum and power.

Many members of our own speakers bureau are consultants and seminar leaders, offering seminars in addition to speaking, consulting, and other activities They present and sell their seminars in four ways:

- In-house for corporations.
- As breakout sessions at association conventions.
- Under the sponsorship of companies and associations on a revenue-sharing arrangement.
- Directly to the public, registering attendees by direct mail and/or other advertising.

A major advantage of offering seminars results from the fact that the audience is one that is especially interested in the subject of the seminar and they are therefore good prospects for related or ancillary products, such as newsletters, consulting services, tapes, and other items. The seminar becomes, in fact, a showcase of all the services and products you have to offer.

Recorded and, especially, videotaped, the seminar becomes an album and videocassette that can be sold independently through direct mail and other media. Moreover, the advertising of these ancillary products and the fact of being publicized as a writer and public speaker itself helps build your image not only as a prominent speaker/consultant, but also as *the expert* in the subject. But it also lays the groundwork for still other related and profitable activities. For example, articles and even books are often inspired by experiences in presenting seminars. And, of course, consulting assignments result quite commonly from seminars and the spinoffs, just as speaking engagements result from consulting jobs. It is an endless cycle in which all the individual activities have a synergistic effect—the whole is greater than the simple sum of the parts.

Being a consultant, a writer, or a speaker is one thing; being a consultant, a writer, *and* a speaker is quite another thing; it is the *whole* professional.

(Remarks by Audrey Wyatt, Executive Director of American Consultants League and Editor of *Consulting Intelligence*, the League's Newsletter.)

Workshops and Seminars: Profit Centers or Risks? You have probably come across literature and advice telling you that an excellent form of additional income for consultants is the presentation of seminars and workshops. We offer here a word of warning. The seminar business has fallen on hard times of late. It is no longer an easy task to attract people to expensive seminars. Seminar presenters are losing their investments at a rapid rate and many are going bankrupt. There are numerous reasons for this.

The expense for the attendee is now enormous when the seminar is out of town. Regular, non-excursion airfares keep rising, the cost of hotel rooms is now double what it was five years ago, and restaurant prices keep apace. If the presenter tries to overcome this by bringing the seminar to the attendee's locality, then he or she must bear the travel expenses. But more importantly, people no longer want to go to seminars. In most cases they can get the same information and instruction more conveniently and less expensively via books, monographs, TV, audio cassettes, and even video cassettes. The popularity of the personal computer has also eaten into the seminar business; many PC owners can plug into the required information on their monitors at home or in their offices—and none of this requires travel or great expense.

So if you want to offer seminars and you feel capable in this arena, we suggest two things:

1. Offer them on a sponsored basis, where an organization retains you at a fixed fee plus expenses to present your material to its group. You have no investment or risk this way.

2. Offer your seminar gratis as a means of marketing your consultancy. Do it locally so that you needn't travel. Make it brief—no more than two hours—so that you don't "give away the store" and so that the people you invite will not find it a hardship to be away from their desks for an extended period of time.

But, until the seminar business gets back on its feet (if it ever does), be aware of the enormous risk at the present time.

Silver Spring, Maryland   HERMAN HOLTZ

CONTENTS

1

A BRIEF ORIENTATION IN SEMINARS

Like most English-language words, the term *seminar* has come to have quite liberalized meaning.

A MATTER OF DEFINITION

Although a seminar was originally a group of advanced university students engaged in a special study, the term has broadened considerably over the years, especially in recent decades. A seminar today is a special instructional session, which may range from a couple of hours to several days, and which addresses a specialized subject. It may be led by a single instructor or by a staff of instructors, and may consist of pure lectures or may include demonstrations and exercises (in which case it may be called a "workshop"). It may or may not include "breakout groups"—small groups formed for individual group instruction or group exercises—as part of the format, and may or may not include a great deal of open discussion rather than lectures.

The distinguishing features are simply a specialized subject (and the question of whether or not the subject truly merits the adjective "specialized" is debatable in a great many cases) and a relatively short duration, rarely more than a week and most commonly one or two days, although there are seminars of less than a full day also.

A FEW TYPICAL SEMINAR SUBJECTS

Following are some typical seminar subjects, suggested by the actual seminar solicitations arriving in the mail almost daily. While some of the subjects are indeed rather specialized and would not be covered in any general course of study except, perhaps, superficially, many of the subjects are quite ordinary and raise the question (in my mind, at least) of whether they are justifiably dignified as seminars. But judge for yourself which subjects merit being termed seminars and which programs employ the word as a euphemism for something more pedestrian. Remember, however, that the following are only general topics or subjects, covering a wide range of possible specific studies and instructions. For example, a program in word processing is probably addressed primarily to young women who are or wish to become "word processing operators," a position which pays much better than typing or even many secretarial jobs. However, a program that teaches the more complex programs—spreadsheets, for example—is more likely addressed to executives. Other programs dealing with computers and computer-related subjects similarly may be rather fundamental or rather sophisticated programs of instruction.

- Computer usage
- Computer system management
- Choosing computer software
- Dress for success
- Effective business writing
- Office procedures and management
- Office design/layout
- Word processing
- Proposal writing
- Direct mail techniques
- Writing direct-mail copy
- Creating/managing direct-mail campaigns
- Writing sales letters
- Labor negotiations
- Contract negotiations
- Contract administration
- The new tax law
- Financial management
- Executive stress
- Winning at office politics
- Personnel management
- Writing personnel manuals
- Fringe benefit packages
- Health insurance/group insurance
- Line supervision
- Inventory control systems
- Purchasing practices
- Starting a small business
- Become a consultant
- Your personal image
- Marketing strategies
- Career strategies

AN IMPORTANT DIFFERENCE

Even this is only a small sprinkling of subjects about which seminars are held, and while you might consider these to be *types* of seminars, there is another basis for discriminating between subjects, a basis that divides the subjects into two groups, rather than into many groups. Consider, for example, the following two groups. Study them and see whether you can discover the important characteristic that determines the difference between these two—that characteristic which determines the very basis for the groupings:

Effective business writing	Career strategies
Marketing strategies	Starting a small business
Inventory control systems	Dress for success
Fringe benefit practices	Become a consultant
The new tax law	Winning at office politics

The challenge was probably an unfair one, but it helps make the point, and before you have put these pages aside you will understand why this is a most important distinction, one that will affect the success of your seminar program most directly.

The difference between these two groups is simply the audience to which each is addressed. The subjects of the left-hand column are presumably addressed to companies—decision-making executives in their positions as such—while those in the right-hand column appear to be directed to individuals as individuals. In some cases, the item straddles the dividing line. For example, in the case of a seminar on how to succeed in a small business, the attendee may be a small business owner and attending personally as the representative of his or her business. But the distinction is still entirely valid, as you will see later when we discuss the marketing of seminars.

Why is this significant? For one quite important reason: It addresses the critical marketing matter of the prospect. One column addresses companies as prospective seminar clients, while the other addresses the individual as a prospective client.

When a seminar addresses the concerns of management in business and offers to train employees so as to improve their performance on the job, the employer is much more likely to pay for the training than are the individuals. In fact, few individuals would agree to pay out of their own pockets for learning how to write a better policy manual for the company, manage the company's inventory more efficiently, or otherwise learn how to contribute more to the organization. They simply do not see it as their obligation or to their benefit to do so; they tend strongly to see it as the employer's obligation to pay for such specialized instruction, and employers generally tend to agree with that view.

On the other hand, few employers would pay for having staff people learn how to manage their own careers, become more effective office politicians, or dress for success. *They* do not see it in *their* interests to do so. There have been and are some notable exceptions to this for reasons that are not of concern here (unless you happen to be in placement services, in which case the pertinent discussion arises later). But normally, in these latter types of seminars, you must induce the individuals to pay personally for their attendance. But that invokes other problems, such as when to hold the sessions and how to reach prospective attendees with solicitations. These are other matters we will discuss at length later, when we explore the not inconsiderable problems of marketing the seminars you produce. But do be aware that we are talking about two broadly different kinds of markets and therefore two broadly different kinds of marketing problems.

Eventually, you will be faced with one or the other of these two marketing problems. It may be that you will have a choice and be able to design your seminars specifically for one or the other of these markets, according to your preferences or, perhaps, to some natural advantage in reaching one or the other. But you may not have the choice: It may be that the nature of your specialties inherently compels you to your market. Or it may even be that you can design your seminar programs so that you can accomplish the ideal but difficult feat of appealing to both markets. Again, that is a subject to be discussed and explored at greater length later, but keep the idea on the back burner as we proceed.

ANOTHER REASON FOR SEMINARS

Not everyone runs seminars as direct sources of income. Seminars can be effective marketing promotions, and many organizations use free ones for that purpose. The Evelyn Wood speed reading school advertised weekly free seminars in this area for a number of years, offering a demonstration lesson along with the sales presentation. Albert Lowry, the butcher turned real estate tycoon, has used many free seminars to promote his $500 week-end seminar in how to make money in real estate. In fact, a number of others offering mail order training programs in that same subject conduct free TV seminars to sell their training programs.

It's a superb marketing tool for consultants and other independent professionals, when used properly. But that qualification—"used properly"—is an important one that will require extended discussion a little later.

Interestingly enough, however, even the seminars for which you charge an admission fee tend to produce consulting assignments. In some respects they are even more likely to produce consulting assignments than are the free seminars that you organize specifically to market your services. There are entirely logical reasons for this.

THE MATTER OF MARKETING

Marketing has been mentioned several times already in this brief span of introductory pages. That's because marketing is critically important in making a success of the seminar business, and it is essential that we get this into proper perspective (aside from another significant fact, also suggested several times already, that seminars are themselves an important marketing medium).

In more than one way, at least according to my own lights, nothing in any venture is as important as marketing. No matter how good your product or service, no matter how honest your dealings, no matter how beneficial the results, if you do not market successfully—do not, that is, persuade enough people to buy what you offer—all those virtues and benefits are wasted: You will not have enough clients enjoying those benefits for your practice or any ventures within it to survive.

Consulting, along with the seminar service, is a profession. But it is also a business, and business *is* marketing; you cannot separate the two. Without marketing—without *successful* marketing—there is no business. You cannot disregard that harsh truth if you wish to survive, and you must not ever permit yourself to become confused about either the role of marketing or the propriety of doing your marketing: It is not unprofessional nor is it beneath your dignity to take an active and aggressive role in seeking clients for all your services. You can market your seminars as you do your general consulting services: with good taste, as befits a professional.

Unfortunately, in accepting this truth about the role and importance of marketing in making a success of a seminar enterprise we must recognize that this makes quality a secondary factor. For the truth is inevitable: Marketing has far more to do with business success generally than quality or any other factor. Contrary to what some idealists wish to believe and some advertisers wish you to believe, marketing success does not equal quality. Nor is the reverse true: Great success in the marketplace is not proof of quality nor does quality automatically ensure success.

This does not mean that quality is unimportant. Far from it, quality is of great importance, and often affects the durability of success. But it must be placed in perspective and weighed realistically. Pointing out these truths and many related ones about quality and marketing as factors in success—including consequences that flow from these premises—tends strongly to come across as cynicism. But it is not my intention to offer a cynical philosophy here. Quite the contrary, I shall urge you at all times to pursue the highest ethical standards and provide the most honest and highest-quality services and products you can. But we must not be blind to truth: Nothing, not even quality, sells itself. Quality must be sold as everything else must be sold, despite the indisputable fact that every buyer wishes for and expects quality. But the subject is far more complicated than it appears.

A most important factor is that of *perception*. Or perhaps I should say *truth*. For what is truth? It is a perception, and in marketing your consulting and seminar services it is only the client's perception, the client's truth, that is decisive. For even if the client is motivated by quality, itself a notion we must take up separately, it is the client's perception of quality that makes the difference.

Unfortunately, *quality* is an abstract term, not a concrete one. It is both relative and subjective. There are exceedingly few reliable measures of quality except in a most limited sense. It is possible to run tests for resistance to rust, for resistance to abrasion, and for other absolute qualities, which may or may not have some relationship to quality. But who can say which is the best seminar, the best book, the best toaster, the best automobile? Your choice of best is probably not my choice. Nor do people necessarily think that the one they bought is best; many buy whatever they can afford, or whatever is most convenient, or whatever they can get fastest.

But there is still another consideration, one that should come as no surprise to experienced advertising experts and marketers, but one that often astonishes and dismays those who are not so knowledgeable: Quality and allegations of quality are poor sales arguments; they rarely motivate people to buy. (If this is a surprise to you here, you will learn more of it later.) Clients must be motivated—that is a central responsibility of marketing—but quality is a rational reason, and rational reasons are rarely good motivators. Quality is not the reason people buy, even when they tell themselves that that is why they are buying! People buy for emotional reasons. The military services must recruit both officers and enlisted men, for example, and that is marketing—selling young people a military career. If you observe marketing by the military organizations you'll note the stress on the benefits: free training, a lifetime of security, pride and prestige in wearing the uniform, and other such appeals. Several recent books that make flying Navy airplanes appear romantic and exciting have had a salutary effect on Navy recruiting. Associations make membership drives, and that is marketing too, since people join to get benefits—e.g., make "contacts," learn others' secrets of success, improve their social lives, and make friends.

If you believe that buyers act rationally and make decisions on the basis of reason, consider my somewhat astonishing experience when I produced my first seminar as a consultant. I had attended many seminars and spoken at others' seminars. In fact, it was my most recent experience as a guest speaker at another consultant's seminar that inspired me to produce my own first seminar. I had been distressed by much of what I heard from other speakers while waiting my own turn on the platform. I was sure that they were misinforming the audience, although probably not deliberately; I think that they were simply not well experienced in the subject and believed what they were saying. But that did not change the fact that the information they offered was distorted and misleading. They were preaching a number of popular myths, fallacies propagated by those who are, for whatever reason, unsuccessful in writing proposals and who busily proliferate the fantasies they concoct to conceal their failures from themselves as well as from others.

The more I pondered on this the more outraged I became. I was aware of these myths; I had heard them many times in idle conversations and was largely amused by them, since I recognized them for what they were and my personal experience was the surest possible proof that they were fantasies. But I had never heard anyone deliver this nonsense from a public platform to trusting listeners who had no way of knowing that they were being grossly misinformed. It was this sense of outrage and frustration that finally led me to organize my first public seminar.

The theme I chose was the promise of "the real truth" about proposal writing—sorting fact from fiction, inside tips, little-known facts, etc. To dramatize that theme the cover of my brochure advised the reader in quite bold type that this was "the graduate course" in proposal writing, or "proposalmanship," as I called it, and was therefore definitely not for neophytes.

The response was excellent. A small mailing brought checks and registrations for 54 attendees. However, whereas my planned presentation was based on the assumption that all attendees would have a good basic knowledge of proposals, I was stunned to find a generous proportion of beginners seated before me. It was quite apparent that they were beginners, since as they asked the most naive questions about the art of proposal writing.

Obviously, no one had taken my warning seriously. My statement that the program was designed for only experienced proposal writers was taken as a challenge and, more important, probably, as an indicator that highly specialized insider knowledge was to be revealed. And so I was forced to improvise a hasty modification to the program to accommodate these eager beavers! Unwittingly, I had dramatized my claims that I would provide advanced and specialized information— the *truth* about proposal writing—and lent those claims credibility by my warning that it was a graduate course. My effort to discourage attendance by the wrong kinds of participants was taken as some kind of proof of my claims!

Once again the buyers' perceptions were different than the seller's and took precedence. I had sincerely planned to confine my presentation to the finer points of proposal writing, but many of those who received and read the literature and who were beginners perceived the seminar as an opportunity to leap from the bottom rung to the top rung of proposal writing in a day, and they turned out enthusiastically.

LESSONS TO BE LEARNED

That was not the only lesson to be learned from that experience: I assessed the market and decided that since there were a number of seminars being offered in the basics of proposal writing, I might find it difficult, as a newcomer to the field, to attract attendees. On the other hand, there were no seminars focusing on the advanced arts of turning out winning proposals—e.g., strategy formulation and ideas for countering typical problems in proposal writing. I assumed that those who were already experienced proposal writers would not turn out for yet another seminar on a subject they were already skilled in, but might turn out for one designed especially to make their attendance a worthwhile investment. I thought, that is, that I would be pioneering in an unexplored and hitherto unexploited area where there was little competition. But the results demonstrated that while there were a few experienced proposal writers who would turn out to see if they could pick up a few little-known pointers, by far the majority of the attendees were individuals who wanted the most basic knowledge of proposal writing. I had misjudged the market itself, as well as the reactions of respondents. Despite the established competition of other seminars offered regularly, some of them by well-established and well-known proposal consultants, there was still an abundant market for seminars in proposal basics. With my excellent 20/20 hindsight I could see what I had done that was right, although I had simply stumbled into doing the right thing by sheer luck; my original assessment had been all wrong.

I thus learned that you should never take anything for granted in marketing. I was to learn this lesson many times, as I learned how to base my marketing actions on this truth. (It is a lesson that most of us have to relearn periodically when we forget and come to grief because of that forgetfulness.)

WHAT IS MARKETING?

Marketing is not a well-defined term, although it is often used as a synonym for *selling*. Getting into extended and/or philosophical discussions of marketing is well outside the scope of this book. And yet we cannot ignore the subject, for it is of little use to present seminars if you do not induce people to attend them. We must probe the subject to at least some extent.

For our purposes let us say that marketing includes selling. But marketing also includes deciding what to sell and to whom to sell it. The success of the sales effort depends heavily on how well and how wisely the marketing effort has been carried out (although occasionally it depends also on dumb luck, as I have just shown you!). It was part of my marketing function, however right or wrong it was to prove to be, to decide that I would organize my seminar and the advertising literature to appeal to experienced proposal writers.

Marketing a seminar, then, should include at least these five functions:

1. Surveying your assets re a seminar venture.
2. Assessing available markets.
3. Making decisions about the above.
4. Planning the sales/promotion campaign.
5. Carrying out the campaign.

For the moment we will review each of these most briefly, although they deserve and will later get far more thoughtful and considered exploration and discussion.

Surveying Your Assets

There are two main assets you are likely to have with regard to a seminar venture: subjects and prospects. That is, you have your areas of special expertise, and it is likely that you have more than one such area; most of us do. You may also have special access to some population of prospects, be well known to some such group, have a special mailing list, or have some other asset with regard to that matter of *whom* to sell to.

Although the foregoing are the usual assets to consider, it sometimes happens that a consultant has some very special asset that can be influential and thus should be considered in the planning. Have you a claim to fame of some sort, some special qualification (Rhodes scholar? former public official? former head of some prominent organization? etc.), or something else that will help materially to sell you and your seminar? If so, consider this also.

Unless you are sure that you know in advance exactly what you want to do, a good idea is to sit down and actually list these assets in a descending order, most impressive or decisive asset first in each list.

Don't overlook the cross-fertilization aspects of this. Study the items in each list for their correlations with items in the other list(s). Items from different lists may support and reinforce each other and may even achieve a synergy—a result greater than the simple sum of the parts—but they may also oppose and detract from each other.

Assessing Available Markets

Markets may be identified as industries, types of organizations, kinds of businesses, neighborhoods, or perhaps other groups. But in the end markets are people, because people are the buyers, regardless of their circumstances. This is particularly true for the marketing of seminars, for rather obvious reasons. (Those other things are merely identifications of the places where people may be found or reached with a sales appeal.)

It is necessary to determine what and where the possible markets are and how easy or how difficult it will be for you to reach them with your offer. Again, you must identify all those possible markets and rank order them in terms of availability.

Making Decisions

So far the chores have been almost mechanical; studying, assessing, and making lists. But now the most difficult marketing chore begins: making decisions. Now you must decide what your seminar will be about. But you do not decide that in a vacuum. You must make a tentative decision and then see whether it can be properly integrated with and supported by items from your other asset list(s). You must try for a synergy. It is of little value to come up with a great seminar idea if you can not reach the right set of prospects with it. Perhaps a secondary choice of seminar topic would be a stronger product when combined with other assets. In short, it is the final *package* that is significant, not some mere part of it.

Of course, you must also make judgments as to what the *need* is— what, that is, prospects will *perceive* as a need. We will explore this in much greater depth later, but bear it in mind as a most important consideration in marketing decisions.

Planning the Sales Campaign

Once you have made the final decision as to what kind of seminar you will offer and to whom you will offer it, you must begin to plan how you will actually launch and carry out your sales campaign. That entails several facets that will be covered extensively later. These include deciding how you will reach your prospects with your sales appeal, although presumably you must have had some ideas about that when you decided who your prospects were to be, what your basic sales strategy is to be—e.g., what you will offer to induce their registration—and all the mechanical details that must be arranged to make your marketing campaign a success.

Carrying Out the Campaign

Of course, once you have made all those decisions and drawn up your plan, you must execute it. You must prepare your literature, place your advertisements, have the printing done, rent or compile your mailing lists, and prepare and make the mailings.

Your main attack will ordinarily be either via print advertising, usually in the daily newspapers, or via direct mail. Most seminar promotions pursue one or the other course principally, with supporting activity in the alternative course and supplemental support via news releases, radio spot commercials, and/or other such peripheral advertising and publicity. Undoubtedly the majority of seminar sales promotions are made via direct mail, and almost always via the mailing of an 8-1/2 × 11-inch brochure of four or six sides or pages. These are generally sent as "self-mailers"—without an envelope (the post office people refer to these as "flats")—and usually at bulk-mail rates. These are approximately one-half the first-class rate. Many promoters go beyond this and arrange for mailing at the special rate offered nonprofit organizations, which is even less than the bulk rate.

The reason that the majority of seminar promotions are made via direct mail is simple enough, but it is also significant so note it carefully: Direct mail is far more effective for attracting seminar attendees, than is print advertising. (One reason for this is that direct mail may be targeted to the right prospects selecting the right mailing lists.) Fortunately, the majority of seminars are addressed to business organizations and their key personnel. Since it is possible to get suitable mailing lists of business organizations and their key personnel an abundant number of mailing-list vendors, direct mail is a practicable option for most seminar promotions.

On the other hand, when a seminar is such that the individual must pay personally for attendance, there is a problem in getting mailing lists. It is, in fact, quite difficult in these circumstances to get mailing lists of good prospects, except under special conditions. Therefore, the alternative is to turn to the less efficient mass media, such as newspapers and radio (primarily newspapers), to seek out the prospects.

Even so, acknowledging that these are basic truths about marketing seminars, there are exceptions. It is sometimes possible to get suitable mailing lists of individuals. (In fact, we will later discover that it is quite possible to seek out suitable mailing lists of individuals, once you understand list management and brokering.) You will also discover that although bulk-mail rates, and especially nonprofit bulk-mail rates, are far lower than first-class rates, it is not always less expensive to use bulk mail. And although it is simpler and perhaps less costly in some respects to mail large brochures as self-mailer flats, it is not always the most efficient way to make your mailings.

Remember this: We live in a fast-changing world. Traditionally, the two major inevitabilities are death and taxes. But let us add another inevitability to those: change. We live in an era of rapid change. Look back a few years, to your youth or even to your childhood: Has the world now changed beyond belief? Is not the old conventional wisdom, the wisdom of your parents, passé or at least of questionable truth today? What happened to the idea that modern railroads were impossible because no one could breathe while traveling at more than 30 miles per hour? Or that skyscrapers were a ridiculous idea because such tall buildings would sway in the wind and crack wide open? Or that superhighways were absurd because no automobile tire could be operated safely at more than 35 miles per hour?

Success demands that you keep your mind open, that you not only accept new ideas, but that you also question old, established ones and think hard about whether the time for change has come. Personally, I have found success more often in trying new ideas than in clinging to the rules of conventional wisdom.

This is not to say that all established methods are wrong or even outmoded. Not by any means; many are as sound as ever. But it is to say that you must be willing to try new ideas that appear sensible to you. If this were not sound advice we should all still be living in caves and throwing rocks at each other.

One thing I abandoned, for example, was the 8-1/2 × 11-inch flat. I reasoned that the tradeoff was this: Bulk mailing a huge quantity—at least 50,000—of those large brochures meant a low unit cost, but many would be discarded by recipients without even a glance. (Even with my special interests I often discard such brochures without bothering to learn what they are promoting.) I reasoned that a small mailing at first-class rates in business envelopes, although far more trouble to mail, would be more effective and more efficient. Results achieved indicated that this was true, since it was a consistently successful method. (I have learned from experience that convenience is costly. Doing things "the easy way" has been at some sacrifice in results, whereas being willing to labor hard at the task has often made the essential difference between significant success and failure or, at best, only marginal success.) Still, I must admit that my approach to this has not been widely emulated, probably because it requires a great deal more effort; most seminar promotions are still conducted via the self-mailer brochure, sent out in great quantity under bulk-mailing permits.

ONE SEMINAR OR MANY?

There are consultants who develop a single seminar and market it aggressively and successfully. There are others who develop a number of seminars, sometimes a series appealing to the same prospects, and sometimes an unrelated group requiring appeal to different prospects.

For example, you might develop a single seminar with broad appeal, as I did, on marketing to the federal government, with focus on proposal writing, an important key to government sales. In time, I developed some variants on that theme—e.g., marketing to state and local governments and marketing to government agencies under minority-preference provisions—but the main theme was unchanged. (Only much later did I get into totally different themes, such as becoming a consultant.)

You might also develop a series of seminars for secretaries, for executives, for architects, or for other identifiable prospects, and stick to your customer/original-prospect mailing list. There are some excellent arguments for pursuing that course, such as the obvious benefits of addressing your appeals to an established customer list.

On the other hand, you might take your original seminar and develop modifications of it for different prospect lists, as I did (although, in truth, my variants came about as a result of client inquiries, rather than through any preconceived design on my part). For example, a course in computers could be modified and adapted to different kinds of prospects almost infinitely. That approach has the advantage of easy development of new seminars, and equally easy modification of marketing literature to suit each new seminar variant.

Or you might develop a series of seminars, all different, for different prospects. That has the advantage of totally fresh campaigns to fresh prospect lists, trying out new and different ideas that may pay off well.

Each approach has its advantages, and I am not going to urge you to any of these because you must decide what is best for you. But I will discuss the many alternatives in the hope that this will help you make the decisions that are right for you.

STILL ANOTHER ALTERNATIVE:
THE CUSTOM, IN-HOUSE SEMINAR

There is one important market for seminars that we have not yet discussed seriously, but one that we certainly ought to mention now before our discussion in greater depth later. That is the custom market, the one in which you present your seminar on a custom basis as an in-house session (in the client's "house," that is) for a client organization.

In general, most subjects that are suitable for attendance by employees under the sponsorship of the organization are good candidates for custom, in-house presentations. For example, my own seminars in government marketing and proposal writing fit that category, and I have presented them to the staffs of many companies and non-profit organizations, including federal, state, and local government agencies and organizations funded and sponsored by such agencies.

The economics favor the organization in such an arrangement. It is not unusual for an organization to send a half-dozen of its staff to such a seminar. Registration alone for a one-day session runs on the order of $1200 to $1500. If the session is out of town, travel and other expenses for a six people can easily amount to a grand total of $3000 to $6000.

Bringing the seminar to the client and presenting it in-house, which is not necessarily literally on the client's premises but is often at a nearby hotel meeting room or other facility, is far less costly. It usually means the cost of the room, a luncheon (often a simple buffet), and a fee plus expenses for you, the consultant. That typically runs to one-half or less of the cost for sending the staff to a public seminar.

But even that is not all of the benefit because most organizations utilize such sessions to have from 10 to 50 employees trained. In fact, my own recommendation to clients is that they should consider such a custom, in-house seminar only if they have at least 10 employees they wish to have sit in attendance.

Many organizations send only one or two key people to a seminar, and then expect those people to return and train others in the organization, passing on what they learned at the seminar. This is obviously a compromise with the ideal, which is to have the others trained at the original seminar by the original trainer (you, in this case). The in-house approach provides a way for the organization to achieve this ideal at a relatively low per capita cost. Typically, instead of costing $200 to $500 per individual, an in-house session can bring the individual cost down to about $75 to $100, and often even less, depending on the various factors of numbers being trained, travel, and other items.

That is a major argument for this approach, of course, but few seminar promoters work very hard at selling these kinds of sessions. They generally offer custom, in-house sessions as a kind of afterthought, evidently preferring the public seminar, with registration open to all. Presumably that is because the profit potential is much greater in that mode.

The tradeoff, for the client, is total cost versus per capita cost and staff-training efficiency. The tradeoff, for the consultant, is risk versus total income. There is the potential for much greater income in the public seminar, but there is also greater risk because you must commit money to guarantees for meeting rooms, to printing, and to postage costs, as well as to all the labor attendant on carrying these things out. Custom seminars all but eliminate that risk, but they limit your seminar income to whatever fees you can command for such presentations, a subject to be discussed seriously a bit later.

THE MARKETING CHOICES

This provides you with numerous marketing choices. You can market to individuals or to organizations, and you can market public seminars or you can market custom seminars. You can also market to several or even all the options suggested. But before even attempting to reach decisions on marketing you must consider many other facets, such as why you should present seminars at all.

2

WHY SHOULD A CONSULTANT PRESENT SEMINARS?

The pros and cons of whether/why a consultant should present seminars are the same as those of whether he or she should be a consultant at all.

WORKSHOPS AND SEMINARS: PROFIT CENTERS OR RISKS?

Consulting Intelligence, the American Consultants League newsletter, takes a stand against seminars as profit centers for consultants. It headlines the question "Workshops & Seminars: Profit Centers or Risks?" (See the foreword by Audrey Wyatt, Executive Director of the American Consultants League.) The story argues that great increases in travel and hotel costs have brought about some reluctance to attend seminars when travel is required. Moreover, the story continues, if you, the presenter, do the traveling, bringing your seminar to the attendees, you have merely shifted the cost burden to yourself, for an implied net gain of zero. (I confess to some difficulty in following the logic of this train of thought; it appears a non-sequitur to me.) But that is not the main cause of what the writer believes to be a major decline in seminar attendance; the main cause, says this article, is that "people no longer want to go to seminars" because they can get the same information at less cost and greater convenience from books, audio and TV cassettes, and personal computers.

It soon develops that the writer is not counseling against all seminars, but only against public or open-registration seminars. The conclusion drawn by the author of the article is that if you wish to offer seminars, do so either free, as a marketing program, or do so under contract to a client organization for a fixed fee. If you do it free to market your services, the counsel continues, do it locally to avoid the travel expense and keep it to two hours so that you do not give away too much free information. At least, the author concludes, keep your seminars on this basis until and unless the seminar business recovers from its alleged current state of morbidity.

I must confess to a certain ambivalence about this. There is some truth in these arguments, and I agree that the writer offers sound advice for the most part. But I also believe that the writer has not diagnosed the state of the seminar business correctly nor made an accurate prognosis of its future.

First of all, the seminar business is far from moribund, in my opinion, although it does appear to be somewhat depressed at the moment. But this has happened before. Seminar business has its good and bad times as most businesses do, and so far there has not been a single announced failure of any of the organizations whose main business is seminar presentation. (I cannot help but be reminded of

Mark Twain's wry observation that reports of his demise were greatly exaggerated!) And since I can find no slackening in the number of seminars offered, the established presenters obviously continue to invest in promotions of future seminars.

Secondly, there is no evidence that books and cassettes are in competition with seminars. Quite the contrary, each has its own market: Many people find it difficult to learn from reading alone, for one thing, and many find it difficult to learn in solitude; they have a need to be in a classroom environment, with a live instructor and other learners. Many have a need for the dynamics of the classroom, a need to be able to ask questions and to listen as others ask questions and open discussions take place. These people often do buy books and cassettes, but they buy them in addition to attending seminars, to supplement and reinforce learning gained and information gathered at seminar presentations.

The fact is that a $20 book or $50 TV tape cassette may very well contain twice as much information as a $200 seminar, and yet for many people the inequality lies in the opposite direction as far as learning effectiveness is concerned. Perhaps a professional educator or psychologist can explain this, but the explanation is irrelevant; the fact that this is so is all that matters here. It's a common enough phenomenon and a problem that troubles sellers of correspondence courses, as they see two-thirds of those signing up for their courses drop out long before they complete them. Books, TV, audio, and other media rich in valuable information simply do not take the place of the small-group (classroom size) and instructor atmosphere.

Despite my disagreement with this portion of the *Consulting Intelligence* article, I do agree that there is substantial risk involved. I do therefore recommend a conservative approach to all seminar ventures, especially initial ones, when you are operating primarily on estimates and fond hopes, and in a later chapter on costs and income projections we'll look more closely at what you can do to minimize the risks. At the same time I believe that you must examine your motives in launching a career as an independent consultant, which is certainly not the easiest career you might choose; consulting as an independent venture is itself a risky enterprise. However, it is easy to reduce the risk by pursuing seminars as a marketing venture and as a custom consulting service for organizations, as recommended by *Consulting Intelligence* and by this writer also.

THE PROS AND CONS

Despite the fact that I personally endorse the notion of seminars as an integral element in a consulting practice, I cannot deny that there are valid arguments that can be made against their use, including and in addition to those already mentioned. Among the drawbacks or potential drawbacks are these:

- Financial risk
- Investment in time and effort
- Dilution of effort
- Diversion from main goals
- Necessity to speak publicly

The Cons

The arguments for seminar presentations have already been stated—aid to marketing direct consulting services, added income, and, ironically, diversion from main goals as a plus, rather than a minus. Although these have been stated, they require extended discussion. But let's consider the arguments against seminars first.

Financial Risk

Financial risk is a relative factor: A large firm may consider a front-end investment of $25,000 a modest sum to explore a new area, whereas $5,000 may represnt a serious investment for an individual practitioner. Therefore, the question of financial risk becomes a rather personal consideration, contingent on your own resources and your own views of relative risk. However, to put things into perspective, here are a few rough ideas of minimum financial commitments you must make. Bear in mind, however, that many of these costs vary widely from one part of the country to another, and the variation has no consistent pattern. For example, you will usually find rates for renting meeting rooms quite high in New York City, as compared with many other localities. But on the other hand, printing is offered at highly competitive prices there.

That is not the only factor that affects costs. Your own resourcefulness and energy in seeking the best prices and services is important too. In printing, for example, I discovered on one occasion that steering away from the printers with the large yellow-pages advertisements and seeking out those with one-line announcements led me to excellent printing services at modest rates. But that is not automatically true, for some of those who do not spend money on advertising may have inflated ideas of what their printing services are worth; you must still do some comparison shopping. (And there are still other considerations that enter into this, but you need not concern yourself with the causes; just do the comparison shopping for prices and quality to find the best sources.)

There is the matter of scale. You do not have to shoot for a major production, especially the first time you present a seminar. Start with modest efforts. You can learn as much from a $1,000 initial effort as you can from a $10,000 one. Remember that you are *testing* with your first efforts, trying to learn what works *for you*. What works for others is of interest, but may not work for you. Trial is the only way to learn.

Finally, there is the question of what you can and are willing to do yourself versus what you will pay others to do. Today, especially if you are equipped with a modern desktop computer system and proper software, you can do a great many things for yourself that you would have been forced to vend out only a few years ago.

With those understandings, here are some typical costs I have experienced in promoting my own seminars:

Meeting room rentals: From $35/day up (for rooms in hotels and motels).

Coffee service: $10–$20 per gallon.

Typesetting brochures: $25–$150 (depending on size of brochure and other factors).

Printing: $25–$100 per 1,000 copies (depending or total quantity and other factors).

Postage: I prefer to use first-class mail (currently 22 cents), although most use bulk mail (currently 12.5 cents).

It is difficult to mount even a minimal seminar-marketing effort today for less than $1,000, unless you are willing to do a great deal of work personally. If so, there are ways to shave the costs, even to halve them, ways that will be explained and discussed later in a chapter devoted entirely to marketing the seminar. However, for argument's sake, let us assume that you will probably undertake a minimal financial risk of $1,000–$2,000.

Investment in Time and Effort

To some degree your investment in time and effort is the inverse of your investment in dollars, as pointed out only a few sentences ago. Still, even if you make the maximum financial investment and pay others to do most things, there is an irreducible and unavoidable investment of your time and effort required to produce a seminar, especially your first one. For example, there is the need to conceive and plan the program in detail. It is difficult to do anything else prior to doing this, for you can't even prepare an adequate promotional borchure before you have planned the seminar program in some detail—in enough detail, at least, to describe it in your brochure and present a reasonably detailed outline of the promised coverage. It would be difficult to persuade anyone to attend without at least this much information. It is almost impossible to plan an effective marketing campaign before you have your seminar design well advanced, as you will see later when we discuss marketing in depth.

Theoretically, it may be possible to pay someone else to conceive and design your seminar program, but you will find this difficult to do in practice; there are some things you simply must do yourself. It isn't really *your* seminar if someone else designs it. Even when I have presented seminars under contract for sponsors who attended to all the marketing and business functions I have had to spend time providing suggestions and guidance about many things.

Very much the same truth applies to the development of your marketing literature, even if you follow the popular practice of mailing many thousands of a large brochure and nothing else. Again, you can hire a specialist to help with this, but even then you cannot avoid spending much of your own time on it.

There will be inquiries to respond to also, many of them by telephone, and although many such inquiries can be handled by someone in a secretarial or clerical position, you will have to respond to many of them personally.

Finally, although anyone can handle the details of registering applicants and other administrative chores, you would be foolish to forgo the opportunity to study the results of your marketing and learn from them. However, once you have set up the system for collecting the relevant data, you need not spend much of your time personally in scanning the results. (Systems and models of relevant forms for collecting and studying the necessary data will be suggested later.)

At best, a seminar venture will consume a significant amount of your time. Whether that is well-invested time is something you will have to decide, although you probably cannot decide that without first gaining some first-hand experience—actually launching your first seminar adventure. But you must consider how else you would have spent that time: Would it have been spent profitably?

Dilution of Other Effort

The possibility that seminar production will seriously dilute your efforts to accomplish other aims is one to be considered gravely. (It is again a question of where and how to spend your time most profitably.) There is no question but that this is one of the chief potential hazards. But, again, this is a matter that is most personal: Only you can decide what your most important aims are and how single-minded you wish to be about pursuing them. Only you can decide whether you are willing to divide your time among several interests and activities. (Or whether developing a seminar program is a dilution, rather than a reinforcement, of your effort.)

Diversion from Main Goals

The possibility that seminars represent a diversion from your main goals is a consideration that is closely related to—perhaps even synonomous with—that of dilution of your effort. While it is my view that conducting seminars *is* a consulting service and properly belongs in a consulting practice as an integral element, that may not suit your own ideas of how you wish to "proceed" as a consultant. In that case, seminar presentation probably represents for you a diversion, and therefore an undesirable activity. Again, the decision is yours alone.

Necessity to Speak Publicly

Perhaps the fear of public speaking is, for a great many consultants, the greatest deterrent to the development of a seminar program. An astonishingly large number of people experience emotional petrification at the mere thought of standing before and speaking to an assembled audience, no matter how small an audience. It's a common enough fear, and an almost countless number of books have been written to try to indoctrinate such individuals into fearless public speaking, most to no avail. Most such books try to teach public-speaking techniques, and they try to explain psychological techniques for overcoming the fear. Unfortunately, such devices rarely work because they do not attack the main cause of the fear: The traumatic impact of dozens — sometimes hundreds–of pairs of eyes fixed on the speaker, with all his/her imperfections, physical and otherwise. The psychologist tends to attack this problem indirectly, rather than directly, by trying to "condition" the subject, rather than by proposing specific measures and expedients.

Later, in an appropriate chapter, some suggestions for overcoming the basic problem will be made, but they will address and suggest practical measures, actual *methods*, to surmount this seminal problem of being the center of attention.

There are other ways out of the dilemma, of course: You can present a procession of guest speakers (they are easier to recruit than you may imagine, and methods for doing so will be revealed later) and you can hire professional speakers. This latter measure increases the investment and thus the financial risks, of course. It also reduces the benefits of enhancing your personal image and so lessens the promotion or marketing of your direct consulting services. Again, the inevitable tradeoff.

The Pros

The major arguments for seminars are two and they have been suggested already: The contributions to your marketing and the income that can be produced directly. But those are not really arguments per se; they are, rather, *promises* of what may result from seminars properly utilized. We have yet to explore the basis for these promises in this chapter on *why* you, as an independent consultant, should offer seminars. Let's look first at seminars as a marketing tool.

Seminars As Marketing Tools

Marketing consulting services—winning clients—proves for most beginning independent consultants to be a most difficult task and a most frustrating experience. In doing research for this and other books I have written about consulting, as well as in personal discussions of problems with many independent consultants, this has become obvious. Those launching independent consulting ventures are baffled to find that conventional marketing methods—handing out business cards and brochures, mailing out literature, and running advertisements in trade journals—do not work well at all. Prospects do not buy consulting services the way they buy commodities. For example, a manager writing on the subject ("Picking a Good Computer Consultant," *MIS Week*, January 26, 1987), advocates the use of "networking" as an effective and productive first step in finding good consultants. That means asking associates and acquaintances for recommendations, which in turn means finding consultants with established reputations. But what is "reputation?"

The Prestige Effect

Experience has taught me that those who recommend you to others are not necessarily clients or former clients—not necessarily those who have had direct experience with you as a consultant! I have found an amazing number of people who will recommend you on the basis of what you *appear* to be—on the *image* they have of you as a consultant. If you have created a favorable image as a competent and dependable consultant, many of those who so regard you will retain you on that basis alone. They will also recommend you to others even when they have not had direct experience with you and your services (except, perhaps, hearing you speak).

In short, one of the most effective approaches to marketing yourself as a consultant is to do those things that create, build, and enhance your professional image. Presenting seminars is certainly one of those things. The mere fact of your offering seminars (with yourself as the presenter preferably) itself tends to be a prestigious activity. Also in the seminar program you conduct you will get many more opportunities to market yourself effectively. (I would guess that about 70 percent of my platform appearances have produced at least one consulting assignment without follow-up marketing efforts on my part, and even without overt selling in the program.)

There are both direct and indirect benefits resulting from seminar ventures. That is, you may (and should) win clients and assignments as a direct result of your seminar presentations, but there are also indirect or peripheral benefits, such as that of support in building and enhancing your professional image.

The Publicity Spinoff

PR, the colloquialism for promotional publicity, can be described as unpaid advertising, which is its greatest virtue; the fact that it is not the typical paid advertising makes it much more credible to prospects. In presenting seminars you should take advantage of the PR you can get. Even those who do not attend your seminars but merely read about them will learn your name and become acquainted with who you are and what you do. For example, although I know absolutely nothing else about Fred Pryor or what he does, I know his name quite well as a result of having received literally dozens of his Fred Pryor Seminars brochures over the years. In addition to the name recognition, it also establishes a strong impression of dependability because of the number of years involved. His is obviously no fly-by-night venture, and that is itself a plus for his image.

I must presume from this that Fred Pryor has achieved similar name recognition and image-enhancing benefits with thousands of others who are on his mailing lists and receive his brochures frequently.

Additional Enhancements

Many seminar producers arrange to use a nonprofit organization, often an institute or a university, as a sponsor. The chief benefits are contributions to prestige and image, especially when the sponsor has a well-established national reputation. (A secondary benefit is a great saving in postage costs under laws that subsidize postage for nonprofit corporations.) In a great many cases the sponsoring organization actually does nothing except lend its name, for which it is paid a share of the receipts.

Some seminar producers believe that any prestigious-*sounding* name is a valuable asset. So consultant Peter Smith may choose to call himself National Professional Training Institute, Inc. when he presents seminars. (Incorporation is inexpensive and easy in most states these days; anyone can do it without special training or qualifications.) You can incorporate yourself as a nonprofit organization too, if you wish, although that imposes certain legal obligations and restrictions on you.

Paid Versus Free Seminars

Many entrepreneurs use free seminars as marketing initiatives because conventional marketing is not effective for their purposes or because their marketing requirement is such that it requires lengthy presentations that would be prohibitively expensive if made via commercial media. In fact, free seminars are thinly disguised sales presentations, and the attendee knows that and so must be somehow induced to attend.

Despite this, a great many people will turn out to attend a free seminar, although they would not agree to attend an acknowledged sales presentation. Free seminars are advertised on the basis of some promised benefit. That is, despite being free they must be *sold*, just as anything else is sold. The word *free* is one strong inducement to attend, of course, but few, if any, would attend if they were not promised some benefit they find attractive enough to merit the expenditure of their time.

All the principles that apply to marketing anything apply here and so we won't pursue them here; another chapter will be devoted to marketing in detail. However, it is necessary to note that at least one major benefit must be promised to induce attendance, and there must be enough rationale or proof to make the promise credible—to persuade the prospect that the benefit will indeed be delivered. (The promise is not enough by itself; some bona fide must be included to persuade the prospect to believe the promise.)

The benefit is usually a sample of whatever it is that the free seminar is designed to market. A free seminar held by one of those promoters who propose to teach you how to make your fortune in real estate, for example, always offers to reveal at least one or more of the "secrets" that allegedly made the seminar promoter a wealthy tycoon. A free seminar by a hypnotist who wants to help you stop smoking or overcome a phobia generally promises to entertain and educate you by providing a demonstration of the hypnotic technique and the magical results obtained thereby. A free seminar in how to increase your effectiveness as a sales professional would promise a few tips, a demonstration, and/or an inspiring lecture by a renowned (allegedly) sales professional, and perhaps even a useful booklet on the subject as an extra bonus. (Most free seminars will offer relevant free literature of some kind.)

Typically, a free seminar will be one to two hours long, with at least another hour or two for peripheral activities, such as taking orders. For in most cases direct sales appeals are made from the platform, after the basic presentation and fulfillment of the promise, and it is desirable to make as many sales on the spot as possible, while the prospects are still under the spell of the presenter and the enthusiastic fervor for whatever is being offered. But the sales effort does not end there, for in many cases the seminar has as a major purpose the development of sales leads, as well as closing sales on the spot. Therefore, follow-up marketing is employed. Each attendee is required to sign in, either at the door or as the first order of business when the seminar begins, and that provides a prospect list to follow up by mail, telephone, and/or personal visits.

In that connection it is necessary to point out that selling professional services of any kind is not a one-call business. That is, selling such services usually requires at least two stages, or phases, of marketing: prospecting, to generate leads, and follow-up, to close the leads with sales. However, the follow-up is itself usually a multi-stage or multi-phase effort, involving a series of appeals by mail, telephone, and/or personal visits, and may include luncheons, proposals, presentations, and negotiations.

With only a little imagination the free seminar can be used in a variety of ways and for a variety of purposes. For example, it can be used to market your services, another seminar for which attendees must register and pay a fee, or other "back-of-the-room-sales" items, such as books, newsletters, or training manuals. From that viewpoint alone the free seminar may prove a profitable venture in addition to promoting your image and winning clients for your basic consulting services. Later, in discussing marketing, I will tell you about still another approach I used which proved to be an excellent way of reducing the risk and improving the profits.

So far we have been talking with reference to free seminars offered the public at large. But let us not forget that other approach in which seminars are offered to a client's staff as in-house or custom presentations made under contract. The approach can be adapted to the free seminar too. You may offer free in-house seminars of an hour or two to organizations as sales presentations made more palatable by the inclusion of valuabl information.

You may consider this to be analogous to any firm offering free samples of its merchandise: You are offering samples of your consulting services or of your regular, paid-attendance seminar, if that is what you wish to promote. In any case, where you would probably meet with resistance in asking prospects to grant you time to make a sales presentation you usually meet with a different reaction when you offer to present a free seminar and demonstration.

What you must do in "selling" your free seminars, whether you are trying to persuade the public at large to attend or trying to persuade a corporate prospect to assemble a group of executives, is to be highly specific about the benefit you promise. "Learn the secrets of making money in real estate," for example, may motivate some people, but "Learn how to buy property with no money down" is almost certain to appeal to and attract a great many more people because it is specific and addresses the problem that deters most people: the lack of investment capital. And that is no less true with corporate prospects than it is with the public generally. Compare these two possible promises, for example:

1. Learn what and how the government buys.
2. Learn how to win government contracts.

The difference between the two approaches is the same in both cases cited. It is the difference between asking the prospect to translate your promise into a specific benefit and articulating the promise to spell out the specific benefit. If you are not specific, you are, in fact, asking the prospect to do your selling job—to sell himself or herself. Don't expect prospects to do that; they won't. You must be specific in the promise, it is far more effective to promise a single, specific benefit than to generalize about a host of nonspecific possible benefits.

Effective promises are those with great emotional appeal. They are promises that paint vivid images, promises that get directly to the point and warm the heart. The prospect does not really care or want to learn what and how the government buys; he or she wants to learn how to win government contracts. Don't point to the rainbow; point to the pot of gold that is at the end of the rainbow.

Marketing Is Based on Strategy

If it is a major objective of your seminar program to serve you well as a platform for marketing your services and/or other products, you must bear that in mind while designing it. It is possible to develop an appealing program and an excellent marketing scheme for your seminar, and yet miss the boat completely with regard to spinning off other sales. The design of both the seminar program itself and the plan for marketing it must reflect a comprehensive strategy that considers your ultimate goals as well as your immediate one.

For example, suppose that I were to promote seminars in government marketing by promising that I not only would reveal all the closely held secrets of the most successful government-marketing professionals, but would also supply each attendee a manual that would contain everything needed to succeed in that field. Or suppose, as an alternative, that I were to offer that all-powerful, all-inclusive, final-word manual in a back-of-the-room sale following the formal seminar. In either case I would have foreclosed virtually all possibility of winning consulting assignments. At the least, I would seriously have reduced that possibility because I would have convinced attendees that they did not need my personal help, since the manual would do the whole job for them. And even later, when they discovered that no manual can do the job I promised and that they probably did need more direct help, I would have compromised my integrity—and my chances for assignments—by having so misled them.

As an alternative, suppose I planned my entire seminar-marketing appeal as promised training to individuals aspiring to get into the marketing field, but not yet in it—as qualification training, that is. Since these would not be people already engaged in the field in companies, they would not be good prospects for consulting assignments; they simply could not arrange to retain me. And even if I appealed to and drew in junior people engaged in marketing in organizations, they would not be the best prospects for me; my best prospects are executives—managers and specialists—who are *responsible* for achieving marketing success and who truly feel the need for such help as I can offer.

The point is, of course, that you must first have a clear and well-defined objective—know precisely what you want the seminar to accomplish for you—and that you must design your seminar, as well as your seminar-marketing plan, so that the latter two items are a true fit for the objective. Think about the logical next step for the attendee: What should he or she do after attending your seminar? Attend another seminar? Buy back-of-the-room items? Retain you? Other? And think about who that attendee should be to match your objective, to be a good prospect for whatever you seek next.

This is a consideration entirely in accord with all sound sales practice. To avoid wasting your time in selling you must qualify your prospects. And qualifying a prospect means satisfying yourself that there is a reasonable possibility of that prospect becoming a buyer. But there are two facets to that: You must satisfy yourself that the prospect has at least a potential interest in, need for, or desire to buy what you are offering and that the prospect has the power or capability to buy—has the money or access to the money (authority to buy or influence in persuading a superior to buy, in the case of the prospect who is an employee of an organization). A good example of this is found among automobile salespeople, who know that many, if not most, men will not buy a new car without a wife's approval, and therefore think a married male buyer is not fully qualified if his wife is not present.

Therefore, consider the attendees of your seminar as prospects, and design the seminar and its marketing to produce as many qualified prospects as possible.

There is one more point that should be made here: You may decide that you want to or need to present a series of related seminars, and plan them so that at least some of the attendees of the first one will want to attend the others. For example, I could create a seminar of several days in government marketing, each day devoted to a separate subject, or I could plan several individual seminars. (Prospecting the government, how the system works, selling commodities, selling services, writing bids and proposals, and negotiating contracts could be portions of a single several-days seminar or each could be a single day.) Were I to do so, I would organize them into a logically consecutive string and design each to help in selling the next one.

Mini-Seminars

It is particularly useful to think of free seminars as sales presentations, for it is much easier to persuade prospects to give their time to a seminar than to a sales presentation: Whereas you must ask— sometimes even plead with—prospects to suffer a sales presentation, you make an *offer* of something having value when you invite them to attend a free seminar. However, two hours is probably a bit too long for the in-house, informal presentation suggested earlier. You will probably meet with greater acceptance by busy executives if you ask for only an hour of their time in offering your free seminar/sales presentation. (I found this to be true in presenting regular, paid-attendance seminars. When I tried offering two-day seminars I learned that many executives were willing to "lose" one day from their regular responsibilities, but were reluctant to be absent from their desks for two days at a time.) With a carefully fashioned design you should be able to deliver a hard-hitting, sharply focused presentation in that time.

Despite that, you would be wise to allow yourself an extra hour for follow-up questions and discussions. If you capture enough interest in the original hour, your listeners will keep you in that conference room for at least another hour with their questions and comments, which is highly desirable from your viewpoint, of course.

Paid Seminars Are Good Marketing Tools Too

You must not conclude from all this that you must offer free seminars to get a marketing-benefit spinoff nor that only free seminars produce other business. Far from it, in some respects paid-attendance seminars are even more powerful as marketing media than are free seminars. For one thing, the attendees who pay to attend a seminar are serious prospects. They are prospects who are qualified at least to the extent of having demonstrated serious interest in the subject, whereas at least some attendees at a free seminar are curiosity seekers with nothing better to do that afternoon or evening.

This is balanced by the heavier attendance at the free seminar, which may produce a greater number of good prospects, if not a better ratio of good prospects to curiosity seekers. That is, there is a *presumption* of heavier attendance, for there is no guarantee of heavy attendance, even at a free seminar.

There is a compromise position possible. You may opt to subsidize your own seminars by keeping the cost of attendance low by comparison with others, which should produce a good attendance, while still screening out the idle curiosity seekers. I believe that at least some of the immediate success I enjoyed in presenting seminars was due to my keeping costs low and passing the savings on to my attendees in the form of modest registration and attendance fees. It is probably true that all of us have an increasing consciousness of rising costs and their depressing effect on business in general.

Are There Too Many Seminars?

The seminar business has been a burgeoning one, and because it is so easy to organize a seminar venture—the capital investment is really comparatively modest and the required technical skills not very forbidding—there have been many seminars offered that are probably not worth attending. But that is no more a problem than are the many books and newsletters not worth reading and the plays, movies, and TV shows not worth seeing. The substandard products and cheap imitations of get-rich-quick vultures are a familiar phenomenon of every burgeoning new industry. Every industry has suffered through this phase (the latest has been the personal computer industry) and endured as the ultimate and inevitable shakedown finally took place, with the worthy services and products the survivors.

The challenge is to demonstrate that your seminar *is* worth attending, but that is and always has been the challenge of all marketing. You must meet that successfully in all cases if you are to succeed in whatever you undertake. But there is still another side to this question of "too many," a side that deals with the broad question of competition generally. It is, in fact, a question that goes to the heart of the free enterprise system that characterizes our entire society and our entire philosophy. It may be summed up simply enough: Competition is healthy in a free society. Competition is the factor that produces quality and efficiency, squeezing out the fakers and charlatans. It is what enables free societies to become economic successes. (Restrictive legislation has rendered our own society less free than it once was, which may account for at least some of our modern economic problems.) It is, in fact, a survival of the fittest—survival of those who are the genuine article. It is true in marketing that the weak perish, but in the long view that is not tragic, for the weak cannot serve society well; only the strong can. So it is entirely fitting that the strong survive in the marketing wars; society benefits, as it should.

However, on the more modest scale of your own marketing problems, consider it this way: Alone, you cannot hope to "make a market" for what you sell. It is the competition—all those other little independent entrepreneurs shouting their wares—that, together with you, make the market. You *need* each other. Yours is, in the marketing sense, a condition of mutual support. Informal and tacit although that support is, it is a force that enables you to survive against the big-league competitors. Competition in a free market is an asset to every one of you; without it you would all perish. Welcome the competition; the market is big enough for all to share.

SEMINARS AS INCOME PRODUCERS

Despite the negative aspects—the risks, the rising costs, and even the alleged overabundance of seminars—many succeed in making seminars a profitable venture, even a major source of income. We have spent some time now in discussing seminars as a marketing tool, itself a thoroughly legitimate justification for the time, effort, and cost involved. In those discussions we inevitably were forced to make frequent references to the profit-making possibilities in seminars, even those presented for the primary purpose of marketing your consulting services. But the other side of that coin, which we are about to explore and discuss, is that of seminar ventures undertaken for their income potential, with their potential for marketing your consulting services a secondary consideration. And we must consider the full potential, which means considering the use of seminars to market those other, ancillary information items described earlier.

Costs and Markup

Everything costs something, although many of the costs are "hidden," as an accountant might put it. That means simply that some costs are not readily apparent or easily assignable. Accounting systems are designed to reveal all costs, however, even those. Later, in a chapter devoted to costs, we'll get into some revelatory details, but for now we want to look at costs and markup in general terms.

Markup is what you add to the cost of whatever you sell to recover all your costs and produce a profit. The markup is itself a *gross profit*, but that is not money in your pocket; it is used to pay back all your costs, even the "hidden" ones, and to produce a *net profit*, which is the money left after all costs, *including your own draw or salary*, have been paid.

A great many small businesspeople come to grief in the matter of costs and markup. If something costs $1,000 and is sold for $3,000 they consider that a large profit. One thing wrong, however, is that they often fail to count many cost items, such as their own salaries, which they regard as part of the profit. Any competent accountant will soon steer you away from that error of judgment: Your salary is as much a cost of the enterprise as are the salaries of any employees. (You must treat yourself as an employee, if you want to follow sound business practices.) In general, people operating service businesses tend to fall into the same trap because their primary item of sale is their own service, and they see a large markup as a large profit.

Even when you sell information products, such as manuals and tape cassettes, that you have published and produced yourself, what you are really selling is a service, not a product. The seminar attendee who buys a manual or tape cassette is paying for your knowledge and counsel expressed therein, not paper, ink, bindings, or vinyl. All of the time and energy you have put into developing those items and producing them represent costs; you must translate that time into cost dollars and value the item accordingly. You may very well (and probably will) invest many thousands of dollars worth of your time to create a single manual.

Much of the investment cost for producing a seminar program is therefore a *development* cost. You have, in fact, created an *asset* with a distinct value, and an accountant would probably put that cost into "inventory" as an asset. You are going to *amortize*—recover—that investment only bit by bit, as part of the markup on that item. And you are going to have to sell a great many copies of the item to recover all that investment and produce a profit. Never lose sight of that; it's a basic business consideration.

Let's apply that principle to estimating the costs of the seminar itself: Here are a few of the costs.

Your time and/or that of employees:
- Planning
- Developing the seminar content
- Designing and writing the brochure
- Preparing the seminar manual or handouts
- Preparing and executing the marketing campaign
- Registering attendees, responding to inquiries, other administration
- Presenting the seminar

Other direct costs:
- Printing and mailing
- Rent of the meeting room
- Refreshments
- Travel for you and staff, if applicable

Even without projecting estimates of dollars for each of these you can see that the costs in time are almost surely much greater than the other costs. However, there is this to consider also: Many of these costs in the first category are essentially one-time costs if you continue to make presentations of your basic seminar, because much of that cost is development cost, creating an asset, as in the case of a manual, tape cassette, or any other product. The marketing materials and handouts will not change materially, but will be useful for all subsequent presentations of the seminar. So the labor is reduced greatly for subsequent presentations, and much of your labor costs—that portion needed to develop the seminar package—will be amortized over many seminars. That means that if you present the same seminar program regularly, you can assign a relatively small portion of that development cost to each presentation. You thus enjoy an "economy of scale."

Most seminar producers take this a step further by scheduling several seminars, usually in different locales, and marketing the whole schedule. That means a much heavier printing and mailing cost and more administrative time required to handle the details, but it also means reduced unit costs—another economy of scale—and probably greater response overall.

The Need for Long-Range Planning and Commitment

The foregoing considerations are a powerful argument for a well-thought-out, long-range program of seminars and the commitment to a full schedule. The typical investment necessary to develop a seminar program, along with its marketing plans and materials, requires reasonably frequent presentations to recover the investment and show a profit. (Certainly, you cannot recover it all in one session or even in a single series of sessions.)

There is no question but that the first sessions should be test sessions. The program itself must be tested and probably revised until it is as effective as you can make it. It is necessary to validate your marketing materials, identify the markets that work best for you, and test all other factors before you make up the full schedule and your commitment to it.

No matter how well you think you know your subject and your market, you will almost surely get some surprises when you put your ideas to the test. In my own case, for example, almost the first change in the presentation was an expansion on the subject of costs, when

I found attendees far more interested in learning about that subject than I had anticipated. (It was obviously not the dull subject I had thought it to be!) But tryouts also brought about more than a few other changes to improve the presentation.

In the matter of markets, I knew that defense-oriented high-tech companies were good targets, but I was surprised nevertheless by several unexpected findings. Electronics R&D/manufacturing companies were not my number-one markets, as I had expected them to be; software developers responded best. Those who needed help most in my opinion, minority contractors, did not respond quite as enthusiastically as I expected them to. Perhaps that was a budgetary problem with many, but regardless of why it proved to be a lesser market than I had wished for, the result was the same: It simply did not respond as well as many other markets I tried.

I was also surprised by the response to my appeal. I had announced a "graduate course" in proposal writing, and stated plainly that the session was for experienced proposal writers, not neophytes. But evidently not many took that seriously, for the questions from attendees forced me to present much primer-type of information, which I had not planned to include. In fact, that caution probably stimulated interest in the seminar and became a positive influence in inducing response.

I learned a great deal from the first seminar presentation also. I had arranged for a series of speakers to supplement my own presentation, and I included a luncheon with a pre-lunch cash bar and a luncheon speaker from a government office. The luncheon and the luncheon guest speaker were great successes; the other speakers presenting portions of the seminar not so great. (I had not previewed them, which was a great mistake on my part, but accepted them on recommendations of others.) Several times I had to find an excuse to take over the platform and rescue a speaker who was stumbling, unable to respond sensibly to a question, or otherwise floundering in some manner. So although my first seminar was a great success in some respects, it was also a near disaster in others. Certainly it was not the smooth, professional presentation it should have been.

I also found the need to put my theories to the test and to learn therefrom when I first attempted to sell my services in presenting my training seminars to organization. The idea of selling to groups had not even occurred to me until I received an inquiry from one company, a well-known Midwest electronics manufacturer. I failed completely to win a contract there, as I did subsequently in following up several similar inquiries from other firms. It wasn't until later, when I analyzed the situation and tailored my approach to this type of business opportunity that I learned how to succeed in winning such contracts. I learned that such inquirers were rarely prepared to meet the expense of developing a truly custom seminar, but yet they did want my seminar tailored for them and presented them in-house without the typical R&D cost. I developed a system to adapt my regular seminar to each such prospect without incurring special R&D expense. I established a set method of responding to such inquiries that enabled me to henceforth close such prospective sales regularly.

Do expect, at the least, to have to "fine tune" your presentation and your marketing before you freeze the design and "roll out" your entire program. Few of us are ever wise enough or fortunate enough to plan and organize anything, much less a complex program, most effectively on our first try.

3 CHOOSING THE SUBJECT(S)

Both practical and psychological marketing aspects of seminar offerings must be considered in conceiving, planning, developing, and marketing seminars. Choosing subjects is alone an exercise in learning to use and balance these considerations.

SEMINARS VERSUS WORKSHOPS

Almost without exception, today seminars are staged as learning sessions, each focused narrowly on a single subject, such as negotiation with labor unions, contract law, copywriting, speed reading, or other practical topics. In most cases the approach overall is one of how to do it—how to write a contract, how to use a computer, how to negotiate with labor, how to develop software, or how to market services. But within that general framework many variations are possible, and you must think out your design rather carefully.

There is, first of all, a major distinction to be made between the seminar and the workshop. The seminar is essentially a lecture or series of lectures, although sometimes supported with demonstrations and other aids. The workshop is a practice session or series of practice sessions, usually guided directly by the presenter(s), to assist attendees in gaining actual skills, as well as knowledge.

In the actual case, presenters opt far more often for "pure" seminars than for workshops, and workshops are rarely "pure" workshops, but are sessions that are part seminar and part workshop. However, few issues in this world are black and white, and seminars are no exception. Even those seminars that make no claim to being workshops are often designed to include at least some degree of direct participation by attendees, such as open discussion, individual responses to questions posed by the presenter, brainstorming, or group participation of another sort. So whether a session should be referred to as a seminar or workshop depends on what the *principal* activity is, although there is a distinct tendency to refer to all such sessions as seminars, regardless of the format and nature of the content.

SEMINARS ARE BASICALLY "HOW-TO" PRESENTATIONS

The almost universal tendency to designate every session a seminar, rather than a workshop, may appear to be a bit anomalous, because the most dominant emphasis in seminars is on the "how-to" approach. That is plainly apparent in seminar descriptive literature, even in the titles, such as the following listed in a number of announcements received in the mail:

"How to be an Assertive Manager"
"How to Buy Printing and Related Services"

"Training & Computers Seminar: How to Teach People to Use Computers"

"How to Work with Customers"

"Proposals & Competition: How to Develop Winning Proposals"

"How to Supervise People"

"How to Get Things Done"

"How to Write and Design Sales Literature"

Even when the words "how to" are not used in the title, the how-to nature of the coverage is clearly implied:

"Developing Applications with dBase III Plus"

"Networking IBM Personal Computers"

"Writing Effective Advertising"

"Designing & Preparing Camera-Ready Artwork"

"Basic Supervision Seminar"

"Advanced Supervision Skills"

"Strategic Planning for Data Base"

"Logical & Physical Design for Relational Data Base Management Systems"

"Analyzing and Improving Direct Mail"

"Desktop Publishing: A Practical Tutorial Featuring Product Comparisons"

"PC LANs: Hardware, Software & Applications"

"X.25: Evaluating and Selecting Offerings and Options"

"The IBM PC XT/AT and Compatibles: Maximizing Their Potential"

"Performance Measurement Systems and C/S Data Usage"

"Power Communication Skills for Women"

To confirm the how-to philosophy of the design, the descriptions of the seminar content—and every one of the 23 programs listed is described and referred to as a seminar—contain many more how-to lists, such as these lines taken at random from many of the 23 program descriptions:

How to test your own assertiveness.

How to settle disputes.

How to configure your machine.

How to evaluate vendors' products.

How to delegate for success.

How to overcome obstacles.

How to assure that the design supports the message.

How to avoid major copywriting errors.

How to make the right decisions.

How to get the facts.

How to use photos and illustrations to sell.

How to deal with sabotage.

How to deal with people who intimidate.

How to deflect unfair criticism.

WHY THE EMPHASIS ON "HOW TO" AND WHY ON "SEMINARS"

It's easy enough to understand why there is so much emphasis on the how to in seminar programs: People come to seminars to learn how to do certain things, to acquire skills—*practical* skills. Most adults do not return to the learning process to further their general education; they tend to believe that they have had quite enough of that. (Even those adults who return to college or other formal courses of general education usually are motivated by the desire for diplomas and degrees, rather than for the knowledge per se.) Attendees at seminars want to learn how to win contracts, how to win promotions, how to use a computer, how to survive office politics, how to write good advertising copy, how to be an effective manager, etc. It is that specific end-result for which they will pay hundreds of dollars and spend days of their time. Employers will spend thousands of dollars to train their staff people to become better managers, write more winning proposals, use computers more effectively, manage payables and receivables more efficiently, and otherwise contribute more to company success. Thus the need for the focus and emphasis on how to—on practical skills: It is the nature of the market; the seminar market is a market for the teaching of skills with direct applications to success of one kind or another. The goal that attracts attendees and motivates employers to pay for employees to attend seminars is not learning per se but some specific, promised benefit that appears to be a likely result.

From a training viewpoint, the discrimination between seminars and workshops ought to be determined by the nature of the skill to be acquired, for some skills require a different kind of learning exposure than do others. Some skills are purely the result of knowledge — are simply the possession of the appropriate knowledge. A medical student, for example, can learn medical principles and much anatomy from lectures, demonstrations, and reading. But other medical skills, such as surgical procedures, must be learned in the laboratory and clinic, from exercises and practice (and, later, in internship and long-term hospital practice). But it is not only the acquisition and mastery of motor skills that require actual practice; facility in many other kinds of skill — writing and illustrating, for example — requires practice under expert guidance.

So much for the training viewpoint and considerations. There are also the marketing viewpoint and considerations to take into account. Unless you keep the marketing requirements in mind in conceiving, planning, and designing your seminar programs(s), your attendance will suffer and may make the entire idea unfeasible. Your seminar cannot be a practical success in any sense — not even as a learning experience — if it is not first a marketing success.

For one thing, in connection with the marketing considerations, the very connotation of the terms used plays a role: The word *seminar* connotes an advanced learning session, usually of a professional or para-professional nature, whereas the term *workshop*, especially when used alone, has more of a blue-collar connotation. Therefore, a "seminar" has far greater appeal for most people than does a "workshop" — unless the *workshop* is distinctly subordinated to and used to denote some portion of a seminar. There it becomes far more acceptable. But even then relatively few seminar brochures make reference to workshop sessions, although the seminar may, in fact, include such activity. Instead, most seminar brochures list and sometimes describe the skills and end-results promised, but do not specify how the results will be achieved, although the implication is plain that revelation by knowledgeable presenters will itself do the job of imparting the knowledge and skills promised.

That is not by coincidence nor is it an evasion. It is the inevitable result of the entire seminar idea, which is geared primarily to what might be called intellectual skills or skills that are the simple and direct result of knowledge. Take note again of the seminar titles — "How to be an Assertive Manager" or even "Designing & Preparing

Camera-Ready Artwork," both of which programs deal with rationales and strategies, and not the basic skills of the fields.

There are exceptions, of course. A week-long seminar in value management held in Washington for government employees consisted of about one-third workshops in "breakout" groups. That is, the audience of about 60 attendees was periodically broken down into five- or six-person teams that moved into separate areas to work on value-management problems and get some experience in actual application of the methodology. However, this was a 40-hour program, and although it was referred to as a seminar, would more fairly be designated a training course. Again, a weekend seminar for parents of difficult children, offered frequently by a Pennsylvania couple, tends to attract about 150 attendees, and much of the weekend is spent practicing the methods in breakout groups of about 10 or 12 people.

Despite this, these are exceptions. Most seminars offered rarely require very much in the way of workshops or other hands-on experience. In fact, given that few seminars run more than a week—and by far the majority are for one or two days—there is simply not enough time to develop basic skills, such as illustrating, but only to enhance existing skills with special knowledge, tips, insight, new ideas, and other specialized data and methods not commonly available to the general public. This, coupled with earlier observations made in this chapter, sums up the nature of most seminars. It thus establishes the baseline to guide you in choosing suitable objectives and subjects for your own seminar program(s). In general, your program probably ought to follow at least these general guidelines for content and basic organization:

1. Have as a specific and most clearly defined goal a direct, practical benefit for the attendee and/or the employer who pays for the attendance.
2. Be a definite "how-to" session, with careful planning to impart practical skills necessary to realize the promised benefit.
3. Include all materials necessary as presentation aids, learning aids, demonstrations, and handouts.
4. Include exercises and practice sessions, if and as necessary.
5. Provide ample opportunity for attendees to ask questions and participate in open discussions.
6. Identify the credentials of presenters and materials promised.

Let's look a bit more closely at each of these.

The Promised Benefit

Only a few pages ago we looked at a list of seminar titles and even some how-to lines from within several of the brochures. Each of these described what the seminar producer regarded as a benefit that was likely to motivate recipients of the brochure to register for attendance. And, yet, a response—actual registration—of one out of every hundred recipients (or even one out of every 200 or 300 recipients) is considered good. Why? Is it reasonable to suppose that with a carefully selected mailing list of *qualified* prospects only one per cent (or even less) should respond?

Of course it is not reasonable. It is supportable because the price of the item sold is high enough to support a grossly inefficient effort. A mass mailing of perhaps 50,000 pieces (brochures) might cost $10,000 and produce 250 registrations distributed over a half-dozen sessions announced and listed. That means a gross revenue of $25,000–$50,000, depending on various circumstances, so the proposition is viable, if not ideal. But the real problem is that "How to be an assertive manager," and "analyzing and improving direct mail" are not truly *benefits*. Managers don't worry about being "assertive" (whatever that means); they worry about being *successful*. Marketers don't worry about "analyzing and improving" their direct mail; they worry about *getting more orders* from their direct mail operations.

You can argue, of course, that the seminar titles do address those needs and goals because an "assertive" manager is a more successful manager. The problem with that argument is that the prospect does not make that translation of "assertive" into "more successful". *The prospect will not do your selling for you. You* must make the translation. Title your seminar "How to be a more successful manager by being more assertive," and see the difference in response for yourself. Promise your addressee to demonstrate how to increase sales via direct-mail, and explain the method or rationale later.

That is at the heart of the matter. The brochures cited are selling the wrong thing. They are trying to sell the rationale, rather than the benefit. As the late Charles Revson, founder of Revlon cosmetics, reportedly put it, "In the factory we manufacture cosmetics; in the stores we sell hope."

That sums up neatly the essence of all marketing strategy: Sell the benefit itself, what the prospect will want, not the rationale or "proof" of the promise. The problem arises because so many advertisers believe that they can promise the benefit on a rational basis and be effective. For example, suppose that you plan to present a seminar in which you will teach the methods of market research. Here are a few possible headlines or seminar titles to consider:

1. "Effective market research"
2. "Modern methods of market research"
3. "How professionals carry out market research"
4. "The 'tricks of the trade' in market research"
5. "Shortcuts to effective market research"
6. "An expert reveals his secrets of market research"
7. "A graduate course in market research"
8. "Discovering market truths"
9. "How to find your true market"
10. "Little-known tips on market research"

Study these and decide which are most appealing and most likely to motivate prospects to register for the seminar. Then check below for my own opinion about these.

My opinion is that most of these are pedestrian, unexciting, unalluring titles and headlines. Numbers 4, 5, 6, and 10 are just a bit more alluring than are the others, but not by much. Why? Because all are lines that might support the main headline or title as follow-up lines, but they fail to address *directly* the prospect's real desire, which is to *succeed* in the market. The way they are worded they require the prospect to *translate* the words into success in the market. But prospects rarely do that; you must do it for them. You must use titles and headlines that do it. People go to college to become marketing experts, but they go to seminars to learn how to succeed in the markets. You will attract some attendees by promising to teach market research, especially if you promise to teach the "secrets of the experts," the "little-known truths," and "inside tips" on market research; people do find the prospect of getting "on the inside" and learning closely held "secrets" most alluring. But you will normally do far better by avoiding the forbiddingly academic term *market research* entirely (except as follow-up copy, and even there you should use it sparingly) and on success in the marketplace.

Consider some of the following titles and headlines as alternatives to the first set:

"Finding your most productive market"
"Finding the right prospects"
"Taking the risk out of marketing"
"Minimizing failure in marketing"
"The certain route to sales success"
"The rifle-shot approach to the RIGHT markets"
"Finding your market"

Note the more direct approach to and identification of desired results: sales success. This does not mean that you will not teach market research in your seminar; not at all. You may teach the exact program envisioned in that first set of titles and headlines. But it means that you will focus your program on what the attendee wants—why he or she is there. That is an absolute must if you want your seminar to be a success. You must understand the attendees' desires. . .what brought them there. . .what desire and anticipated result persuaded them or their employers to go to the expense of their attendance. In this case, they really do not care for the academic theories of market research, or even for the methods, except as the latter are useful to their direct goals (which are sales success, not passing grades, diplomas, and degrees).

Even those latter titles and headlines are not the most direct appeals possible. Even those require some interpretation by the prospect. Some introspection may produce even more effective headlines and titles. Consider some of the typical problems of everyone engaged in marketing:

1. Finding and targeting the *right* prospects, not always an easy task.
2. Beating the competition, often the most serious problem.
3. Creating the most effective marketing materials, a problem in creativity.
4. Carrying out an effective campaign within the budget allocated, almost always a problem.
5. Keeping up with all new developments in the industry, often extremely difficult to avoid a losing battle.
6. Keeping up with new developments in marketing methods, materials, media, and techniques.
7. Keeping up with what competitors are doing.

Your success in choosing seminar subjects to headline is a reflection of how accurately you estimate major concerns of prospects and how well you manage to "strike a nerve" in them as a result of your estimates. Suppose, for example, that you estimate number 6 above as a major concern of your prospects and therefore build your seminar and seminar literature around that conclusion. If your estimate is accurate, you will get an enthusiastic response and a well-attended (and profitable) seminar. But if you have miscalculated and your prospects are not really concerned much about the factors of number 6 above, you may lay an egg with your seminar campaign.

An Inverse Kind of Benefit

The promise of positive benefits is not the only kind that produces the kind of results you want. Neither is relying on the prospect's own perceptions of need the only way or the best way to motivate prospects. You do not have to depend on your ability to estimate the *felt* concerns of your prospects, those concerns they sense spontaneously. Instead, you can do something to *create* the concerns. You can alarm the prospect about the problem (many who use this technique prefer to express it as "educating" the prospect about the problem), and then offer the solution. It is a technique that works in many situations. Insurance, for example, is almost invariably sold in exactly that manner, using that strategy. It is a marketing/advertising approach that is sometimes referred to as the *fear* technique. Advertising by companies selling security devices and services usually find it necessary to use this approach, as insurance companies do. It is, of course, a "natural," for those kinds of advertisers, since most insurance is a hedge against expensive disasters, while for those selling security services and devices the strategy is dictated by the very nature of what they sell.

Fear as a Motivator

Fear is a powerful motivator. Insecurity and the fear of failure are most common, even among the top executives and most successful individuals; appeals to fear "find a home" quite readily with most of us. In some cases, such as those just cited (insurance and security), the fear strategy is dictated by circumstances—is inherent in the nature of the service or product. However, even when this is not the case, the method lends itself to the advertiser as an option. In those cases the technique is to direct the prospect's attention to some potential hazard and offer a solution—*promise*, that is, that whatever it is that the offeror is selling will solve the problem or overcome the hazard. (In fact, it is the promise itself that the offeror is really selling!) A few examples of that type of appeal to fear appeared in an earlier list. Read the following few examples of that kind of appeal and then, to be sure that you recognize and fully understand this approach, go back and see if you can identify the other, earlier examples:

"Don't let competitors get the jump on you"

"Learn how to avoid failure in the marketplace"

"Some are winners, some losers; which will you be?"

"Here is what you NEED to be successful"

"How to find your way around the booby traps in the marketplace"

MOTIVATIONAL RESEARCH

The advertising industry has made a great thing of motivational research, research into what moves individuals to buy or not to buy. And the research has demonstrated many things, not the least of which is that subtlety is usually self-defeating; people habitually are either totally puzzled by or draw the wrong meanings from subtle messages. When a major brand of cigarettes depicted its package bursting a chain, for example, the intended message was "break the hot smoking habit," but most viewers got the message "stop chain smoking," which was certainly not what the advertiser wanted.

Every day we see examples of advertising messages that miss their mark because they are subtle and, quite often, because the copywriter was more interested in displaying cleverness than in conveying a clear message. A computer-printer manufacturer takes a two-page advertisement in an expensive medium to advertise its laser printer, and devotes one of those two very expensive pages to a headline that says POWER OF THE PRESS. The body copy then rationalizes that headline by claiming that this new laser printer will bring "the power of a printing press" to the prospect's office. The headline is a play on words that offers nothing to arouse the reader's interest, aside from being totally cryptic. If, in fact, the advertiser expects the bringing of "the power of a printing press" to one's office to be motivating (which is quite doubtful in itself), the headline should have said so. Burying the prime promise in the body copy defeats the whole purpose of the advertisement itself, let alone that of the headline!

Another manufacturer does slightly better when it headlines for its color-copier advertisement, IF YOU WANT TO GET READ, USE RED. The motivational strategy is not a bad one, but its implementation could stand some improvement. Were it my copy I would use the headline to stress one or more of several outstanding and attractive features described later in the body copy. Or, at the least, I would follow up and strengthen that rather weak headline with an *immediate explanation* of those other features. (Even better, I would use a subhead to do that.)

Another printer manufacturer runs an institutional type of copy, with a photo of an egg as the centerpiece and the headline WE HATCH ORIGINALITY. The body copy goes on to brag about the company's superior ideas, designs, and products in copy that turns out to be all claim with no proof—without even a single illustration of that claimed originality and inventiveness—making it weak copy indeed.

Important although titles and headlines are—and we will discuss these again at the appropriate place—every line of description is, in fact, advertising and motivates the prospect for or against attending your seminar. And those lines of description are inevitably linked to the subjects and orientation you have chosen for your seminar. Ergo the need to think always in terms of marketing and motivation when conceiving your seminar content. That is, it is not enough to make the right pledges, descriptions, and explanations in your advertising materials; you must plan and design your seminar with those features as design goals.

Professionals writing user manuals make the mistake of estimating the prospective user's need in terms of their own interests. The engineer writing a maintenance manual, for example, typically wants to include reams of engineering data that is not needed by the maintenance technician. And often those designing seminars fall into the same trap of letting their own interests and biases prevent them from thinking in terms of their prospects' interests.

The common error is to design a program that you think is "right" for whatever purpose you have in mind, and then rationalize a promotional campaign to persuade prospects to register and attend. That appears to many to be a logical procedure. But that is, like a great many ideas accepted as conventional wisdom, a false trail. Ironically, the fact is that the opposite is the truth, and the procedure described by the late Joe Karbo reveals this clearly.

Karbo was the gentleman who ran those full-page advertisements you may have seen headlined THE LAZY MAN'S WAY TO RICHES. He sold a reported 600,000+ copies of a 70-page paperback book for $10 each through those advertisements. And he ran the first advertisements before he wrote the book!

According to his own account, he first wrote the advertisement, constructing it to appeal to what he judged to be a felt need, with a general idea of the book in his head and the knowledge that he could write it in a few days. But he was wise enough to want to test his idea first. Had he received only a few orders after his first advertisement, he would have returned the money and dropped the idea. But when the idea proved viable as a business proposition, he wrote the book, had it printed and rolled out his campaign.

What he did, in fact, was first estimate a need that he thought he could satisfy, as well as sell to prospects. He didn't write and publish a book that he thought was "right" and then try to sell it; he determined, by his test, what prospects wanted—whether they agreed with what he proposed to them as a need—and then created the product to satisfy that need.

NEEDS: HOW TO "FIND" THEM

Karbo's method is, of course, the ideal way to go about selecting subjects for and designing your seminar program. There was no question here of the basic "need," for the vast majority of individuals would agree quite quickly that they have a need for more money. But Karbo had to test the public reaction to his proposition—his offer of a slender paperback book that would present his own advice on the secrets of getting rich. He did not have to ask anyone whether they wanted or needed more money; he knew the answer to that question. But he needed an answer to the more sharply pointed question he was asking: Do you have a need for this book I offer?

It is an example of the often heard "formula" for success: Find a need and fill it. But it is also much like the ironic advice for stock market success attributed to financier Bernard Baruch ("Buy low and sell high"); it's a goal to pursue, not a method for doing something. There is one more observation that ought to be made about needs, an observation best illustrated with a true story about an inventor who studied the problem of persuading ketchup to flow out of its traditional narrow-necked bottle and invented a simple device for making it do so.

Having perfected his little device, this bright young inventor trotted off to the executive offices of the world's leading ketchup manufacturer, convinced that his fortune was assured. To his dismay he found the executives of this company became horrified and were thoroughly prepared to throw him down the stairs in response to his offer of the invention. Finally accepting defeat, he went off licking his wounds and determined, as he later explained, never again to offer people what they need, but only what they desire.

Had he understood marketing better, he would have realized that his prospect not only did not desire the product but did not need it. In fact, its use would have been a disaster to a company whose advertising focuses on the thickness of its ketchup, as illustrated and "proved" to consumers in countless TV and print advertisements by the graphic representations of its slowness in pouring.

You cannot unilaterally decide what a need is; a need is not a need unless the prospect agrees that it is. Still there are immutable needs, when you get down to basics. There was no question about the perceived need of most people for more money, for example, but there was a question of whether that could be translated into a perceived need for the book Joe Karbo offered. You must discriminate between a *basic* need, such as the need for security, love, warmth, clothing, and self-esteem, and the recognition or acceptance of potential methods for satisfying these requirements as needs in themselves.

The needs for warmth and protection from the elements satisfied at an early time by animal skins and natural shelter, such as caves. Many thousands of years later we are still satisfying those *identical needs* by better methods, methods that are still being improved. We have needs for clothing and shelter by today's standards, and animal skins are used more for decorative purposes than to satisfy basic needs for clothing.

In short, all basic human needs are immutable. It is the ways of satisfying those basic needs that change constantly, as we search for and discover newer and better ways.

"Finding a need," then, actually means finding a *better way to satisfy a basic need*. Movie attendance is enormously reduced today because the videocassette recorder and movies on tape are perceived by many as a better way to satisfy the basic need for diversion (although TV had already made great inroads into attendance at playhouses). To find a need you must consider the basic needs, the ways in which they are being met today, and better ways in which they can be met.

But even that is not all of it, for while there are many cases in which the prospects readily perceive an offer as a better way even without persuasion, in many cases they must be persuaded to that view, if you are to be successful in your venture.

Of course, there is no denying that what is offered as a better way may or may not be one, and what is accepted by prospects as a better way may or may not be so. Thus Joe Karbo's method for determining public acceptance before committing a great deal of money and effort to the venture made sense, and many others use similar methods. (I have used it myself, with similar success, I am happy to report, in both seminar and direct-mail publication ventures. In fact, the testing that is standard practice in direct-mail operations today is philosophically quite similar to this, in that its strategy is to make small mailings and test public reaction to the offer before "rolling out"—committing substantial resources to the major effort.)

A FOR-INSTANCE

In my own first seminar I was trying out three ideas, at least one of which (the third one below) was radically different and in direct contradiction to the established methods and practices used almost universally by others. (Many might argue also with the strategy represented by the first item below.)

1. Representing the session as a "graduate" course, designed for only those already experienced in government marketing and proposal writing.
2. Promising to reveal many "inside tips," including my own strategies for winning.
3. A different mailing technique—small brochures and a cover letter, mailed first class in a conventional business (number 10) envelope.

I therefore made a small, 1,000-piece initial mailing as a test. To my surprise, the response was so great that I made only one additional 1,000-piece mailing and filled the meeting room to bursting! (In subsequent seminar promotions I tried out many more ideas, some of which worked out quite well, and which will be described and explained later.)

GENESIS OF THE IDEAS

There was no question in my mind, based on my direct experience over many years, that there was a need for training proposal writers. I regarded that as a basic need that was not being satisfied nearly as well as it could be. In fact, my decision to offer a seminar of my own was provoked by a growing sense of dissatisfaction with what I was hearing from other lecturers on the subject. Even in casual conversations with others who are involved in marketing I heard many remarks that disturbed me. There was a great and unjustified cynicism, for one thing. I heard many opinions (which were stated as fact, however) that the game was rigged and no amount of marketing or proposal-writing skill would make a difference to anyone who had not been on the inside of things earlier. My personal experience was the opposite of this—I had won many contracts strictly on the basis of my proposals—and I believed these kinds of stories to be sour-grapes rationalizations by those who couldn't or wouldn't make the necessary effort to turn out winning proposals. (Perhaps this view was also the result of observing but not understanding the entirely different process of awarding the major contracts for multi-billion-dollar projects that resulted only from lengthy negotiations directly involving governors and members of Congress.) Even from those who were not so twisted in their views I heard much that I disagreed with.

In addition to this I thought that there was much too much emphasis on proposal *writing*, and not nearly enough on marketing skills and strategies. I therefore decided to deemphasize writing per se and coined an awkward term that never caught on—"proposalmanship"—but did help me make attendees understand that writing skill alone is not enough to turn out the winning proposals but needs the addition of a good knowledge of marketing.

The result was the little brochure illustrated in Figure 3-1. Note that it does not even mention proposal writing, but focuses attention on *winning*. And if you observe the next figure, 3-2, you will see how the theme was carried out in follow-up text and the program outline. The third item in my list was at least partly the result of my experience in direct-mail marketing, in which it is considered

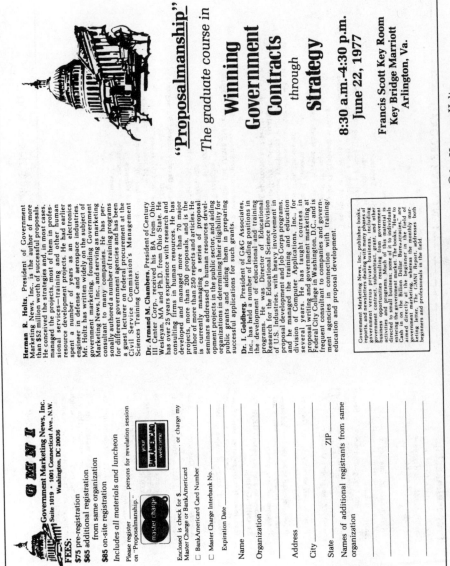

Figure 3-1. Front panel of seminar brochure. Copyright © by Herman Holtz.

Proposalmanship:

The Graduate Course in Winning Government Contracts— through STRATEGY

A fact-packed, one-day workshop that will graduate you from proposal writer to a contract winner.

In just one day, you'll receive the benefit of years of experience from government marketing experts who have won millions of dollars in contracts. And they did it by employing the proper strategies.

How to sell directly to the Government—"across the counter."

How to appear to be the low bidder— and how to win even when you're not the apparent low bidder.

How to make your proposal THE OUT- STANDING ONE.

How to analyze the requirement—iden- tify the critical, key point on which award will hinge—develop a WIN- NING STRATEGY.

A word of caution. This workshop is not for neophytes. This is not a course in proposal writing. It is a strategy session in winning contracts.

You'll learn many strategies that can be employed to persuade proposal evalua- tors to select YOUR proposal.

Innovation instead of imitation . . . pricing strategies . . . program strategies . . . presentation strategies.

Learn the art of Proposalmanship vs. simple proposal writing.

And come prepared to work. This is a workshop, not a lecture session. This will be a shirtsleeves workday, during which your questions, relevant to your organiza- tion's specific problems, will be addressed.

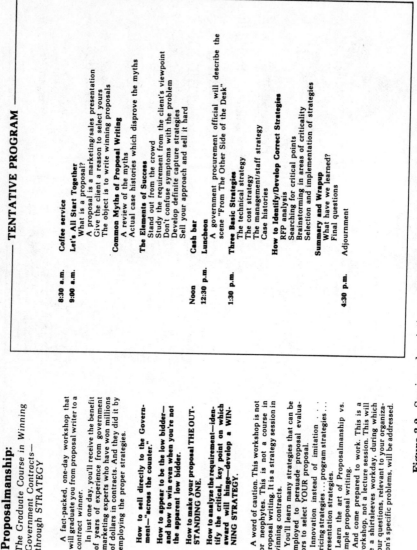

TENTATIVE PROGRAM

8:30 a.m. Coffee service

9:00 a.m. Let's All Start Together
What is a proposal?
A proposal is a marketing/sales presentation
Give the client a reason to select yours
The object is to write winning proposals

Common Myths of Proposal Writing
A review of the myths
Actual case histories which disprove the myths

The Elements of Success
Stand out from the crowd
Study the requirement from the client's viewpoint
Don't confuse symptoms with the problem
Develop definite capture strategies
Sell your approach and sell it hard

Noon Cash bar

12:30 p.m. Luncheon
A government procurement official will describe the scene "From The Other Side of the Desk"

1:30 p.m. Three Basic Strategies
The technical strategy
The cost strategy
The management/staff strategy
Case histories

How to Identify/Develop Correct Strategies
RFP analysis
Searching for critical points
Brainstorming in areas of criticality
Selection and implementation of strategies

Summary and Wrapup
What have we learned?
Final questions

4:30 p.m. Adjournment

Figure 3-2. Seminar description and outline. Copyright © Herman Holtz.

essential to build the mailing package around a sales letter. The very idea of sending someone a brochure without a covering letter disturbed me badly; it was simply contrary to my views of what is proper procedure. Moreover, my experience with bulk mail and mailing to rented lists was not encouraging: I had found more success in mailing first class to lists I had compiled myself. And so the instincts I had developed in direct-mail operations guided my actions. However, I might mention another factor that I believe to be an important one: I have never been impressed with the sanctity of "We have always done it this way" or "Everyone does it this way." Quite the contrary, I have found in many situations that a totally new and different approach— even one that is the diametrical opposite of the conventional one—is often much more successful than the conventional one. And I do like to experiment; I prefer to try various new ideas and I happen also by nature to be somewhat skeptical of that which I have not personally verified. So I prefer to try for myself and to form my own conclusions from my own observations.

Of course I am often wrong and the classic way to do something proves to be still the best way. But trying alternatives and new ideas works out often enough to be worth trying again and again.

I also happen to abhor waste, and the very thought of mailing thousands upon thousands of brochures that would be discarded with hardly a glance distresses me greatly.

Given all these factors I had little hesitation about turning to first-class mailing of brochures and letters that would fit into a number 10 business envelope.

SOURCES OF IDEAS FOR SUBJECTS

In my own case the first idea I got for seminars was imposed on me by chance, as was my very entry into consulting. Because I had enjoyed a great deal of success in writing proposals that resulted in contract awards, more than a few people came to me and urged me to help them with their own proposals. This led me into consulting in the first place. But I knew that proposal writing is a group effort, and in most organizations all the professional staffs are called upon to help. Therefore, I knew there was a large potential audience for seminar programs on the subject. That knowledge, combined with the stimulus just described, set my feet on the path to presenting my own first seminar.

Some consultants will object to presenting seminars on the very subject upon which their consulting service is based. They see this as detracting from their consulting service, as selling their expert knowledge and services at bargain-basement rates and weakening their practice.

I think that attitude is a mistaken one. First of all, if you find your basic consulting services well received and appreciated, you already have an excellent clue to a successful seminar subject. For everyone who needs and wants your services enough to pay your direct hourly or daily rate, there are almost surely many others who will never retain you directly but who would be happy to learn from you in a seminar where they would pay only a fraction of your individual rate. And as for injury to your consulting services, it has been my personal experience that my seminars have not only never injured my consulting practice, but have supported and aided it. Nor am I alone in this. Nido Qubein, for example, one of the most successful consultants and sales trainers in the country, conducts seminars, delivers lectures, writes books, and publishes both a newsletter and series of audio tape cassettes on the subjects that are the focus of his consulting. And he is not alone in this. It is a common practice among successful consultants to deliver their knowledge and wisdom via a variety of media. Of course, you are entitled to differ with this opinion. You could devise a seminar on a related subject, but you might thereby risk losing the seminar-promotion asset of your reputation as a consultant in your specialty.)

As you proceed, you will surely find yourself getting ideas for other seminars. For example, I appeared as guest on a local TV talk show and was literally flooded with calls and letters for some time later. Talking to these individuals led me to stage a series of what I called "mini-seminars" for these inquirers, many of whom were not interested in proposal writing but were interested in other aspects of marketing. I also developed a seminar program on how to become an independent consultant and build a practice as a result of later developments, especially after having written extensively on the subject.

I found, in fact, that just as writing books often provoked ideas for other books—i.e., a chapter in a book often lent itself to expansion into an entire book on the subject—topics in seminars may be seeds for entire seminars. For example, because attendees surprised me by demonstrating far greater interest in cost analysis and cost estimating than I had anticipated, I expanded that portion of my seminars, and could easily have developed that into a separate seminar. (In practice

I found it sensible to bring in an expert on the subject to conduct a complete seminar on costs, contracts, and negotiations.) As a further example, inquiries about marketing to state and local governments led me to research and develop an entire presentation on that subject.

The possibilities—ideas for additional seminars—propagate rapidly, once you condition your instincts to be alert for them. (In my case, for example, an idea for a magazine article often provokes an idea for a complete book even before I write the magazine article.) Think first about the most basic needs, as they relate to your special field, and then about how they are satisfied conventionally today, and finally about how they might be satisfied more efficiently, more swiftly, more cheaply, or more effectively using some special knowledge, techniques, or materials that you can supply. Think particularly of how-to ideas— how to get a better job, handle everyday problems better, stop smoking, reduce stress, write more effectively, program a computer, become a powerful leader, win promotions, get along with others, learn value engineering, lose weight, or how to do any of many other things.

Consider the kinds of questions you are most commonly asked at meetings, at conventions, at any kind of contacts with others. Sit down and make a list. Sort the list in order of frequency: What do people really want to know about what you do and/or how you do it? What kinds of things appear to trouble them? What kinds of problems are they trying to solve? What are they most unhappy about?

Don't limit yourself to these people. Include the questions asked most often by your clients. What are they most often worried about? What kind of help do they want from you most often? What kinds of things do they know they must do and yet find that they need your help in doing? What do they think their staffs ought to be trained to do?

THE PROCESS

Perhaps you will have a beginning idea virtually thrust upon you by circumstance, as I did, although it is more likely that you will have to apply some of the kind of observation and meditation suggested here to come up with the basic idea. But in either case, you will probably start with a general idea, such as a field or broad goal. You will then have to think it out, extrapolating from it a program and strategy. You will have to ask yourself some basic questions to develop the general idea into a set of specific ideas necessary to flesh out a program. Suppose, for example, that you are a marketing specialist and you propose to develop a seminar program in marketing. Of course, marketing is a rather broad field, and you will have to narrow your goal somewhat. A first step would be to determine just what it is in the broad field of marketing that you will address.

Among the first steps in narrowing your focus might be research into what is either standard or recent in the literature—books, articles, journals—and in training—manuals, other programs.

A second step might be listing various specialties in marketing (the choices undoubtedly influenced by your own specialties), such as marketing research, demographics, direct mail, or other.

A third step might be evaluating each item listed in terms of whether it offers you advantages of some kind, for while you are trying to devise a useful program, it must also be an attractive one.

Here are some of the kinds of questions you must ask yourself as you study the various options and the pros and cons of each:

What are the most common and most serious marketing mistakes you see people make every day?

What are the problems or needs these people themselves recognize or believe are most critical?

Do you agree with these insights into their problems and needs?

What areas or kinds of marketing—in terms of product, services, or prospective buyers—appear to offer the greatest opportunities?

What kinds of organizations or individuals appear to be best prospects to attend your seminars?

How many others are offering seminars in this field?

How do those other seminars compare with what you are trying to do?

What special and/or exclusive ideas, tips, knowledge, insights, angles, strategies, or materials do you have to offer?

What other special inducements can you offer?

How can you structure your presentation to be different, superior, and special?

SPECIAL FEATURES

In studying the potential for offering special and/or exclusive features, you should consider several different possibilities: special and/or exclusive information, ideas, materials, demonstrations, presentation techniques, and guest speakers. And "special and/or exclusive" does not mean that the features must be of earth-shaking proportions: So much in the world is mediocre—as much of your competition is likely to be—that simply being *excellent* is often being momentously superior and exclusive.

What that means, in practical terms, is that you must measure the qualities of your presentation in terms of the competing offerings, rather than on an absolute scale, for that is the way the world measures you. (There is no absolute scale for what must inevitably be judged subjectively. Even the critic who purports to measure you absolutely is actually comparing you to whatever else he or she has observed.)

By all means avoid being a "me, too." It is not enough to be as good as your competition; you must be better, far better.

Many of those special features that can make your seminar program an outstanding one are not especially difficult to acquire, and not even particularly costly in most cases. In fact, many such features are available free or virtually free.

Guest Speakers

Consider getting guest speakers as a special feature of your program, for example; it is usually quite easy to do. Government agencies—federal, state, and local—will often provide a speaker without cost to you. (My cost for guest speakers from government agencies was usually only a lunch!) Business clubs, such as the Rotary and the Lions, often supply speakers, as do many other nonprofit organizations. Many companies, especially large and important corporations with large public relations and public information departments, maintain rosters of executives and staff specialists who are members of what the company terms a "lecture bureau," and who are usually available without charge. These are services government agencies and other organizations—companies, associations, labor unions, and others—provide as public relations activities. All they seek in return is the opportunity to make their name and activities known to the audiences they address: the PR. In fact, many corporations will gladly supply movies, videotapes, equipment, and personnel to operate them, all as part of their public relations programs.

It is not only the sizable organizations who can and will contribute. Individual entrepreneurs—fellow independent consultants and other professionals in private practice—will often agree to appear on your platform and make presentations without compensation or for small honoraria and the opportunity to make themselves and their professional offerings more widely known (and the opportunity to possibly pick up an occasional new client!). Usually such seminars include a literature table, and all guest speakers are invited to deposit thereon a supply of their business cards, brochures, and/or other promotional literature. And, of course, you can often strike deals with others who present seminars where each of you makes guest presentations at the other's seminars. The benefits are then mutual in more than one way, for you may also occasionally acquire a new client through your guest appearances.

Presentation Aids

Just as guest speakers are often available at little or no cost to you, so are many presentation aids. Governments at all levels have many audiovisual aids available—movies, slides, film clips, audiocassettes, and videocassettes—for use, usually without charge. Public libraries alone are a good source, but the federal government also has thousands of such programs, most of which can be borrowed. The Government Printing Office publishes a directory of these, copies of which can be consulted at a well-stocked public or government library. (Most government agencies of size have libraries, and most of these are open to the public.)

Many companies, associations, and other nonprofit organizations will also lend such materials and may even send someone out to help. And if you happen to be in or near Washington, DC or the capital of any state government, there will be many lobbying offices of large organizations that often have audiovisual materials useful to you.

Handout Literature

Printed literature in quantity sufficient to hand out freely to attendees is the easiest kind of support to get. Governments, large and small businesses, associations, community groups, lobbyists, labor unions, and even individual entrepreneurs have an abundance of printed materials and are generally quite eager to supply as much as you need. Many consultants presenting seminars hand out large portfolios bulging with useful information (printed literature) supplied from such sources.

Demonstrations

Depending on what it is that you are presenting, you may be able to get models and/or demonstration kits, or get others to offer demonstrations for you. The motivation for organizations to do so is the same: they do it in the name of public relations.

FINDING THE SOURCES FOR SPECIAL AIDS

Your own local telephone book is an excellent place to begin searching out sources for materials and other aids. You will find all local offices of federal, state, and local government listed therein. Be sure to visit the local Small Business Administration Office personally and talk to the officials there. They have a volunteer force of retired executives and professional specialists, for one thing, and they are an excellent source for literature. They usually keep in touch with local businesses and other organizations, as well as other government agencies, and can often steer you in the right direction for additional help. You might also benefit by visiting other large government offices to inquire into the possibility of such assistance as that noted here.

Inquire also into the location of the nearest Government Printing Office bookstore. You can often find books there dealing with subjects and offering information not available anywhere else. Moreover, in most cases the publications are in the public domain, which means that you can duplicate them or portions of them freely.

The telephone directory will also furnish you a list of associations, corporations, nonprofit groups, and other organizations. Call and visit these. Seek out marketing managers in for-profit companies, and public relations managers (sometimes referred to as "public information officers") in all organizations.

Turn to local professional societies—and you should belong to at least one or two yourself—to find other independent entrepreneurs and professionals in private practice. Make your needs known in these associations. You may also want to consider announcing your needs in their newsletters.

You need not restrict yourself to local organizations or local offices of organizations. Quite often you can write to main offices of organizations headquartered elsewhere and get what you need by mail.

If you carry out this research vigorously enough you will not only find your program enormously enriched by what will be almost an embarrassment of such assets, but you will also avoid a great deal of expense and thus increase the probability of economic success.

4 PLANNING DETAILS AND DECISION CRITERIA

Overall seminar success depends in a large part on the quality and completeness of your advance planning. In fact, planning here has a special significance.

THE FACTORS REQUIRING DECISIONS

By now, presumably, you have made the major decisions on subject matter and sources and have at least roughed out a program, including notes on seminar content, materials, speakers, marketing, and other major details. Now you must begin to make the final, firm decisions, most of which are so interlocked that you cannot begin to implement your plan until it is complete.

There are a number of things to be done. Some of those listed below may not apply, depending on your decisions and final designs, while others, such as reserving the meeting room and having a brochure made up, are absolute musts for all seminar promotions. Here is a list of most of the major items that must be carried out in preparation for a seminar or series of seminars:

- Have a descriptive brochure and, possibly, other materials made up, typeset, and printed in whatever quantity you will need.
- Set the date(s), reserve the meeting room(s), and make arrangements for the amenities (refreshments, lunch, or other) and equipment (e.g., slide or transparency projector and/or audio equipment).
- Prepare and print handout materials in time to ensure that they will be available in sufficient quantity at the right time.
- Make firm arrangements for guest speakers.
- Firm up marketing plans and arrangements—mailing lists, news releases, mailing materials, print advertisements, etc.

HOW THE FACTORS INTERLOCK

Of course, you can't begin marketing without having the marketing materials ready—the brochure, most importantly. But you can't write and print the brochure until you have set the date(s), made the room reservation(s), and finalized the seminar content, speakers, and other such details. This is especially true if you have decided to offer seminars to the public at large, as compared with selling an in-house seminar-presentation service to client organizations. So administration—especially marketing—cannot truly begin until you have completed most planning details and committed yourself to them firmly. Nor can you mail too closely to the planned seminar dates. You need to allow time for your literature to reach prospects and circulate in organizations until they reach the right individuals. My own experience tells me that the announcements ought to be planned to give prospects at least six weeks before the seminar date. On the other hand, the lead time must not be too long, either, and my experience here tells me that eight weeks is about the longest time to allow.

Of course, this assumes that you have decided to ask for advance registrations, as most seminar producers do. But you do have to decide on that matter. Usually, you must offer an inducement, such as a "discount" or lower price for advance registration (you accept at-the-door registrations, but you charge a bit more for them).

This has its downside, however: At least some prospects consider it risky to make plans so far ahead if they have to pay in advance. You must state a policy for cancellations, therefore, and most seminar producers do. Most offer a refund if the cancellation is made at least a week or two before the seminar, but I found registrants willing to accept a "rain check" for a later seminar, which eliminated the refunds. I found, also, that it was a productive policy to permit registration by telephone, with the remittance to follow in the mail or even be paid at the door.

There are other considerations. You have to decide how you will mail brochures before you can design, develop, and print them. If you choose to follow the convention and mail them in bulk as "flats" and self-mailers, you will need to print them in full-page format and in large quantity. If you opt for a 3×9-inch size and first-class mailing in a business envelope, you will not need nearly as many, but you will need a salesletter. And if your goal is to persuade client organizations to retain you to present seminars to their staffs, you will need a direct-mail package designed for that purpose. (The marketing will be quite different, requiring at least a two-stage proposition of mailing and other activities to develop leads followed by pursuing the leads to close them.)

In either case there are many matters you must decide before getting your marketing materials ordered:

- Will you offer an inducement to advance registrations with payment in advance? Refunds for cancellations?
- Will you offer an inducement (especially if your appeal is to organizations who will pay for employees' attendance), such as a discount, to groups of attendees registering together?
- Are you announcing seminars or offering them? That is, are you shooting for individual responses from the public at large (open

registration) or trying to sell custom, in-house presentations? Or perhaps both? Of course, if you are pursuing custom, in-house presentations only, you do not *announce* seminars; you *offer* them. And if both, you have still another matter to decide: Will you use a single brochure, with or without accompanying pieces, to offer your seminars, or will you design two different mailers? (Normally, the latter would be far more effective, for the two sales appeals have a number of points at which they ought to differ.)

For the rest of this chapter we will consider the many alternatives from four perspectives:

1. *Presentation and learning efficiency.* The objective for the attendee is to learn information or skills of value, and your presentation will be judged at least partially on how effectively that happens.
2. *The appeal of your program.* No matter how skillfully you or someone else writes the sales copy, your success in marketing the seminar inevitably depends on what prospects think of your proposed content and design.
3. *Costs and risks.* There is no way you can fail to consider the front-end investment and total costs and what they mean in terms of what you must charge and how they affect your probable margin of profit—or loss.
4. *Practicality.* A grand plan that would be attractive, economical, and effective is of no value if you can't bring it off because it is overly complex or it presents serious problems and obstacles of other kinds.

Here again you will find some interlocking and, perhaps even more significant, tradeoffs of several kinds.

A FEW OF THE TRADEOFFS

Almost everywhere you turn you find yourself forced to make tradeoffs in reaching decisions. For example, the most effective program usually proves to be the most complicated and most costly, and the most attractive program proves to be less than the optimal learning design. You have to search between the alternatives to find the most acceptable compromises.

The same problem occurs when trying to market the seminar both for individual registration and for in-house presentations. Having guest speakers for a session planned in your own locality is one thing, but transporting a staff to a distant location for a custom presentation becomes impossibly expensive. There are obvious disadvantages in having a different program for a seminar conducted locally and for the same seminar conducted elsewhere, so it is necessary to keep the basic design simple enough to transport the seminar easily. Probably the sensible solution is to design it so that you can control it yourself, using a single presenter. This consideration applies both to the custom, in-house seminars you present for clients and to open-registration seminars, if you want to "take them on the road" to other cities. That, too, would incur far too much expense if it required you to transport a staff to each location. If you study the typical multi-city seminar announcements you get in the mail, you find that most include a single speaker and many are quite noncommittal about the speaker.

Again, even this is a tradeoff. There is a benefit in presenting a brief biography in the descriptive brochure, extolling the qualifications of the presenter, but you will pay a price for this in flexibility: This locks you in to a given presenter—even if you plan to be the presenter yourself in all cases—and creates a problem if you have to change presenters or if you find it necessary to use different presenters for different locations.

PRESENTATION, MATERIALS, AND EQUIPMENT

Except for that matter of presenters, there is little difficulty in standardizing your seminar program for repetitive presentations in many locations. Printed materials and other supplies can be shipped ahead to the meeting site, if necessary, and equipment—slide projectors, for example—can be rented at each location. (Each hotel where you rent a meeting room can handle this for you if you specify it.)

Materials are typically printed handouts, writing pads and pens or pencils, and presentation aids. In my own case I generally use some materials that I have created and others that government agencies make available to me without charge. My own materials are usually a copy of a seminar manual of about 40 pages, with a table of contents that serves as a general outline of the day's presentation. I have designed the manual to provide space for making notes, as Figure 4-1 illustrates. This is a copyrighted publication of my own that I pro-

VII: THE TRUE ESSENCE OF SALES STRATEGY

Every trade has its "tricks" and proposal writing is not an exception.

THE KEY TO SALES TECHNIQUE **NOTES**

Despite all the elaborate theories of marketing and selling, in the end it all comes down to just two factors: *promise* and *proof*. People buy what things *do*, not what they *are*, and smart marketers sell results (some call them "benefits"), not things. That's why no one sells beer; they sell good times at the beach or at the corner tavern. They don't sell laundry detergent; they sell freedom from embarrassment and the admiration of others. They don't sell insurance; they sell security and the freedom from guilt.

It works just as well in proposal writing as it does in selling soft drinks or automobiles. Government agencies and other customers who request proposals award contracts because they want certain results–problems solved, headaches ended, programs implemented, costs reduced, profits increased, images improved, waste ended, criticism stilled–and they are eager to listen to promises of delivering those results. *That* is what they really want to buy.

THE PROMISE

The promise is always something much to be desired, and is an emotional appeal. (Virtually all human motivation is emotional, not rational. Humans want love, prestige, security, appreciation, and other such ego-gratification, even more than they want food, warmth, and material possessions, and material possessions are themselves valued to the extent that they provide the emotional needs.) And even the government executives evaluating your proposal react to emotional appeals, because they have personal stakes in the projects, as well as a duty to their employers, and they usually have little difficulty in finding that their personal

20

Figure 4-1. Page of seminar manual.

vide each attendee as the main handout. However, the Small Business Administration, the Department of Commerce, and the General Services Administration publish numerous brochures of direct interest, and they are usually highly cooperative in supplying enough copies for your needs without charge. (Depending on the nature and subject matter of your own seminar you may also find these or other government agencies to be valuable sources of handout materials, as well as of information.)

You can buy an inexpensive folder or portfolio at any good stationers to hold all of the handout material, and most seminar producers who have a quantity of handout materials opt to assemble them in this way.

Many seminar producers who provide a copyrighted manual of their own creation state plainly that the manual is not for sale and is available free of charge, but only to attendees of the seminar. That exclusivity is an inducement to attend, but it requires that some effective effort be made to "sell" the free manual itself as a valuable benefit of attending the seminar. That means describing the manual's content in suitable terms, pointing out content that is itself exclusive—perhaps "inside" information or "tips" from experts, detailed how-to guidance, or whatever else you believe will appeal strongly to prospects. The quality of the handout materials, particularly of carry-away materials valuable for future use, can be decisive in persuading many prospects to register and attend. And a copyrighted manual of your own is much more prestigious and perceived to be far more valuable and desirable than is even a large package of what are obviously government pamphlets and advertising literature from various sources.

The manual I created for my seminar on proposal writing is designed to be used by attendees as a useful post-seminar reference, a tool to be used in applying the principles and methods taught in the seminar. Many authors list only chapter titles in their table of contents. I have made it a usual practice to list some descriptive information—headlines from within the chapter—under each chapter title in the table of contents, as shown in Figure 4-2.

That practice has more than one spinoff benefit for you. For one thing, it can serve as a conveniently available basis for a content outline. For another, it helps the attendee understand the content and use the manual effectively. And for still another it is a guide to selecting the most persuasive items for your brochure and other marketing literature.

TABLE OF CONTENTS

Figure 4-2. Table of contents for seminar manual.

MAKING THE PRESENTATION

You have a number of options in making the presentation, which include doing it yourself, wholly or in part, and getting others to do so or help to do so. There are various ways of involving others, from hiring a presenter to inviting other consultants to be guest speakers and taking advantage of services offered by many organizations, as discussed earlier. Of all the options, however, none offers the same benefits and advantages that doing it yourself does. Admittedly, there are problems in this sometimes.

Platform Fever

For some reason, a great many people (perhaps even a majority of people) would sooner face a charging rhino than face an audience. Perhaps it is a fear of appearing inadequate or even making a fool of oneself, but whatever it is, it is a true problem for many. They cringe at the thought of being exposed and alone on the platform, the object of attention by an audience whom they regard as critics who may jeer or smile indulgently at best. That fear alone prevents many consultants from gaining the many benefits of speaking publicly and presenting seminars themselves.

Why You Should Do It Yourself

In fact, the benefits of producing seminars are far greater when you make the presentation yourself. Aside from the obvious benefit of minimizing costs, there is the prestige and image-building that results from your appearances on the platform. Even if your prime purpose in offering seminars is income and profit resulting directly from the seminars, the spinoff benefits of gaining clients is maximal only when you have personally conducted the seminar. Moreover, the more you do of this the more confident and professional you become on the platform, and that also spins off in several ways: As you gain confidence and win applause for your presentations, you begin to enjoy speaking and you find yourself doing more and more of it. You soon find that you can earn fees as a speaker, another welcome addition to your overall income. You find yourself becoming a better marketer, making better sales presentations. And soon you find that as you become more skilled at making presentations, something you are required to do at least occasionally as a consultant, you inspire greater confidence in the client and thus become a better consultant. It is therefore very much in your interest overall to learn how to overcome your fears, if you have them, and to develop platform skills. It takes experience and practice to do so, of course, but there are a few devices that will help you greatly.

The Stress Extremes

The most difficult—most stressful—situation in public speaking is standing on a bare platform, with or without notes in hand. Unless you are an experienced and confident professional, you don't know what to do with your hands, you fight to resist slouching, you smile nervously, and you wish you were anywhere but where you are. That is a situation to avoid, especially when you are still new to speaking publicly and the shock may inhibit you for a long time after.

At the opposite end of that spectrum is the least stressful situation for a speaker. That is sitting comfortably behind a table as a member of a panel along with several other speakers, making extemporaneous, casual, and informal remarks as they occur to you. Early experiences like these help build your confidence. However, in practice, if you present your own seminars, you will most often be alone on the platform, and that is usually not literally a platform but the front area of a meeting room. You will usually be standing, but you can always arrange to have a lectern there and stand behind it. That relieves you of the problem of what to do with your hands. (Later, you won't be conscious of having hands, and you will use them expressively to add to your delivery.) It also puts a barrier between you and your audience, which gives you a psychological shield.

Some speakers sit at a table and deliver their remarks. It's easier on the speaker, but I do not recommend it. You lose much of your force when you sit, instead of standing, if you are the single speaker (as contrasted with a panel). Start by shielding yourself behind a lectern; with a little seasoning you will come out from behind that lectern and stand boldly and confidently before your listeners. You will stride back and forth, and even "invade" their space to add drama and emphasis to your remarks. You will gesture, raise your eyebrows, shout, grin, act out a role, and sit casually on a corner of the table in front of the audience. And you will do these things unconsciously, almost instinctively, as you begin to forget about yourself and concentrate, instead, on your audience, what they are there to learn, and how to get your information and ideas across with greatest effect.

There are also other ways to overcome that self-consciousness and fear. Remember that part of the paralysis you are experiencing is the result of being the center of all that attention. Anything you can do to divert that attention away from you personally will help greatly. And you can do something along those lines, something that actually makes your presentation itself more effective: Use presentation aids freely.

Presentation Aids

Today there are several forms of presentation aids, including these:

Transparencies and overhead projectors.
Slides and slide projectors.
Filmstrips and filmstrip projectors.
Movies and movie projectors.
Videocassettes and videocassette players.
Posters.
Blackboards.
Flip charts.
Models.
Demonstrations.
Exercises.

Some of these aids accomplish the same result as others so the differences are cost and convenience. For example, transparencies and slides can both be used to present charts, graphs, and other such items, but there are differences in the ease and cost of preparing them and in that of presenting them too, since they use entirely different equipment. Transparencies, which use overhead projectors, are by far the more popular aids because they are easy to prepare—a good office copier can be used, for example, to make transparencies—and because the overhead projector has another convenient use: The projection surface can be used as a blackboard, on which you can write with a marker and project the result on a screen.

Another alternative to the blackboard is the easel, with its large sheets (about 3 × 4 feet), which can be flipped back and forth, unlike the blackboard, which must be erased for each new use. (You can also use this with previously prepared charts.)

Each aid has its own advantages, according to what you wish to accomplish. In discussing costs and cost analysis, for example, I could save myself a great deal of effort by bringing previously prepared charts to the podium, but I prefer the spontaneity of creating the chart, while asking rhetorical questions, making observations, and inviting questions and comments from attendees. I believe it to be more effective than a "canned" chart would be, since the attendees can participate actively in the creative process, as they must do in practice.

Not only are these aids of use in helping attendees grasp your points, but they help you too: The more you direct the attention of the audience to such aids as these the less stress you feel, and so at least during the time that you are building up your confidence and developing a platform presence use as many of these as possible. Bring in models of whatever helps get your points across, if possible. Make demonstrations or get some of that outside help to put on demonstrations. Ask questions of your attendees: Make them think and volunteer their ideas. Do exercises on the blackboard and easel, and make them group-participation exercises. Challenge your listeners, and invite them to challenge you. Finally, encourage questions and discussions. In many cases attendees can contribute valuable ideas and information. It is wise to encourage them to do so. (To this day I use ideas and material I get from attendees of earlier sessions.)

An amazing synergy soon takes place: Attendees overcome their reluctance to volunteer answers, and you forget about yourself and how you feel. You soon find yourselves—all of you—working together in quest of answers. At that point it may occur to you that you are not merely a lecturer or instructor; you have become a leader also, another role a good seminar presenter should play.

QUESTION AND ANSWER SESSIONS

Many seminar programs have scheduled question and answer sessions. I list such sessions at appropriate points in my own seminar programs and outlines. In pursuit of this philosophy, many presenters, when questions arise spontaneously during their presentations, ask for them to be held until the scheduled time for that session arrives. Presumably, they are reluctant to break the continuity of their presentation, and sometimes they believe that since the answer will surface later, the question will prove to be unnecessary.

It is in this latter matter that I depart from the practice of many others. First of all, it is my opinion that it is far better to accept the interruption than to permit confusion to persist. And it is likely that for everyone who interrupts with a question there are others who are also confused or uncertain. That is, I interpret the mere fact that the question was raised as a sign that I have not covered the subject adequately or have misled my audience somehow. I believe this so strongly that I not only accept spontaneous questions, but I invite them. At the beginning of my presentation I announce this policy and invite questions, challenges, disagreements, and comments.

It makes for a lively session, I find, which is a bonus for all of us, audience and speaker. It keeps the audience alive and alert, and makes them conscious participants, while it creates a positive atmosphere. (It also forces me to be on my toes!) I believe it to be an essential ingredient of my own presentations and far superior to the totally controlled setpiece seminar.

USE OF BREAKOUT GROUPS

In some situations it is useful to break up the audience into small, separate groups for exercises. This is a useful simulation when the work for which the attendees are being trained is normally carried out in small groups, as in the case of value engineering. It is a necessity in the case of very large audiences—150 attendees, for example—which makes whole-group participation difficult and of limited value.

To do this you need room for the groups to form and separate. Preferably, each group should be in a separate room, but that is not always possible. Therefore, this is frequently carried out in a large ballroom, where each group occupies a ring of chairs well separated from the next group.

Of course, this calls for planning, since you cannot continually break up the audience and reassemble them without losing continuity. The pattern is usually first a group presentation and preparation for the breakout exercises, then the breakout, and finally the reassembly for reviewing and critiquing results. This sequence can be carried out for a morning and an afternoon session, but not more frequently than that.

THE TYPICAL AMENITIES

It is a common practice to provide coffee and tea at seminars, often accompanied by breakfast pastries. This is catered by the hotel, which normally forbids bringing your own refreshments onto their premises. This is often followed by cold drinks served for the afternoon session. Some hotels also provide pencils and small notepads gratis.

LUNCH BREAKS AND INCLUDED LUNCHEONS

Since most seminars are held in hotel meeting rooms, at least one eating facility is normally available on the premises, and there are often other restaurants close by. The presenter normally describes the available facilities to the audience before the lunch break, which is usually about an hour and one-half. Other than that, there are at least three plans in common use for the midday lunch break:

1. A simple announcement of the lunch break and the specified time for reassembly for the afternoon session.
2. A cold or hot buffet served in an adjacent room as part of the formal program, included in the registration.
3. A sit-down luncheon, served in another room—possibly in the hotel dining room—as part of the program. This often includes an address by a speaker other than the presenter.

The formal luncheon is often preceded by a cash bar set up in another room. Many seminar attendees find this a most welcome few minutes of relaxation before lunch, as well as an opportunity to meet and chat with other attendees. For you, as the seminar producer, it is also an excellent opportunity to meet and chat with individuals who may very well become new clients or an avenue to new clients.

Probably the simple 90-minute break, with each individual on his or her own for lunch, is the most commonly used option, and there is no doubt that many attendees prefer that arrangement. Seminars spon-

sored by organizations as custom, in-house programs for the staff tend
to include the buffet luncheon. The formal, sit-down luncheon is probably the least frequently used choice, but it does have some advantages.
The inclusion of a cash bar and formal luncheon has definite appeal
to many prospects, and is probably a factor in attracting at least some
of the registrations. Too, a good speaker included in the luncheon portion of the program is a definite asset that helps make the seminar
a pleasant memory. For the first seminar I presented, for example,
I dragooned an acquaintance in the Department of Labor as my luncheon speaker. He happened to be a good speaker with a wry sense of
humor and yet with an understanding of the interests of his audience,
and his address was easily the highlight of the day. But be careful:
The luncheon should be a light affair, a break from the serious and
perhaps tiring business of the main program. It should be a pleasant
interlude in the middle of the day, so your speaker must be reasonably
entertaining or at least interesting for this feature to be of any help.
A boring speaker will do only damage to your program. It is far better
to have no speaker at the luncheon or to restrict speech-making to a
very few light remarks of your own than to offer the wrong speaker
to the group. They will not soon forgive you for spoiling their lunch!

SPECIAL FEATURES

When I plan a seminar I consider all local organizations and individuals who may have something of value to offer my attendees. For seminars on consulting, for example, I am likely to invite such experts as
Hubert Bermont, J. Stephen Lanning, and Audrey Wyatt, who have
already made an appearance here in forewords to this book. I usually
invite them to supply their own literature as handouts and/or make
personal appearances, if they can manage to make time and wish
to do so. Individuals who would serve similar useful roles for your
own seminars have obvious interests of their own and hope to benefit
directly by making personal appearances and/or supplying handout
material. So you need have no hesitation about inviting them to participate; they are generally pleased to do so. The benefits are mutual:
They, you, and your attendees all benefit.

In the case cited here, since I happen to be acquainted with the individuals, my invitations to them are on a quite informal and friendly
basis. But, because of the mutuality of interests and benefits, you
need not hesitate even if the individuals are total strangers who have

never heard of you. However, it will probably be necessary to provide a fairly detailed explanation of the background of your invitation. Probably a letter along the general lines suggested by Figure 4-3 would be in order. Remember that in this case you are inviting someone to support you and your program when you are totally unknown to the other party. This person would want to be sure that participation in your program would be beneficial and not harmful would need to know who your attendees are and what both their and your interests are. Therefore, you will normally have to provide enough information about yourself and the planned seminar both to describe the objectives and content of your program and to assure the other party that you and/or other presenters are qualified and that the seminar program is one with which they are willing to be associated. Possibly some people might be casual about this, or their eagerness for advertising and promotion might overcome their instincts for caution. But others are likely to be quite cautious, and so these measures of qualifying yourself and your program are very much in order. They are also necessary from another viewpoint: Your respondent needs to understand exactly what your seminar program is all about to respond intelligently to your invitation—to know what literature and what remarks are appropriate. Misunderstanding about this can cause both of you great embarrassment, and that, unfortunately, generally results in hostility. Be sure to provide as much information in as much detail as possible.

YOUR OWN BROCHURES AS HANDOUTS

Even if it is not one of your main objectives to use seminars to market your consulting services, there is certainly no harm in including among your handouts literature that describes your services and provides inducements or at least reasons for retaining you directly as a consultant. And, if you have other seminars, manuals, reports, or other items to sell, you should include appropriate literature about these also. You should, however, restrict your marketing and advertising to that literature unless specifically asked by attendees to speak about your other services and products. Even then the proper procedure is to respond directly and briefly to the question, preferably with a smiling and self-deprecating apology to the others for the "interruption for a commercial." It is definitely not in good taste nor even very

Independent Consulting Associates
3333 Hopeful Lane
Chicago, IL 60606

Jan 6, 1989

J. J. Norton, Executive Director
Health Professionals Association
1333 Gold Coast Blvd
Chicago, IL 60602

Dear Dr. Norton:

We are planning a training seminar for entry-level careerists in health services, to be held in the Chicago area approximately 120 days from now. A preliminary outline of the program planned is enclosed for your information, as is other literature describing Independent Consulting Associates and our qualifications.

While we will provide extensive handout materials of our own creation to each attendee, we will also make attendees aware of local facilities, services, and organizations of direct interest, such as your own association.

For that reason we invite you to supply copies of brochures describing your association and/or whatever literature you think would be appropriate. We anticipate a need for about ___ copies.

We would also be entirely willing to have you or someone else from your organization make a personal appearance to speak to the group and answer their questions and we hereby invite you to do so.

I will be most happy to discuss this further with you at your convenience. Please feel free to write or call to follow this up.

Cordially,

Eager Consultant

Enclosures

EC/dd

Figure 4-3. Suggested format for invitation to participate.

ethical to make a lengthy advertising or sales presentation from a platform paid for by attendees who have come to attend a seminar. Most would probably resent such a cynical misuse of their time and registration fees and rightfully so. You can, however, invite anyone who is interested to stay for a few minutes after the regular session to discuss such matters, or can talk to individuals during breaks. It is quite likely, in fact, that you will be approached during breaks by individuals who often turn out to be prospective new clients or good leads to new clients. Be sure to have your business cards available (although your handout kit should have included a card). Even more important, *exchange* cards with attendees who seek you out individually, and follow up later. The paid-attendance seminar is simply not the place to pursue new clients and to close sales directly, although you may do so indirectly—you will even find it to be a natural fall-out of selling yourself generally through the personal image you create at your seminars. You will get many leads, which you may and should follow up later, for at least some will result in new clients and assignments. (Of course, this injunction is only for seminars with paid registration and not true for the free seminar, where your primary objective *is* winning sales and new clients.)

Despite all the foregoing—do's and don'ts of coverage; materials, general and special; guest speakers; and other embellishments—probably nothing influences an audience more than the personality and delivery of the main presenter. The reaction of the attendees to the speaker has a great effect on how they perceive the materials—their reaction to the entire program, in fact. But it is even more profound in its net effects than that: The presenter creates his or her personal image, partly as a result of audience reaction to the materials and coverage, but far more as a result of audience reaction to the personality and delivery of the presenter. That overall impact can have far more effect than the substance of the presentation. (This potential for creating good leads is what motivates many consultants to appear as guest speakers at others' seminars.)

That is one compelling reason to be the main speaker yourself and to learn how to make a powerful delivery. If you make the delivery well, you will create for yourself a professional image that will surely result in winning new clients and new consulting assignments. That subject—the persona you project and the achievement of a high-quality delivery—is worth at least a brief discussion before closing this chapter.

PERSONA AND DELIVERY

Bear in mind, first of all, that while consulting and seminar presentations are not exactly show business, audience reaction to your style is as much an influence on their opinion of you as is their judgment of the materials and information offered them. There is a great reluctance to think ill of anyone who is likable, and the opposite is equally true: Observers resist admiring someone who "turns them off," even when they do not know just why the latter individual has this effect. So perhaps it is show-biz, at least to the extent that you are on view, that you will inevitably create an impression of one sort or another and that you can and should be in control the image you create.

Obviously, this has a great influence on any judgment an attendee might make as to the desirability of retaining you as a consultant. To be seriously considered for that you must manage to make yourself appear knowledgeable, alert, effective, and easy to work with. The most important word in that sentence, however, is the word *appear*. The attendee will base judgment of you and your qualities on his or her *perception*. And that perception is rarely completely objective. Inevitably, that perception is heavily colored by emotional reactions, by subjective judgment.

What this means is that it is not enough to be totally competent—totally knowledgeable, decisive, imaginative, analytical, creative, and/or otherwise ideal—you must also *project* an *image* of such qualities, while at the same time creating an image of affability and friendliness. Really good presenters do manage to impart such an image, and you can also. Perhaps it's a gift, something that for some "comes naturally," but anyone can learn to project that kind of image from the platform. Adhering faithfully to certain rather simple principles can help you achieve that goal. Following are some starter ideas for doing so. But before embarking on a study of those a caveat:

None of this is intended to suggest that you become "Mr. or Miss Personality" on the platform, smiling incessantly, straining to be humorous, talking down to the audience, dressing extravagantly, and/or otherwise being the TV talk-show host. That is definitely not the objective. The guidelines and suggestions offered here are things you can do in all sincerity, which simply make your presentation appear in its best light.

Visible enthusiasm is perhaps the greatest aid of all. I assume that you do have enthusiasm for your subject, since you have chosen to make a career in that field. However, some individuals are so "laid back" that they *appear* to be bored to death with everything and enthusiastic about nothing. It is, of course, no character defect to be a restrained and undemonstrative individual, but it is definitely a severe handicap in this case. It is important both to display enthusiasm for the subject and to inspire enthusiasm in your audience. Enthusiasm is excitement, and it is contagious; your audience will catch it from you, if it is visible enough. They will see it, feel it, and catch it if, during certain dramatic moments, you pace excitedly, raise your voice, wave your arms. They will catch it from the sparkle in your eyes and from your abrupt shifts from a shout to a hoarse whisper. They will know when a point you are making is an important and dramatic one because your persona and delivery announce it.

A rule in writing fiction is that you if you wish to create an effective mood and make readers *believe*, you do not simply tell the reader that something is the case, that a character is angry, for example; you *show* it by example and description—by having the character smash a fist on the table, or get red in the face and scream. And so you do not simply tell your audience that a given point or bit of information is seminal or of decisive importance; you *show* it by your delivery and the force of your personality in making that delivery. In written presentations you emphasize certain points by underlines, exclamation marks, italics, boldface type, positional significance, wise choice of conjunctions, and other writers' devices; in platform presentations you emphasize by allowing your enthusiasm to take command and exhibit itself unrestrained. You show emphasis by forgetting your inhibitions and abandoning the shield most of us maintain when in the company of and/or communicating with strangers. You show it by your gestures, inflections, facial expressions, and other platform means and devices. These are as much a part of platform delivery as are those devices and techniques used in writing, and you should be the master of them as you should be the master of grammar, spelling, punctuation, rhetoric, and composition generally when you are writing formally.

If you are one of those who is new to and truly nervous about appearing on the platform you will have to make a conscious effort to "psych yourself up" to the task. You can do so by long and careful deliberation and introspection. Bear these following principles and injunctions in mind and think long and hard about them until they are deeply embedded in your consciousness and you have come to truly *believe* in them:

1. You are the expert—the *only* expert—in the room on the subject of your presentation. That is why you are on the platform and the attendees are "sitting at your feet," figuratively, to catch the pearls of knowledge, if not wisdom, from your lips. They begin the session by regarding you with respect, perhaps even some awe, and they are ready and fully prepared to accept you and what you have to say.

2. The attendees accept you as the expert. That is why they have paid substantial fees to spend their time listening to you.

3. Be fully prepared. Do your homework as necessary. Know your subject thoroughly, and speak with obvious confidence in what you say. Remember that you cannot fool an audience for long; if you are not fully prepared—do not truly know your subject—it will show up in subtle ways, and the audience will know it and lose faith in you. The great concert pianist Ignace Paderewski was reported to have said: "If I do not practice for a day, I know it. If I do not practice for two days, my manager knows it. And if I do not practice for three days, my audience knows it."

4. You *owe* these attendees something: You owe them your total effort and dedication both to presenting the promised information and to helping them in every possible way to learn that information. Arousing their own enthusiasm, dramatizing key points in your presentation, and otherwise highlighting those key points with proper emphases is very much a part of getting the information across effectively; it is part of your obligation to the audience.

5. You must therefore forget about your feelings, your inhibitions, your fears, your ego, and yourself generally, and focus totally on what these attendees need to master the subject you have promised to teach.

6. Be careful that you appear confident. If you appear nervous and fearful, an audience is most likely to interpret that as lack of true expertise and competence. Smiling and looking relaxed between shows of great enthusiasm is necessary and important to maintain the mood and sustain the image.

7. Invite and respond freely to questions and comments, but do be careful to avoid being dogmatic or careless with your responses. If you carelessly give an answer that is not true and the audience knows or even suspects that it is a snap judgment or dogmatic response, you will lose their trust. If you are not sure, it is far

better to say something along the lines of, "I would have to check on that to be sure, but I believe...", or even to say flatly that you do not know. If it is a matter that has no absolutes, grant the other person the right to an opinion that differs with yours. Honesty and open-mindedness are necessary to inspire and maintain the image.

If you have any trouble with this—if you are still fearful that you may appear a bit ridiculous when you shout, wave your arms, gesture with your hands, grimace for emphasis, pace excitedly, and otherwise create a *mood*, as well as a personal image—decide to make the supreme sacrifice and do it anyway, *one time only*, as a test.

You will be amazed by the results. You will find yourself applauded, and otherwise rewarded by an appreciative and satisfied audience. You will be reassured and probably never have any further reluctance to throw yourself into the task of making the seminar as productive as possible for your attendees. It will forever change your feelings and attitude toward appearing on the platform.

5 TYPICAL COSTS AND INCOME PROJECTIONS

For the uninitiated, the matter of costs and income appears to be a simple one: Deduct costs from receipts and the result equals income—gross income, at least. In practice it is not that simple. Not at all.

WHAT ARE COSTS?

Seminars cost money in several ways, some of which have been touched on briefly in earlier chapters. In this chapter we will look at costs once again, this time in far greater detail and on an exploratory basis, trying not only to identify all costs, but to understand them and relate them to income and profit. Surprisingly, for those inexperienced in business generally and accounting especially, the matter is not as simple as it appears to be, especially when it includes the entire spectrum of creation, marketing, production, and administration of that product or service that is to be sold.

For purposes of establishing a most basic understanding of costs, their relationships to each other, and their relationships to other matters, it is helpful to recognize that there are different kinds of costs. In this case three general categories can be established first:

1. Development.
2. Marketing.
3. Operating.

These three cost descriptors are phase related. That is, the costs are generally incurred in the order given here, first to develop the product, then to market it, and then to produce it—to make actual presentations of the seminar, that is. But each of these cost classifications is subject to subclassifications, and costs can also be classified and described or characterized in other ways, of which the following are examples.

One-time costs.
Operating costs.
Fixed costs.
Variable costs.
Line-item costs.
Administrative costs.

These characterizations can also be subclassifications. For example, development costs and marketing costs include one-time costs, both for the product (e.g., seminar program and materials) and for the marketing campaign (e.g., brochures and general marketing plans), as well as variable and perhaps other types of costs.

BUT WHEN IS A COST NOT A COST?

If you equate *cost* with *expense*, as the average person is likely to do, you run into another problem in definition. Development costs are not expenses, at least not in the common sense that the cost of development must be recovered immediately from the marketing of the seminar. And here the key word is *immediately*, for the cost of developing the seminar must, indeed, be recovered by marketing, but it can't be done immediately; it must be *amortized*. That is, it must be recovered gradually, rather than immediately, and that can cloud the picture if not carefully designed and fully understood.

Amortization: A Process

To manufacture even a simple device, such as a toaster or blender, the manufacturer invests many thousands of dollars in engineering and testing before the product is ready for marketing. There are meetings, drawings, models, revisions, discussions, and many related activities necessary before a final product is even ready for manufacturing, let alone manufactured in enough quantity to begin marketing it. The manufacturer may thus easily invest $50,000 to create a product that brings in $20 each at wholesale prices. Even if he realizes a $5 net profit on each one sold, he must sell 10,000 of them before he recovers the $50,000 in development costs. However, even then he would not have recovered all the cost because he has also the cost of marketing the item. Suppose, for argument's sake, that it costs $1 each to market the gadget. Now the gross profit is down to $4, and it is necessary to sell 12,500 of the item to recover the costs. (And even that is not all of it, but it suffices for the example.)

There are other problems. The manufacturer is unwilling, for several reasons, including possible problems with stockholders over the figures on the annual report and general business principles, to assign all profits immediately to recovering the cost of development. Instead, the manufacturer will assign some part of the gross profit to recovering that cost gradually—to *amortizing* that cost. He might, for example, assign $1 to amortizing that and take the remaining $3 as gross profit. He would then have to recover the development cost by selling 50,000 units at $20, after which his gross profit on the item would rise to $4. (This is necessarily a much-simplified example, for there are other considerations, but the principle is the same.) And so, on the books, an amortization account is maintained to retire the development cost through those $1 repayments out of sales, just as though a debt were being repaid to another person or organization.

We commonly regard an expense as representing money gone forever, not wasted—expenses may be completely necessary—but expenditures that will not be recovered, except indirectly as overhead or other administrative costs. However, since we do expect to recover development costs through the amortization process, we cannot and should not count the development cost as an expense. Rather, the development cost represents an investment, and in the accounting sense the money was never spent at all, but was converted to another form, representing at least its equivalent value in that other form. In short, the manufacturer has created a $50,000 asset (or perhaps an asset worth a great deal more, representing an immediate profit!) by developing the new product. That $50,000 is now in an "R&D inventory" or some equivalent account (perhaps a "labor inventory") on the books. So while you may tie up your operating capital in developing your seminar program, you must value it as an asset of at least equivalent value, which will produce income and profits for you.

In actuality, you need not treat the investment in this manner if the total amount is small enough. That latter depends on the IRS laws in effect at the moment. When I purchased my first computer I chose to "expense it" by charging it off as an operating expense immediately. I was permitted to do so under the law at the time because the item cost was not in excess of $5,000. It was my choice to treat it in this manner for I had alternatives: I could claim a tax credit or I could establish a depreciation schedule and charge off a portion of the cost each year. (You depreciate property to recover the costs, as far as taxes are concerned, but you usually amortize the costs associated with an item you sell. The two, amortization and depreciation, are quite different things.)

Establishing the Amortization Schedule

The basis for amortization is purely arbitrary. Perhaps your accountant can guide you, but even then the guidance will be based on your own judgments. (Try to remember always that your accountant is, like your lawyer, an advisor; *you* must make the decisions. Therefore, it is essential that you listen carefully and be sure that you fully understand all the implications of what your accountant tells you.) Meanwhile, there are some commonsense principles that ought to apply here, and the first is this: Avoid both extremes, that of trying to amortize the cost too swiftly and that of amortizing it too slowly. There will be tax considerations, which will depend on IRS and local tax regulations that are in force at the time. These will certainly influence your decision, and here you probably truly need your accountant's advice.

You must also consider that the smaller the amount or percentage of gross income assigned to amortize your development cost, the greater your nominal—*taxable*—profit will be. Too, the smaller the amount the longer the payout period will be. That may be an advantage or a disadvantage. Consider, for example, whether the content of your seminar will become obsolete information in some relatively short time, and how that may affect the original investment. If you draw the period out excessively, you may never recover the cost. But even that is not necessarily a disadvantage, tax laws being what they are; it may provide a beneficial write-off. Again, the counsel of your accountant may be decisive.

On the other hand, assigning a large portion of your receipts to amortizing the initial investment may have an opposite effect, retiring the investment too quickly to provide maximum benefits.

In general, you normally would want to amortize the cost in such a manner as to recover the original cost during the useful life of the product. Unless there is some strong incentive to do otherwise, my suggestion is to create an amortization schedule that recovers the original cost over one-half the estimated useful life of the product.

That calls for more than one estimate, of course. You must estimate not only the useful life of the seminar program—how long before you have to abandon it or revise it extensively—but also what income you are likely to be able to realize from it over that period. Those estimates will have their effects on your amortization plan too, and may force you to change your schedule.

IDENTIFYING THOSE INVESTMENT COSTS

Probably the major investment cost for development of the seminar is the cost of your time. You should set it up as a distinct project, keeping track of all costs, including your own time at whatever you believe to be a fair value. There will be other costs, of course, for typing, development of handouts and other materials, travel expenses, postage, telephone calls, and whatever else may have been required to create the program.

The assignment of some of the related costs is arbitrary. The cost of designing and developing a descriptive brochure, for example, can be assigned either to development of the product or to development of the marketing system. My preference would be to establish a separate account for the development of the marketing materials and plan and charge the brochure to that account. You can, however, lump all those costs into one budget for both, if you prefer; there is equal justification for that approach. (Your accountant may have some other ideas.)

In any case, there are development (investment) costs for marketing, whether you lump them in with program development or maintain a separate budget for them. There is the cost of developing the literature, whether that consists of only a brochure or is an entire direct-mail package. There is the cost of research to identify the best mailing lists and/or to develop house lists. (The latter are usually by far the most effective.) And there is the cost of whatever else you must do to develop your seminar program, your marketing plans, and your procedures.

By now we have established the rationale and need for setting up and maintaining records of development costs in such a manner that you get a realistic view of income and profit resulting from the seminar venture. These are presumably one-time costs. But that may not be the case. Unless you are extremely fortunate, the first time or two that you market and present your first seminar you are quite likely to discover that your original designs need some improvement. Things do not work out as perfectly as you thought they would. And so you do some fine-tuning of the program and/or the marketing plans and materials.

It costs money—more money. And it is development money. Fine-tuning the program is a normal development cost, and the books should not be closed on these costs until you have run the marketing and the program at least a time or two and are satisfied with the design. In fact, to recognize and formalize this you should consider the first couple times you run the program as test runs that are themselves part of the development process. Only when you finally freeze those designs can you close the books on the mounting development costs and prepare to amortize and recover those costs.

All of these costs we have been discussing are separate and apart from the operating costs. For example, the cost of developing and designing a brochure or a handout is part of the development costs generally, but the cost of printing and mailing the material is part of the operating costs, although even that can be divided into costs for presenting the seminar and costs for marketing.

MARKETING COSTS

Marketing costs tend to revolve around two principal ones: printing and mailing. Most seminars are sold via mailings of brochures, using rented mailing lists. (Yes, you *rent* these mailing lists for one-time use, and pay the rental fee again if you wish to use the list again.) In time you build lists of your own—"house lists"—but since you normally must mail brochures by the thousands, you usually must turn to commercial list brokers for help in the beginning.

Rental fees for mailing lists vary considerably, from as low as about $35 per 1,000 names to about three times that, with the average roughly about $50–$75 per 1,000 names. Mailing lists are valued according to several factors, such as their age, what/whom they represent demographically, and the demands of the owners of the lists. (Since most lists are rented by brokers, they usually belong to a third party, such as a magazine or mail order firm.)

Postage rates vary too, of course. Most mailings are made via bulk mail, at approximately one-half the first-class postage rate, and many of these are made under the special bulk rates permitted for nonprofit organizations, which are even less.

There are labor costs involved if you do the mailing yourself. Many choose to turn to a commercial mailer, and for large mailings it probably is no more expensive to have it done by a commercial mailer than to do it yourself. And, incidentally, many of the larger commercial mailers offer one-stop service, and can take care of providing the mailing lists and even doing the printing. For a rough average, using today's costs as a benchmark, it will probably cost you from $250 to $300 per 1,000 pieces mailed. But even that figure can vary considerably in either direction, depending on various factors such as the total quantity mailed, the nature of what you are mailing, and the class of postage you use.

That is not all of it; there are other possible marketing costs. You may choose or even be compelled to utilize print, radio, or TV advertising in your marketing. You can assign this expense or part of it to development costs, if you choose to, because the response adds names to your in-house mailing lists. These are a definite asset in more than one way and ought to be valued and carried on your books as such. (Once you build them up adequately, you can rent your own mailing lists to others, either directly or via a list broker, and derive income from them.) That will depend in part on how you advertise, as well as why: Advertising for registrants directly is normally an operating cost, whereas advertising to gather names for your mailing lists is not only a totally different "why," but a different "how" as well; the latter is inquiry advertising, and inquiry advertising is carried out in quite a different way than is advertising for direct sales.

MISCELLANEOUS COSTS AND COST CATEGORIES

The administration and marketing of the seminar program entail many operating expenses, which must be charged against the receipts to the extent that you can identify those costs. There will be clerical costs, for example, for making and keeping records, and it is wise to keep track of these and charge them against the seminar venture as far as it is possible to do so. Of course, some expenses are overhead costs and can't be assigned to specific projects or activities. The rent you pay for your offices, basic telephone service, insurance, and taxes, for example, are among the kinds of costs that you can't segregate. It is for this reason that these and other, similar costs become known as *overhead*. But since it is most definitely in your interests to maintain as low an overhead figure as possible, it is wise to keep track of the costs that you incur directly to operate the seminar venture—to keep those costs from getting into your overhead expense pool and increasing the overhead rate. It is also beneficial if you can keep those costs segregated into operating costs both for marketing the seminar and for presenting the seminar. That is because the chief reason for accounting is to provide useful information for management (and not to please the IRS!) The more detailed the accounting information feedback you get the more intelligently and effectively you can manage the enterprise. You want to know in as much detail as possible where and what all the cost centers are—what everything costs—and what the results of cost expenditures are. Ergo, the more you segregate and identify costs, the better able you are to determine what activities pay out best.

Certain costs, such as printing, postage, and advertising of specific programs, are variable because they are incurred only when and to the extent that you choose. Rent, basic telephone service, and insurance are among those costs that are usually fixed. It is certainly useful to think of costs in these terms, because they affect your management decisions.

OVERHEAD COSTS AND RATES

Unfortunately, there appears to be a great deal of confusion over what overhead really is. But to discuss that intelligently it is first necessary to point to two other terms that are significant. They are *direct* costs and *indirect* costs.

Direct Costs

Direct costs are those specific and precise costs you incur for an activity and which would not have been incurred otherwise. Office rent is not one of those costs, for example, because you will have the office rent to pay whether you do or do not run seminars. Printing a seminar brochure is another matter; it is a direct seminar cost. In fact, it is a direct seminar-marketing cost.

General telephone service is not a direct cost. But toll calls made in behalf of or for a given activity are a direct cost *if you record and keep track of them*, which I suggest you do.

Ultimately, you should know the total of direct costs for each seminar presentation and for its marketing as well. The price you establish for attending your seminar must take these costs into account, for you must recover these costs if the venture is to be profitable.

Indirect Costs

All other costs, costs you incur but cannot assign specifically to any given activity, are indirect costs. You must recover these too, but you have a somewhat different problem here because you don't know precisely how much overhead cost should be charged to the seminar. You therefore must use some other means for charging off the overhead and recovering it.

Establishing an Overhead Rate

To recover those indirect costs, most of which are known as *overhead*, your accountant will establish an overhead *rate* for you. That is a percentage of direct costs. In some cases it may be a percentage of direct labor costs, in others of all direct costs, depending on whatever the accounting policy is. But in a consulting practice, which is usually "labor intensive," the usual practice is to charge it as a percentage of direct labor. For example, suppose that during the year you incurred $50,000 for labor cost on billable projects. And, during that year, you also incurred $30,000 in other, indirect costs—rent, taxes, insurance, postage, telephone service, and other such items. Your overhead rate is calculated

$$30,000/50,000 = 0.60 = 60 \text{ percent}$$

That means that the burden for recovering the indirect costs is distributed equally on all activities that are part of your practice by adding that 60 percent figure to all projects when calculating their cost. That is, if you calculate that you invested $10,000 of labor in designing a seminar program, you add 60 percent of $10,000 to the figure to get a $16,000 subtotal. Then you add any other direct expenses to get a final total.

Obviously, that overhead rate is going to vary, possibly being different each year. With care you can manage to keep it as low as possible. And that will help you in more than one way. For one thing, it will help you to be maximally competitive in your pricing, since that overhead rate has a pronounced effect on your quotations. For example, suppose that a prospective client asks you to furnish a quotation for presenting a seminar. Let us suppose that you have decided that you must earn $750 for your own services—must pay yourself that much, that is. And let us suppose further that you have gotten into the habit of lumping all "miscellaneous" costs together as overhead items, so that you now have a working overhead of 125 percent. (That is not an unusually high overhead under the stated circumstances.) You will therefore not charge the client separately for handout materials and other miscellaneous items, but will include all those miscellaneous items under your direct labor, overhead, and profit—you expect to earn 15 percent profit—so that the final figures tote up about as follows:

Direct labor:		$750.00
Overhead @ 125%:		937.50
	Subtotal:	1,687.50
Profit @ 15%:		253.13
	Grand total:	$1,940.63

On the other hand, suppose you keep your overhead rate to about one-half that—say 65 percent—by managing things carefully and going to the trouble of identifying all possible direct costs. When that request for a quotation comes in you estimate that you will need to provide a small fund of about $150 for miscellaneous direct costs—toll calls, postage, copying, and other such items. So your estimate now takes the following shape:

Direct labor:		$750.00
Overhead @ 65%:		487.50
Other direct costs:		150.00
	Subtotal:	1,387.50
Profit @ 15%:		208.13
	Grand total:	$1,595.63

The figures speak for themselves, of course; a lower overhead means a more competitive position, and that alone is reason enough to strive for a lower overhead rate.

Typical Overhead Rates

For service businesses (i.e., labor-intensive businesses), such as consulting, typical overhead rates range from lows of approximately 40 percent to highs of about 150 percent. It is usually difficult to live with a rate as low as 40 percent, however, since there is virtually no margin for error. And rates of over 100 percent are also hard to live with because they tend to become burdensome and an obstacle to effective marketing. Probably 65–85 percent is a true middle-road overhead rate for consulting practices, and I would recommend that you work for an overhead rate in this bracket.

It is also possible to establish separate ledgers and rates for different activities—to set up seminars as a department or division of your practice. It is an additional expense, of course, but it may prove to be in your interest to consider it. It is sometimes a solution for the entrepreneur who happens to have an unavoidably high overhead rate in one department or division. In such cases that high overhead, if used as the universal overhead for the entire organization, acts as a drag on other departments and activities.

A Few Typical Costs

Costs for a hotel meeting room vary widely, according to the size of the room, the day of the week, the season of the year, the location of the hotel, the general cost structure in the area, and what's "in it" for the hotel. That is, the seminar producer who reserves a large block of rooms for attendees can often get a much reduced room rental rate, and may often even get the meeting room at no cost! Certainly you should bargain with the hotel, for most are quite flexible, and some have quite surprising standards, as the following experience of my own will illustrate.

Of course you must reserve your meeting room at least six to eight weeks in advance to allow time for printing announcements, mailing them out, and registering attendees. Ordinarily I plan a seminar of that kind at least 60 days ahead, and I generally prefer 90 days. Usually there is no difficulty; most hotels are delighted to have meeting rooms booked up months ahead. However, on one occasion I called a hotel in Virginia and attempted to reserve a meeting room 60 days ahead. To my utter surprise I was refused quite bluntly. When I asked why, I was told quite frankly that the hotel management preferred to leave rooms open for near-last-minute reservations for social occasions because they could demand a much larger room-rental fee than for a seminar! Needless to say, I have never done any kind of business with that hotel since.

I am happy to say that that was some kind of aberration; I have never had another experience even remotely resembling that one. However, some hotels may charge more on a weekend than they would during the week, whereas in other hotels the opposite condition will prevail. That depends primarily on the location of the hotel. A hotel in the business district in center city tends to have little action on weekends, and so is eager to rent rooms for whatever they can get on a weekend. But a hotel in a suburban area has the opposite situation, and so will ask a larger figure for a Saturday or Sunday rental than for a weekday. (But most will rent a room for a seminar at whatever their rates are!) Also, hotels in or near vacation areas usually have much higher "in season" rates than they do the rest of the year.

Of course, rates vary in different areas of the country, and a meeting room in a New York City hotel will obviously cost a great deal more than in Dubuque, Iowa. And a room in a large and expensive hotel will cost more than one in a modest hotel.

In any case, the room rental is generally not a significant cost factor in the overall operating cost. In general, for a small meeting room, adequate for seating perhaps 35–50 people, expect to pay anywhere from $40 to $100 a day. You will probably pay about $15–$20 per gallon for coffee. Strangely enough, it has been my experience that when I paid high room rentals the amenities were modestly priced, and the reverse was also true.

Normally there is no additional cost for a blackboard and lectern; most hotels can supply these, and most appear to have built-in public address systems, should you need one. But you usually do have to pay rental fees for projectors and other equipment, and most hotels (in my experience) simply order these from a local supplier.

People coming from out of town usually prefer to stay at the hotel where the seminar is being held, and you should discuss this with the hotel management. You probably will be (and probably should be) reluctant to guarantee anything to the hotel, at least until you have run your seminars long enough to feel some confidence in your ability to estimate the number of out-of-town attendees. (However, as a service to advance registrants, you should offer to make their hotel room registrations for them.)

Should you take your seminar on the road to several different cities, you can arrange to ship your materials ahead to be stored and held at each hotel. There should be no extra charge by the hotel for this little service. Caution: Things do go wrong (Murphy's Law never takes a holiday!), and it is wise to check up carefully on such arrangements to be sure that they have been carried out properly. There is nothing quite as discouraging as arriving for your seminar and finding that your materials are somewhere in limbo.

REGISTRATION FEES AND INCOME PROJECTIONS

Registration fees for most seminars today range from lows of about $95 per day to highs of $300 per day. In general, however, those lower fees are usually for seminars held on subjects that are not really highly specialized or "advanced." Such low-priced seminars tend to include seminars on office skills, writing, work procedures, and other rather mundane activities. On the other hand, the higher fees are generally charged for attendance at seminars dealing with highly technological and high-level subjects, such as utilization of the latest and most complex computer programs, engineering subjects, financial management in large corporations, and investments. But even in this latter class of seminars, registration fees in excess of $200 a day are, at the time of this writing, much more the exception than the rule. In fact, $200 per day appears to be close to the average for seminars of this type.

To consider the net effect of all this and give you an appreciation of possible results of various approaches, let us hypothesize a case or two, as it might apply to you or any other independent consultant operating on a modest budget.

Case Number 1

Let us assume, for this case, that you are a busy consultant who chooses to utilize outside help for the detail work, while you do the master planning of the program. Your costs are likely to mount up along the following lines:

Program Development

Your own labor, 40 hours @ $100/hour:	$4,000.00
Support services–typing,illustrating, etc.:	2,500.00
Vendor support:	500.00
Total Marketing Plan investment:	$7,000.00

Marketing Plan Development

Marketing consultant:	$2,000.00
Inquiry advertising:	750.00
Compiling of responses:	300.00
Total Marketing Plan investment:	$3,050.00
TOTAL FRONT-END INVESTMENT:	$10,050.00

You decide that you can run that program essentially unchanged (for purposes of illustration we will assume that these figures include testing and revision costs) for four years, presenting it 12 times a year. That means that you must recover the costs in 24 payments (using the formula of amortization over one-half the estimated shelf-life), which amounts to $418.75 per presentation. That is, each seminar presentation has an advance cost of $418.75 added to all other costs.

The cost of the seminar can be estimated along the following lines:

Amortization payment:	$418.75
Printed materials:	200.00
Room rental and amenities:	150.00
Mailing-list rentals:	650.00
Travel and related expenses (averaging between local out-of-town presentations):	350.00
General administrative expenses:	200.00
Your presentation fee:	1,000.00
Total:	$2,968.75

You must take in that amount to pay all expenses, including your own fee. If you pro rate that across an estimated 25 attendees you find that you must charge a registration fee of at least $118.75 to pay all expenses. But even that entails some risks, for although an estimate of 25 attendees appears to be a modest one, you will find that while one mailing will produce 50 or 60 attendees, another will produce only 10 or 15. And you should be aware that in almost every session you will get a certain number of "no shows," individuals who fail to appear, so that even when you ask for and get advance registrations you cannot depend totally on those numbers.

Consider the necessary minimum fees for the following estimated total registrations. (These numbers are rounded off to the nearest dollar and reflect only what is necessary to recover all costs.)

No. of Attendees	Minimum Registration Fee Necessary (per day)
10	$297
15	198
20	148
25	119
30	99
35	85
40	74
45	66
50	59

You can see that a well-attended seminar can be quite profitable, even at the relatively low figure of $95 per registration per day. However, the number of attendees is normally a direct function and result of the effectiveness of your marketing, particularly the size of the mailing. For the typical modest mailing of 5,000 pieces you ought not expect large numbers of attendees. Those who specialize in seminars as a sole activity and therefore present many more sessions per year than you are likely to undertake are likely to mail out as many as 50,000–100,000 brochures, announcing seminar sessions in a half-dozen cities. Of course, that calls for a relatively large investment, easily $20,000 or more, for the marketing effort alone.

One seminar producer with whom I work—he handles everything but the actual presentation, and pays me a fixed fee to do that—operates on the modest scale that is probably typical of the independent consultant. He charges fees of about $125, and requires an absolute minimum of 20 attendees to realize even a small profit. When a mailing fails to produce that many registrants for any session he simply cancels the session. He must then write off all the costs of the mailing and room-rental—paid in advance—as a net loss. But it is less of a loss than he would experience by continuing, for he would then have to meet the cost of my fee plus some incidental expenses such as refreshments and equipment rentals.

Referring to the chart again, you can see that on the basis of the costs projected here you would have to attract at least 35 registrations to make your seminar a success at $95 per head, and even that would leave you a rather thin margin between profit and loss.

There are three things you can do about this. You can cut the costs by doing more of the work yourself, you can charge the program less for your own services—pay yourself less, that is—and you can charge more than $95 for registration. My suggestion is to do all three in the early period, when you are feeling your way and trying to establish a pattern and a modus operandi. Time enough later to experiment with higher prices, greater costs, and less of a burden on yourself. But let us now consider a second case.

Case Number 2

Here is what happens to costs when you charge yourself a "wholesale" rate and do more of the work yourself:

Program Development

Your own labor, 60 hours @ $70/hour:	$4,500.00
Support services—typing, illustrating, etc.:	200.00
Vendor support:	100.00
Total Program investment:	$4,800.00

Marketing Plan Development

Your own labor, 16 hours @ $70/hour:	$1,200.00
Inquiry advertising:	750.00
Compiling of responses:	300.00
Total Marketing Plan investment:	$2,250.00
TOTAL FRONT-END INVESTMENT:	$7,050.00

Using the same amortization formula, the payments are $293.75 in this case, and the total of expenses to be recovered undergoes considerable revision. The cost of the seminar for the second case can be estimated along the following lines:

Amortization payment:	$293.75
Printed materials:	200.00
Room rental and amenities:	150.00
Mailing-list rentals:	650.00
Travel and related expenses (averaging between local out-of-town presentations):	350.00
General administrative expenses:	200.00
Your presentation fee:	750.00
Total:	$2,968.75

Let us now consider what happens to the table of number of attendees versus registration fees required under these changed conditions:

No. of Attendees	Minimum Registration Fee Necessary (per day)
10	$259
15	173
20	130
25	104
30	86
35	74
40	65
45	58
50	52

You can see that even under these latter conditions there is not a great deal of margin for error if you fail to charge enough for attendance: It becomes quite easy to lose money on the venture. But this does not mean that seminars are more risky than are other entrepreneurial ventures; far from it, properly managed seminars are relatively risk-free, and one of the ways to reduce the risks is to present the seminar on a custom basis as a consulting service.

The Custom Seminar

There are two sides to every matter, and usually they are opposites, so that while one side is a liability the other is an asset. The rising cost of attendance is a liability that has tended to depress the open-registration seminar business a bit. But at the same time it has encouraged organizations to sponsor custom, in-house seminars, which are much less costly on a per capita basis. Where an organization may easily spend $2,000 to send two or three people off to an open-registration seminar somewhere, it is often possible to bring that seminar in-house to present to a dozen or more attendees for approximately the same cost. So more and more organizations are bringing those seminars in-house.

It is cost that drives this business. One of the lessons that I learned early on in the training business—and make no mistake about it, seminars are part of the training industry—was that, totally unlike the government, few private-sector organizations are willing to pay for custom development. Most organizations assign a relatively low priority to training needs, as far as budgets are concerned. They are convinced, apparently, that suitable training materials and services are or should be available "off the shelf." It was a lesson I had to relearn.

Rather soon after I began to offer open-registration seminars on marketing to the government generally and proposal writing especially, I began to get inquiries and requests to quote prices on presenting my seminars on a custom, in-house basis. Early requests came from large and successful companies.

I forgot the lessons of earlier years and prepared quotations that included full customization of my seminar program for each prospective client organization. The result was dead silence in response to my quotations. Nor was the problem really the prices I quoted, for my prices were still modest ones. The problem was that my quotation described full customization, and that frightened the prospects: They reacted almost automatically and with immediate hostility to the very idea of paying for a customized program.

I soon realized that I had committed a tactical blunder, and I began to mend my ways. I decided that I would not revise my program for custom presentations, except spontaneously. Instead, I asked for information about the organization, including copies of their relevant literature, and "customized" my standard seminar program as I spoke from the client's own platform!

From that point on I succeeded in closing virtually every prospect who expressed serious interest in having an in-house seminar program. In fact, several large organizations had me return several times to present my program to a different department or division of their corporation, while some assembled representatives from different companies of the corporation to attend my seminar sessions.

At first I charged these clients my standard daily consulting fees (plus expenses, of course, where appropriate). But I soon learned that I was well below the market, even for those earlier days, and I ultimately doubled my fee for custom seminars. I experienced no problem in doing so, as long as I did not alarm the client with elaborate explanations of the cost structure.

(There are occasional exceptions. One very large multidivisional corporation requested a formal proposal, for example, very much as government agencies do. It appeared obvious to me that they were motivated by their experience with federal agencies, and so I responded to them with a fairly elaborate formal proposal as I would to a federal agency, quoting a substantial five-figure sum for a full-blown, custom-designed seminar program.)

Of course, you do not have special preparation and development costs in such cases as these. In my own case I furnish a single reproducible copy of a copyrighted seminar manual I wrote a few years ago, and grant the client the right to reproduce as many copies as are needed for the seminar. I charge the client a single fee plus expenses. The fee includes my profit markup, of course. The seminar is thus a totally risk-free venture.

It is difficult, perhaps impossible, to furnish specific standards or even clear guidelines for pricing the custom, in-house seminar. There are many individuals who can command $5,000 and even more for a full-day's presentation, due largely to the reputation they have built in their fields. On the other hand, the unknown presenter is not likely to command that figure.

I believe that as an individual you must feel your way, beginning modestly and, as your reputation grows, growing with it. However, it is apparent that clients do base their opinion at least in part on price, and are likely to be swayed considerably by how you value yourself. I doubt that any client can get or would want a seminar session in which the presenter was willing to appear for less than $1,000 per day. I therefore suggest using that as a starting figure for offering your seminar as a custom, in-house presentation.

6 MARKETING THE SEMINAR

Cynical as it may seem at first glance,
quality and value are never absolutes and
never as important as *perceived* quality
and value. But marketing deals primarily
with perceptions. They are the basis
on which all sales are made.

IS THERE NO JUSTICE?

Let us hypothesize a case: You are going to offer a seminar on your favorite subject: management. You are a true expert, you have had lots of experience training others in the fine art of management, and you know how to put an effective program together and how to present it. You have an excellent seminar manual, terrific handouts, superb presentation aids, and several marvelous guest speakers, all widely recognized authorities on the subject. You have also a handsome luncheon with a prominent official as speaker. And to top off all this magnificence you have managed to offer this outstanding program at a most modest price. So yours is far and away the finest seminar on the subject being offered by anyone. Who could want more?

There is only one, small problem: Your marketing leaves something to be desired. Your brochures are quite ordinary—*pedestrian*, some might call them—and your mailing is to a somewhat indifferent set of lists you rented, relying entirely on the broker's representations and advice.

You do not have the field to yourself. You have one immediate competitor. He presents a seminar on management that is acceptable, although mediocre compared with your own offering. He has nothing very new or different to say about the subject and a rather ordinary program overall. But, on the other hand, he has a terrific marketing program. His brochure sparkles, he has worked hard at getting the most appropriate mailing lists and has also his own house lists. And he also pursues several ancillary promotions, including several effective PR initiatives.

Obviously he is going to outsell you by far, despite the fact that his program is inferior to your own, and despite the fact that your program costs attendees less and represents a much greater value from every conceivable viewpoint. Those who attend his session in preference to attending yours are much the poorer for it, but they will never know that.

It doesn't seem fair. You offer great deal more for less money and yet your competitor succeeds where you fail. Is there no justice?

The harsh truth is that justice is, indeed, served here; your rival deserves to succeed, and you deserve to fail. Your high-quality program does no one any good because you failed to persuade people to attend it—you failed, that is, to *educate* prospects in the advantages of your own offering. On the other hand, the people get some good out of the other program because they did attend it.

Only rarely do prospects recognize quality without having it pointed out, explained, and *sold* to them. You must help prospects understand why they need your program or why they need it in preference to other, competitive programs. That is as much a part of the service you render as is the content and delivery of the program itself. Modern marketing is itself a consulting function, helping prospects solve their problems, showing people how to satisfy their needs through the services or products you offer. Failing to market properly is letting your prospects down and expecting them to sell themselves. Far too many entrepreneurs expect prospects to be their own analysts, to be discriminating buyers who will study rival offerings and analyze them to choose the best one. But whether prospects can or cannot analyze your offering is not the point; some of them can and some cannot, but you may be sure that few will. They expect you to provide the information, to explain why your offering is better than others' and why they should choose yours.

In fact, doing that is selling. But selling is part of marketing, the final act of marketing. If selling is getting orders, then marketing is deciding what orders to pursue and win, and what steps are necessary to make the sales possible. To understand sales properly it is necessary to first understand marketing, perhaps not in the academic tradition of philosophical discourse, demographic studies, ruminations on psychology, and excursions in economic theory, but in a succinct and practical overview of key essentials, expressed in the simplest language possible.

WHAT IS MARKETING?

In a sense marketing is already defined in the earlier statements 1) deciding what orders (sales) to pursue and win, and 2) doing everything necessary and preparatory to making the successful sales efforts. That says everything, and yet it says nothing because it does not tell you what to *do* to market successfully.

The objective of marketing is sales: persuading your prospective buyers to accept and buy your product or service. And yet, despite the tendency of many to confuse the two terms and use them as synonyms, marketing and sales are not the same, and the two terms do not mean the same thing. At least for our purposes here *sales* and *selling* are the functions of getting orders from buyers, whereas *marketing* includes many steps that are preliminary to winning orders, including the following major steps:

1. Deciding what you are selling—even *what business you are in.*
2. Deciding to whom you will sell—identifying your prospects.
3. Planning and preparing the system for *reaching* those prospects with your offer—making the presentation(s).

It is reasonable to regard *sales* as the final act of marketing, which is what leads to the tendency to confuse the two terms and use them interchangeably. However, for purposes of our discussion it is helpful to keep the two separated, and the discussions that follow should make the reasons for this understandable.

WHAT ARE YOU SELLING?

The question of what you are selling may appear to be a throwaway question, since you are obviously selling seminar registrations. Or are you? Does the question bear closer examination and, if so, does that affect the answer? Let us explore that.

The first response to the question is another question: What does the prospect wish to buy? In this case, that is, does the prospect wish to buy a seminar registration?

WHAT DO PROSPECTS WANT TO BUY?

Put this in personal terms and engage in a bit of introspection. Think back to the last time you yourself paid for and attended a seminar. Or if that is inappropriate, think back to the last time you bought a periodical or a book. Why did you buy it? What was your motivation? What did you expect to gain from it?

Perhaps you bought it to help pass the time on a long trip. Or it may have been a book that you thought might help you in your career or business. Or perhaps one that had received lots of publicity and so aroused your desire to read it as pure entertainment. Or perhaps it offered what appeared to be interesting information about a hobby of yours.

There are many reasons you may have bought that book or periodical. The question here really revolves around whether the seller was selling the same thing you were buying, for you were not buying a book or magazine, were you? Were you not buying something to divert you and help pass the time? Information to help you professionally? Something to satisfy your curiosity? New ideas about an avocation? Or whatever else the publication would *do* for you?

The point is that neither you nor anyone else really parts with money and/or valuable time for the physical object or the service per se, but only for the resulting benefit. Therefore, to sell with maximum effectiveness, you must sell the benefit, not the product or service itself. In short, you must sell what the prospect wants to buy. Unfortunately, however, it requires a good bit of hard thought to do this. Typically, sellers are trying to sell high-quality kitchen appliances when prospects want to buy admiration and high praise for their prowess as cooks, well-made garments when prospects want the envy of less well-dressed friends, quality when prospects want convenience, style when prospects want prestige.

What Seminar Titles Offer

Following are several seminar titles, as they are headlined on the front page of their announcement brochures. Presumably they reflect what the seminar producers are selling. But are they what most prospects are likely to want to buy? Think about this as you study the titles and think too about how you might change them to reflect more accurately the benefits derived from the seminar.

"How to Buy Printing and Related Services"
"How to Be an Assertive Manager"
"Analyzing and Improving Direct Mail"
"Advanced Supervision Skills"
"How to Get Things Done"
"How to Write & Design Sales Literature"

The first of these might appeal to someone who has no experience in buying printing and related services and who is now confronted by a need to do so. In fact, the title itself suggests that the seminar is for the neophyte. It would be entirely reasonable to infer that meaning, and those with at least basic knowledge or experience would be unlikely to have their attention captured by this headline.

Yet the body copy makes it quite clear, under a separate box headed "Who Should Attend," that the producer thinks the seminar valuable to everyone and anyone buying printing and related services, as well as a number of others in related occupations.

The headlined seminar title, therefore, misses the boat because the author of that title failed to ask *why* the prospect ought to register and attend the seminar. What should be the motivational argument reflected in the title and headline? What will be the direct benefit to the prospect, especially he or she is not a complete stranger to buying printing and related services?

How would you change this title to present the motivation—an *argument* for attending the seminar?   Consider the following four possibilities and decide which, in your opinion, would be the most compelling and most likely to induce prospects to register:

1. "How to Become an Expert Buyer of Printing and Related Services"
2. "How to Save Money on Printing and Related Services"
3. "How to Get the Best Prices on Printing and Related Services"
4. "How to Become a Professional Buyer of Printing and Related Services"

In fact, these four suggested titles reflect only two motivational arguments, one focused specifically on becoming more expert or professional, and the other on saving money.

The Motivation Versus the Prospect

Think of yourself as a prospect in weighing the two alternative headline ideas. Unfortunately, the question now arises as to your interests. Are you a company purchasing agent who buys printing occasionally? An individual who wants to be trained as a buyer? An entrepreneur who buys printing increasingly? An executive who is increasingly dismayed by the size of the printing bills coming in?

In short, which is the more appealing idea to you, saving money on printing or becoming an expert in the activity? That obviously depends on who you are as a prospect. It depends on whether you are paying to attend personally and improve your own skills or whether you are paying for someone else to attend and save the organization money. (Or, perhaps, whether you are an independent small businessperson who does your own buying of printing.)

By now it should have become obvious that you cannot separate the first two items listed earlier—what you will sell and to whom you will sell it. They are interdependent. On the one hand, if you have decided what you wish to sell, you must decide who are the most logical and most promising prospects. But then you must decide what will most motivate them—what they will most *want*—for you must sell what they wish to buy.

In fact, you will find an interdependency among all three of those items listed earlier, the third being your planned method for reaching the prospects and laying your offer before them. When we discuss that shortly you will see why that is also linked to the first two items. But in the meantime let us consider the interdependency of what you are selling and to whom you plan to sell it.

WHO ARE THE TRUE PROSPECTS?

Those who offer seminars often tend to assume that their marketing appeal ought to be to prospective attendees. That is one reason so many seminar brochures are relatively ineffective. The individual who must be sold as the *primary* prospect is the one who is *paying* for the registration. And in the majority of cases most of the registrations are paid for by organizations who send employees to learn skills beneficial to the organization. The individual might wish to add to his or her personal skills as a buyer of printing, might wish to go because the subject appears interesting, might be looking forward to a welcome break in a boring job, or might have some other personal reason for attending. The employer, however, has different motivations, and is willing to spend the money to send the employee only if there is good reason to believe that the organization will benefit. For that reason the proper emphasis in the seminar title and headline must address the employer's interest. And few considerations motivate business proprietors more than the prospect of saving money, increasing sales, and adding to profits.

Even so, it is necessary to motivate the employee who is to attend the seminar too, for in most cases it is he or she who suggests it, often making a formal request to do so. Ergo the need to motivate both individuals, the prospective attendee and the individual who must approve and authorize the attendance. For that reason, it is sensible to combine the two motivators and to place them both "up front," but to give the headline to the real buyer, and the subhead or blurb to the attendee, to wit:

SAVE MONEY ON PRINTING AND RELATED SERVICES
You can become an expert. Learn all the tricks of the trade.

Of course, there are many cases where the buyer and the attendee are one and the same. In my own seminars there are often attendees from government agencies and from some of the largest corporations in America, but there are also self-employed individuals and entrepreneurs who must be treated both as buyers and attendees.

This raises an interesting sidelight that is a marketing consideration of another kind: Many executives, especially those running their own small companies, are reluctant to be away from their businesses for two or three days. If your seminars are aimed at this kind of prospect, you may be wise to confine your seminars to one-day sessions. I experimented with several approaches vis-a-vis seminars of one, two, and three days, and became convinced that for me the one-day session was the most satisfactory.

In any case, you can see that defining what you propose to sell and identifying the prospects to whom you plan to sell are not unrelated questions. If you start with a fixed idea about your seminar content and design, you must think out who the proper prospects are to be. On the other hand, if you start out with a fixed idea of who your best prospects are, you will have to develop a design and content package suitable to them.

In fact, developing a seminar is usually an iterative process, as sketched below.

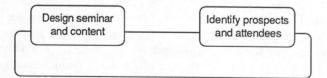

Initial designs and specifications are necessarily tentative ones that must be modified through successive iterations until they are a suitable match with each other, with your objectives, with your capabilities, and with your resources.

But even that is not all of it. There is at least one other major consideration that is related to the first two. It is the matter of reaching your prospects and laying your offer before them. You must not take this part of the marketing task for granted (as too many do); it may turn out to be the most difficult and most critical part of the entire venture. In fact, quite often this proves to be the linchpin upon which the seminar success depends.

This third element must be factored into that iterative loop, for it is linked firmly to the first two elements:

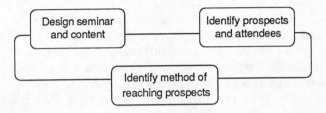

REACHING PROSPECTS

There are not a great many options available for reaching prospects for open registration seminars. Advertising announcements are a must here, and the two main media available for that advertising are print and direct mail.

Pros and Cons of Print Advertising

There are two main problems with print media for advertising seminars. One is that, with the exception of those for daily newspapers, advertising deadlines are generally three or more months ahead of the month of publication. It is difficult to plan seminars that far ahead, especially since tentative early dates often change before they are finalized. You would probably have to plan three to five months ahead, and if you wish to conduct a half-dozen seminar presentations in as many cities, you would be likely to find the coordination and scheduling problems most difficult to work out.

The other problem is that the cost of space, even in daily newspapers, is so high that it is impractical to try to buy enough space to do the selling job and yet not overload the seminar cost burden. The cost of four to six 8-1/2 × 11-inch pages (the typical seminar-brochure size) in a newspaper, for example, would be prohibitive. It would be well over 100 column-inches and could cost you anywhere from $25 to $90 per column inch (depending on circulation figures, primarily) for each paper. We are talking about an advertising budget of well over $2,500 because you would have to advertise in a newspaper in *each city* where you planned to present your seminar.

There are other problems, and one is that newspaper print advertising does not really reach everyone you want to reach: Targeting prospects is most difficult there because newspaper advertising scatters the message to millions of readers in the hope of reaching a few potential buyers.

There is also the problem that newspaper advertising normally reaches only the immediate metropolitan area in which it is circulated. Even those with mail-order editions do not reach great numbers outside their metropolitan area, with the possible exception of *The Wall Street Journal* and *The New York Times*.

On the other hand there are a few advantages: One is that there is a relatively light burden on you once you have developed your advertising copy and placed your order for it to run. The newspaper does the rest. Another advantage is that you do not have to search out or develop mailing lists. Again, the workload is lighter. Still another is that the newspaper does, after all, reach a far greater number of people overall than you could reach with direct mail. And, finally, the newspaper will reach at least some of those for whom you could not have gotten mailing lists in any case.

The Pros and Cons of Direct Mail

Judging by the number of seminar brochures I find in my mailbox and the frequency with which they appear there (as well as the infrequency of media and other print advertising for seminars), I must conclude that direct mail is by far the favored and most widely practiced method. And it is understandable that this is so for several reasons:

1. You can target your prospects with direct mail by using the right mailing lists. Instead of the tiny fraction of the newspaper readers who might be suitable prospects for you, the majority of the direct-mail recipients are good prospects.

2. Since you can mail up to five 8-1/2 × 11-inch sheets—e.g., a brochure of 10 pages that size—for 22 cents (and even less in bulk mail), you can aford enough space to *do the selling job* when using direct mail.

3. You can, through proper monitoring and record keeping, build mailing lists of ever-improving quality, saving some money but, much more importantly, getting an increasingly better response from your mailings.

4. You can use those mailing lists to bring other benefits to your enterprise.

There are cons too, of course. Unless you vend the work out, you are going to have a lot to do. There is labor, a great deal of it, in mailing out thousands of brochures. There is labor in monitoring, tracking, keeping records, and analyzing those records so that you know exactly what is happening and what to do in the future. (There is some of this when you use print advertising too, but not as much.)

There is always a problem in getting suitable mailing lists. With due respect to the list brokers, who do a good job overall, their approach depends almost entirely on probability statistics. This means that results accrue dependably and predictably only from very large mailings. For example, you might garner 1,500 paid registrations from a mailing of 250,000 pieces, a response of 0.6 percent. But since 250,000 is far too large a mailing for you and you are more modest in your expectations and demands, you decide to mail only 5,000 announcements and settle for 30 paid registrations.

Unfortunately, the probability statistics do not work that way since the ratio is not linear: What works for 250,000 mailed announcements is one thing, and what works for 5,000 is another. You may very well get only five or ten responses to a mailing of 5,000 pieces, especially if you rely on the typical rented mailing lists.

THE CHOICE IS NOT ALWAYS YOURS

In a very practical sense, the choice is often not yours; other considerations than your preference dictate the choice. If your seminar addresses a personal concern of individuals—a seminar on losing weight, giving up cigarettes, or starting a small business, for example—you are almost compelled to turn to newspaper advertising because you will have difficulty finding suitable mailing lists. Remember that while a Chicago employer might send an employee to New York or San Francisco for a seminar, individuals paying for their own registrations are far less likely to undertake the cost of travel and lodging. This means that you must rely almost entirely on the local population. Even if you could rent the subscription list of *Income Opportunities* or some similar publication, only the names and addresses of those in your local area would be of great value to you.

For that reason, those offering seminars to individuals paying their own way tend to use newspaper advertising. They encourage prospects to arrive and register at the door, although they also often urge readers to register in advance to assure themselves of a place at the seminar.

Some seminar producers have used local radio commercials to announce their offerings and invite listeners to call in for more information and to register. (So far, TV appears to be too costly a medium for this, except possibly for cable TV.)

Despite the arguments that have been offered—and they were offered in all sincerity and on the basis of practical experience—none of these observations are absolutes. Each represents an extreme of one sort or another, and there are viable positions between the extremes in most cases. For example, print advertising and direct mail are not necessarily in opposition to each other or mutually exclusive; they can sometimes be wedded to achieve a useful and profitable result. The most appropriate and probably most effective way to do this is to use inquiry advertising.

INQUIRY ADVERTISING

The problem of high cost in print advertising was one issue discussed earlier, as was the problem of finding suitable mailing lists when the prospects are individuals who would normally have to pay for their own registration and incidental expenses at a seminar. Effective inquiry advertising can solve both problems by helping you build your own house lists, while not imposing a great burden of cost for advertising. (Normally, unless you can mount a relatively massive effort, it takes time to build mailing lists, even by this method, so you may wish to combine this with rented lists in the beginning.)

The long-range goal of inquiry advertising is to develop sales leads for subsequent follow up. In this case the goal is to develop a mailing list for follow-up by direct mail. When properly done, the resulting mailing lists are usually far better—produce at a more efficient rate of response—than the list you would rent from a broker because they are tailored to your needs.

Where to Run Inquiry Advertisements

For every "general interest" periodical you see on a newsstand, there many more circulated on a limited scale. Every profession, trade, industry, business, vocation, and avocation has its own periodicals, referred to as "business magazines" or "trade journals." Many of these have official circulation figures of only 25,000 or thereabouts, although there are some with much greater circulation than that, but they offer you the advantage that through them you can reach a closely targeted reader group. That is a very important factor in inquiry advertising and list building. The more closely you can target your prospects the greater the rate of response you can expect.

How to Run Inquiry Advertising

Inquiry advertising is relatively inexpensive because what you are "selling" costs the respondent nothing, other than a postage stamp or telephone call. Therefore, the advertisement does not have to be large and costly. In fact, many entrepreneurs use inexpensive classified advertisements to draw inquiries and build mailing lists. Here are a few examples of such notices, taken from recent periodicals. (Names and addresses were given in the advertisements, of course.)

1. *In a magazine for writers:*
   Self-publishers earn big money! Writing and selling books by mail is big money. Free information.
   Senior editor evaluates, helps. Prompt, inexpensive. Free facts.

2. *From a business-opportunities periodical:*
   New imports. Foreign manufacturers offering direct. Free information.
   Enjoy lifetime of homework. 48 years of happy, easy moneymaking. Now retiring. Free secret folio.

Qualifying the Respondents

The idea is to draw the *right* inquiries, inquiries from *qualified* inquirers. And qualified means inquirers who are suitable prospects. Notices similar to the first one—make money as a self-publisher— appear in many periodicals, including those directed to "opportunity seekers," but such notices are much more accurately targeted when they appear in publications read by writers.

Let us suppose that you planned a seminar on the subject of self-publishing as a business venture, and you decided to build your own mailing lists by running inquiry advertisements along the following lines:

1. Publish it yourself! You will probably make more money in the long run doing it yourself. For more information—FREE INFORMATION—write or call_____.

2. Make money publishing your own work. It's easy and profitable. For FREE information call or write_____.

Note, first of all, that these two notices have different focuses. Although both suggest self-publishing as a moneymaking venture, the first one addresses writers' interests—getting one's work published—directly, while the second version addresses opportunity seekers' interests—making money—directly. That is targeting the readers with the opening words so that anyone scanning a list of classified notices can identify a notice of immediate interest.

Were you to develop two mailing lists by running these notices, you would logically expect a higher rate of return from the first list than from the second simply because of more sharply focused targeting. It is logical to assume, that is, that writers would be more likely to find the idea of self-publishing attractive and practicable.

But there is another side to focusing and targeting: Note that neither of the two notices mentions the word *seminar* or suggests in any way what the ultimate item of sale is likely to be. Of course, the reader is intelligent enough and sophisticated enough to know that the free information is going to be advertising literature, but that does not mean that it will not also be interesting. The question is, will telling the reader here and now that the ultimate sale is attendance at a seminar kill the reader's interest and reduce the probability of responses? On the other hand, will the matter of fewer responses be compensated for by a better mailing list resulting from the inquiries?

The question of how much to tell the reader in your advertisement has many pros and cons for each option, and even these will vary from one case to the next. The only way to know which is the best option in any given case is to test them, but trying and keying different advertisements can easily become too burdensome and time-consuming to be worthwhile. And even that would not produce conclusive results, for ultimately the response to your mailings depends on the effectiveness of your copy and other factors, as well as on the quality of the mailing list. Probably your own judgment and instinct for wording, once you understand all the considerations, is as satisfactory a method for developing inquiry advertisements as any other.

There is one other side to the matter of qualifying respondents. One of the problems with inquiry advertising is that no matter how carefully you target your inquiries, you will get responses from children, bored individuals with time on their hands, and other idle curiosity seekers. This is especially a problem when you run inquiry advertisements with special inducements, such as the promise of a free calendar or novelty item of some sort. Such inducements do increase the response to your advertisements, but they also increase the difficulty of qualifying your respondents and separating the true prospects from those who are not.

Among the ways some advertisers deal with this problem is imposing a requirement on the respondent. Some commonly used requirements are the enclosure of a self-addressed, stamped envelope ("SASE"), a business letterhead or a business card when making the inqury, and the remittance of some nominal payment. These measures tend to discourage the idly curious.

Such requirements as these do reduce the general response, and cost you at least some properly qualified responses. That's the trade-off, and you will have to decide for yourself which option you prefer.

Inquiry advertising, properly conceived and executed, is an excellent method for developing house lists, but it is not the only way. There are at least two other practical methods you can pursue. However, before going into that, let's have a brief look at the mailing-list business and where the millions of lists vended commercially come from.

LIST BROKER OR LIST MANAGER?

I have referred here to the commercial renters of mailing lists as "list brokers." That is a designation that regards the person who offers lists for rent from your viewpoint as a potential customer. However, the list vendor prefers to be regarded as a *list manager*, especially by the owners of the lists. That is because the vendor has relatively few house lists; most of the lists the vendor rents out—the assets upon which the entire list-renting venture depends—are the property of others, who receive a percentage of the rental fee. Hence arises the notion of *broker* from your viewpoint, but the desire of the vendors to portray themselves as wise managers of lists, which are a profitable asset to their owners when handled properly.

The list vendor must make two sales: One, the owner of the lists must decide to deposit those lists with and authorize the vendor to rent them. It is for the purpose of making this sale that the vendor refers to his or her function as "list management," a term that implies expert and profitable handling of the lists. The other sale is, of course, to you as the lessee who will pay for each use of the list.

Typical owners of mailing lists are publishers and mail-order dealers of all kinds, but there are others such as associations willing to authorize the use of their membership lists or just about anyone else with a lengthy list of potential buyers.

It is because of these known sources that vendors can characterize and classify their lists, so that you can order a list of electronics engineers, bank vice presidents, buyers of books by mail, people who have spent $100 or more for a mail order item, single males earning at least $50,000 a year, or any of hundreds of other qualifiers. A great deal of effort goes into developing the demographic descriptors. Here, for example, are just a few of the headings, selected at random from a recent catalog published by a leading vendor of mailing lists:

Accountants, accounting
>   Accountants in education and government
>   Certified Public Accountants
>   Self-employed accountants

Engineering and construction
>   Engineering firms, all
>   Civil engineers
>   Consulting engineers

Personnel
>   Administrators and directors
>   Temporary help agencies
>   Training and development executives

Senior citizens
>   High income prime-timers
>   Organizations

Teachers
>   Athletic coaches
>   Senior high teachers
>   Principals, all

Modern computers have made it possible to manipulate these lists in almost any way you might want them—in zip-code order, by state, alphabetically, or other. You can have mailing lists customized for you today, and the vendors' catalogs offer you many options.

In a few cases the owner of the lists also does the renting of the lists. Some large publishers of periodicals, for example, will establish a special department or division to do this, but those owners who do their own marketing are the exception, rather than the rule; for the most part, mailing lists are vended by specialists who are list managers, list brokers, and/or list vendors. Choose your own term.

COMPILING LISTS

The conventional wisdom among many experienced direct mailers is that compiled lists are not very good, in spite of the fact that at least some of the lists rented commercially are compiled. (Association membership lists are compiled lists, for example.) Theoretically, at least, names on a compiled list are unqualified, whereas commercially vended lists guarantee some characteristic—e.g., each is the name of someone who has bought by mail, has attended a seminar, has an income at some stated level, buys books, is a yuppie, lives in the suburbs and owns a home, etc. And by far that which is regarded as the most important characteristic is that of having bought by mail, especially if the vendor can identify what the individuals bought, how much they spent, and how recent the event was.

There are advantages in using commercially rented lists because of the customization possible and because most vendors try to offer helpful advice; many are themselves direct-mail experts and consultants in the field. However, I must confess that I had little success with rented lists. Possibly that was because of that characteristic of probability statistics I referred to earlier. By their nature rented lists are rarely targeted and focused as sharply as house lists are. It is in the interest of the list vendor to keep each list as large as possible—charges are by the thousand names—and so there is an inclination to keep even doubtful names on the list. And perhaps the list brokers were just a bit overly enthusiastic about the qualifying characteristics of their lists.

In any case, rented lists did not work well for me. So I turned to other sources, and I soon began to learn how to compile my own lists,

lists that worked reasonably well for me. Here is exactly what I did:

First of all, bear in mind that I had long ago decided that my prime prospects were those companies who depended primarily on selling to the government. But that was not all of it. My specialty was knowledge of marketing to the government, but my greatest strength lay in a well-established track record of writing winning proposals. That translated into prospects who wanted to sell their custom services and custom-developed products to government agencies—to prospects whose success lay in their ability to write winning proposals, for that is the nature of government marketing. That established the real focus and identification of prospects for me: they had to be people and organizations whose success depended on effective proposal writing.

Armed with that knowledge, my problem was simply this: Where/how could I find sources from which I could compile names and addresses of prospects meeting this definition—prospects who *needed* to learn or to train their people in writing effective proposals?

My success in doing this was due largely to my intimate and thorough knowledge of my field. I knew the kinds of organizations which fitted my prospect specifications, and I could easily recognize such organizations from their advertisements, which appeared frequently in the both the classified and display help-wanted advertising columns of such major newspapers as *The Wall Street Journal, The New York Times*, and *The Washington Post*. These were long among my prime sources, and the lists I derived from them worked very well for me for a long time. (It would be even easier today because there are several special tabloids that carry nothing but such advertising, but they did not exist then.)

This should really present no great surprise. The names on those lists were hand picked, one by one, as I scanned the source materials—newspapers primarily, in the beginning. Later I searched out other sources for such prospects. I found a few federal government publications that furnished lists of contractors, for example. And I found, also later, that for only $75 I could get a copy of the list of 29,000 subscribers to the government's own publication for contractors, the *Commerce Business Daily*. All of it added up to an excellent supply of good house lists in a comparatively short time. And even that is not all of the possible resources that I managed to discover. I found it possible to get membership lists of certain associations. For example, when I was retained to present seminars or lecture at conventions and meetings of various kinds I asked for descriptive literature of the organization, and that often included a membership directory. I found, too, that some associations will sell copies of their membership lists. In that manner I acquired a list of hundreds of venture capitalists, as well as many other lists. There are also many directories that may be useful in public libraries, such as *The Thomas Register* and *Standard & Poor*, both directories of industrial and business firms of various kinds. Even now I buy a current copy each year of a paperback directory called *The National Directory of Addresses and Telephone Numbers*, a publication that grows thicker each year and has proved itself a peerless asset for many uses and in many situations.

Compiling house lists requires a great deal of tedious work no matter what methods you use, which is one of the reasons you do not build up house lists quickly. (It is a great deal easier to do it yourself now, with desktop computers to do much of the tedious work that the list brokers have long done with their mainframe computers.) But there is one method that enables you to expand your house lists quickly. That is swapping lists with others who are not directly competitive but whose lists are relevant and useful. For example, if you are planning that seminar on self-publishing that I hypothesized earlier, you might use the lists of a contemporary who sells typing and/or typesetting by mail. And if the other party can use your lists, you can usually make a swap. In this manner you can sometimes double the size of your house lists quite quickly. I succeeded in doing this several times, sometimes even by mail with people I had never met face to face. All you need to get started is a big enough list of your own to make a swap worthwhile for the other party.

Bear this in mind, too: Although you do not own the lists you rent from list brokers—you usually rent them for one-time use only—you do acquire ownership of the names of any who respond to your mailing. They go on to the most valuable list of all: your customer list. Be sure to maintain a customer list regardless of how you acquired the customer. If the name was originally on another list—a prospect list, for example—simply transfer it to the customer list.

You may want to try radio spot announcements to acquire names. One organization did this and found it reasonably effective and not overly expensive. However, if you adopt some of the ideas just described and adapt them to your own situation, you ought to have little difficulty in beginning the successful compilation of your own house lists.

One word of caution about renting lists before going on. There are vendors of lists at bargain prices, as low as $25 per 1,000 names.

These rarely work well for you. They are names of uncertain quality, usually individuals who would not be good prospects for a seminar. Be cautious in renting any list that is offered for under $50 per 1,000 names. Even that is at the low end of the scale, although you will probably have to pay extra for selecting names by locality or other special grouping. Many brokers have a minimum of 3,000 or 5,000 names, many offer discounts for quantities above 10,000, and some offer special deals, such as rates for three-time use or unlimited use for a year. If you plan to rent names, it will pay to solicit quotes from several of the leading brokers (a list of brokers is furnished later in a reference section) before making a decision.

ADVERTISING VERSUS MARKETING

Although direct mail is definitely advertising, the advertising professionals tend to treat direct mail as a poor relative and focus their own main efforts on print and broadcast media, largely slick-paper magazines and TV. There is, however, a very distinct and dynamic direct-mail industry that tends to be rather specialized and rarely uses the word *advertising* in connection with what it does. In fact, people in direct mail tend to think of what they do as more closely related to and defined by the terms *marketing* and *sales*, and some even use the common abbreviation "DM" to mean *direct marketing*, as well as *direct mail*.

The Cleverness Disease

I happen to agree heartily with this latter philosophy. In direct mail we are talking about marketing, rather than advertising, because the end-goal is sales, not mere publicity. This is something that advertising copywriters often appear to forget in their eagerness not only to be clever but also to demonstrate their cleverness to the world. That is what leads to such ill-conceived puns for headlines as the following.

Bag a mousse (advertising dessert preparation).

Beauty and the beach (advertising motorcycles).

Time after time (advertising watches).

It's better than a partridge. And you don't need a pear tree. (Advertising whiskey named after a common fowl).

Power of the press.

We put our money where our mouse is.

Take the law into your own hands.

In only one or two cases does the headline furnish even a clue to what the advertiser wants to sell; in fact, it was necessary for me to provide definitions here, which is itself revealing and should be alarming. In fact, many of the headlines are actually misleading: What in the world does "beauty and the beach" have to do with motorcycles? And what do you suppose "take the law into your own hands" is supposed to advertise? Try to figure out what product or service each of the last three of these headlines refers to, and then check the answers following to see how well you succeeded.

The copywriter in each case evidently hoped that a pun would intrigue readers enough to make them pause and see what copy followed. Faint chance. Most readers will go on to other copy. Readers do not read advertising copy to be amused; they stop and read advertisements when the copy strikes a nerve. That means when they recognize that the headline or illustration is about something that concerns them. At this moment, for example, I would be interested in any advertisement in a computer magazine about a 24-pin dot matrix printer because I am contemplating acquiring one and I am trying to judge which is the best model for me. But unless something about an advertisement identifies it immediately as concerning a 24-pin printer—or, at least, a printer of some sort—I am unlikely to even pause. Clever puns do not amuse me, and probably most readers hardly notice them for what they are; they just go on to more interesting copy.

But now have a look at those three headlines and see how well you were able to guess at what the advertiser was selling:

Power of the press (laser printer).

We put our money where our mouse is (computer mouse).

Take the law into your own hands (computer program about law for the lay businessperson).

Getting Attention

What leads many copywriters down the garden path is the advertising dictum that you must first get attention. That's a sound idea in the abstract, but clever puns are not the way to achieve the goal. Getting the reader's attention through some gimmick does not guarantee that he or she will continue reading because the second rule, after *Get attention*, is *Arouse Interest*. Appealing directly to the reader's interest—getting attention *and* arousing interest (at the same time)—is the way. Desperate dieters will hurry past full-color advertisements displaying a tempting steak or ice cream cake, no matter how clever the headline, but are likely to stop and read one that pictures a slim man or woman alongside a headline that says, "Here is how I lost 30 pounds in 30 days. "

This is as true in direct mail as it is in advertising. In fact, forget the word *advertising* and concentrate on *selling*. Concentrate on what the prospect wants, but concentrate on the result and not the means. Show a prospect three ways to get a result, equal to each other in all respects, and you will find that the prospect really cares little about the means, but wants only the result.

That's the first concern. The second concern will be which means is most convenient, fastest, and/or least costly, and that is the probable order of priority. Although most people do want to save money, most appear to want convenience and fast results even more. So while a headline that says something such as "Lose weight the easy way" will probably command attention, it will command even more attention if it says "Lose a pound a day" or, even better, "Eat what you want to and lose a pound a day. " And, finally, to really finesse the problem you will definitely strike a nerve if you are able to promise "Lose a pound a day for pennies a day," thereby incorporating three motivators. What sincere and dedicated dieter could possibly pass up a headline that makes that promise?

Some Relevant Principles of Selling

You must remember that advertising, whether it is in direct mail or via any other means, is selling, and the rules of selling apply. The chief difference between selling via direct mail and selling face to face is that in the latter situation you can interact spontaneously, detecting and reacting to the prospect's responses. That offers great advantages, for you can use the prospect's signals to help you judge what you must do next to move the sale along.

In face to face selling you can determine on an individual basis what captures the prospect's interest and attention. That is, in fact, a vital key to selling, for it is a fundamental truth that you cannot sell a prospect anything that he or she is not truly interested in, despite all blandishments and all special appeals.

That is contrary to what you may hear from some who write, speak, and teach on the subject of marketing and selling. Some will insist that you can create a need. That is simply not true if the prospect is truly not interested. However, that does not mean that you cannot arouse an interest the prospect did not even know of or at least did not consciously recognize as being represented by what you are selling until you pointed it out.

When I went looking for a new automobile on one occasion, I visited the showrooms of a dealer who had five different franchises and showrooms in one location. I was driving a Dodge that had seen much better days, and since I was then "on the road" in my work, I urgently needed a car I could trust.

I stopped first in the dealer's Chevrolet showroom. A salesman approached and asked me what I was looking for. I replied that I did not know exactly, but I did need a new car that day. He then handed me his card and invited me to look him up when I knew what I wanted.

I stared at his departing back in amazement. I had told him that I was there to buy a car and that I needed one immediately, and he apparently expected me to sell myself a new car! I threw his card on the floor in disgust and turned to leave, when another salesman approached me with the same inquiry. When he heard my tale, he invited me to look over the cars on display for a few minutes while he had a look at the car I wanted to trade.

When he returned he explained that he could get me a very good deal on a Dodge—a Dodge showroom was included among the others—because I was trading a Dodge, old though it was, and sad though its condition was.

Until that moment I did not know that I was interested in a Dodge. (In fact, I was more or less indifferent to brand name and was concerned primarily with a dependable new car at a price I could afford.) This salesman was shrewd enough to examine my basic need, understand it, and translate it into an interest. He got my attention, and he sold me a new car quite quickly and painlessly. (Painlessly for him, that is; I had to make all the painful payments!)

Note, too, the shrewd statement that he could *get* me a good deal, rather than *give* me one. That established a bond, putting us both on the same side against the adversary, the seller. Had he offered to *give* me a good deal, he would have been my adversary instead of my compatriot!

In face to face selling you can probe with questions and comments to discover what the prospect perceives as his or her need, and then demonstrate how what you are selling satisfies that need. In direct mail you cannot do that, of course; you must estimate or anticipate the most common needs and problems of the prospects you are addressing, and structure your printed presentation to respond to that estimate.

There is at least one other parallel between direct mail and face to face sales that must be drawn: "Closing" is a key tool of selling when used properly. Unfortunately, the term is often not even understood, let alone used properly. Many people who ought to know better believe that closing is getting the order, achieving the sale. Not so. Although the term is often used to mean that (actually getting the sale) in a general sense, it has a *technical* definition in the world of professional salespeople. There it means *asking* for the order.

The rationale for this is simply that most customers will never say, "Write it up," or, "I'll take it" after the salesperson has finished the presentation. This is especially true of "big tag" sales where the prospect is asked to part with a fairly large amount of money, or of any sale where the customer truly has to be sold. It is an accepted premise, therefore, that the salesperson must ask for the order, not directly, but indirectly through innocent questions that assume the order, such as these (and which cannot be answered easily with a simple "yes" or "no"):

"When do you need delivery?"
"What color do you prefer?"
"Do you want to take it with you?"
"How many can you use?"

But there is a deeper strategy to closing. The stories of salespeople who talk too much, talking the prospect out of the order just at the point of success (i.e., *un*selling the order), are legion. But how do you know when you have talked enough and should be writing (writing up the order, that is)? Closing is a way of discovering whether there is a need to keep talking—to do some more selling. If your innocent question assuming the order is rebuffed, you know that you must sell some more. You may wish to discreetly ask the prospect what his or her objection or uncertainty is so that you have a clue for your response. (Frequently the prospect's response to your close will itself furnish that clue, however.) A salesperson may thus have to close many times before getting the order, but that is preferable to the risk of talking too much or otherwise groping blindly in the dark. In fact, it is a good idea to close often, for that minimizes the probability of saying the wrong thing or saying too much.

In direct mail you don't have this advantage of multiple closings and responses to guide you in your selling. And yet many well-designed direct-mail packages do make several closes, anticipating the possible responses of the prospect. Direct mail does this by including in the package several elements that each do their own selling and closing. Of course, there is that same risk of overselling and thus unselling the prospect when you include a superabundance of literature and sales appeals, but that is unavoidable.

As you have seen, the vast majority of seminar presenters take the easy way out by printing and mailing many thousands of large brochures. They are thus "playing the numbers game" or gambling on the statistical probability that if you mail a large enough quantity of brochures, even a small rate of response will produce enough registrations to make the venture viable.

To be honest, there are advantages in this approach. Mailing large quantities of a simple brochure as a "flat"—self-mailer sans envelope—means that unit costs are minimized, for one thing. In printing, the larger the quantity printed the less each copy costs. The same thing applies to mailing services and, especially, to the simplicity of the mailing, which can be done almost entirely automatically in a large and well-equipped mailing house. And, finally, large mailings qualify for the bulk-mail rate, with its greatly reduced costs. Moreover, this approach imposes little burden on you personally, once the copy is prepared.

And so you may very well be able to print and mail 25,000 or 50,000 pieces in this mode for no more than you would pay for printing and mailing 10,000 or 15,000 direct-mail packages at first-class rates, while being put to a great deal less trouble personally. This does not mean that the results will be equal. There are factors other than sheer quantity and probability statistics that affect the outcome.

Among the adages of direct mail is a saying that "The more you tell, the more you sell." I can verify that this is generally true because of my own early experiments in direct mail. Among those early experiments, for example, was one in selling a small program—two booklets and several sample sheets—in resume writing as a home-based business. I got leads through classified advertisements and followed up with a direct-mail package. The initial package included a sales letter and a brochure, which produced fair results. But I then added another brochure and a circular, and responses doubled immediately.

Again and again I found that respondents wanted details, not necessarily for their own sake but as validation. Details are evidence of validity, and detailed explanations are far more believable and convincing than are generalizations. Thus the details make the presentation far more motivating. Respondents tend to recognize instinctively that anyone can make broad claims and generalize in global terms about almost any subject under the sun, but that only someone who knows what he or she is talking about can furnish the details.

I have observed this to be an important truth in all presentations, written and verbal. And in the case at hand, the problem with that mass mailing is that you are severely limited by that brochure, even if it is an 8-1/2 × 11-inches. The problem is not only the actual limitation of physical space—a six-panel presentation of those dimensions actually affords you enough space for 5,000 or 6,000 words—but also the psychological impact of the brochure. The mere fact that it is a single brochure, obvious advertising, arriving without even an envelope, makes it suspect immediately. It does not *look* as though it could offer information of much importance. It is, in fact, surprising that such a simple mailing manages to sell any registrations, when you consider that the registration means spending $200 or more in most cases.

In short, the window dressing is important: Appearance is in many ways as important as substance, and sometimes it is even more important. That is, to put it into terms well understood by most marketing experts, what counts most is the prospects' *perceptions.* All our efforts to sell things are devoted to trying mold those perceptions. Our success in selling depends on how well we succeed in creating the perceptions that will induce the prospects to buy. The marketplace success of a product or service is neither dependent on nor related to its quality or value; it's related entirely to the prospects' perceptions of its quality, value, and other characteristics. Those perceptions are dependent on and the result of several factors. These include the prospects' biases and other unpredictable influences, as well as the effect of the marketer's efforts to shape perceptions. If, for example, the prospects are biased strongly enough by a desire or need to save money, they will tend strongly to perceive the higher-priced offering as a lesser value than a competitive lower-priced one. Consciously or unconsciously, our judgment is heavily influenced by our biases, which are in turn often the result of our needs. If we can't afford the high-priced version of something, we may succeed in convincing ourselves that the lower-priced version is actually a much better value and more desirable. But it can work in the opposite way too, when prospects who are biased in another direction judge quality by price.

Obviously, if you are appealing to a general market there will be prospects in it of each type, and you will find it difficult—but not impossible—to appeal to both. You have probably seen advertising, for example, that tries to explain that the advertiser's relatively low prices do not mean lower quality, and then goes on to explain why that is so. Generally, however, you must decide which market segment you are going to pursue—quality [perceived] or price, in this case—because it is quite difficult to pursue both without compromising your marketing effectiveness overall. (A most common mistake of some marketers, and often a fatal one, is trying to have things both ways.)

What Are You Really Selling?

By now it should be abundantly clear that what you wish to sell is not important; what is important is what the prospect wishes to buy. And it should be equally clear that the prospect really wishes to buy the end, not the means. So in the final analysis what you are really selling is the promise of that result.

In the case of some products, such as automobiles, jewelry, or furniture, much of the prospect's perception is self-induced. That is because the product has its own emotional impact, and the main buying decision depends heavily on the prospect's emotional reaction. But in many other cases the prospect's perception is based largely on what you and/or your literature have to say about the product's benefits—on the prospect's reaction to your promise and the evidence you present to back it up.

In short, there are two main elements to every sales presentation: promise and proof. The promise appeals to a desire—an emotional desire—and the proof helps the prospect believe in that promise. It is that simple—and that complex. If the promise is appealing enough—if it anticipates successfully an ardent desire of the prospects—it will satisfy that first requirement of advertising to demand and get attention. But, with only rare exceptions, that is not enough; the prospect has a certain amount of skepticism (we are all "from Missouri" in this enlightened age) and needs some evidence to make the promise credible.

Let's look again at some of the seminar titles as headlined in their brochures and see how this is handled:

"How to Be an Assertive Manager". This title assumes that the prospect is a manager who has a desire to become assertive or finds the idea an attractive one. Therefore, the promise is that this seminar will achieve that result, with no information on the instructor. The headline is followed up with the details and outline arguing the case and a modest $98 fee quotation.

"How to Buy Printing and Related Services". Again, the headline is based on the assumption that many people already have a desire to learn how to buy printing or will immediately perceive the benefit of learning such a skill. The specific promise to improve the prospect's skills in buying printing is not made until the second page of the brochure. The details elucidating the promise seem valid enough and include mini-biographies of the faculty, but it takes a reading of the small print to discover that the price for the one-day seminar is $245.

"Training & Computer Seminar: How to Teach People to Use Computers". The implied promise of the headline does not specify a benefit of any kind, unless the reader interprets learning how to teach people to use computers as a benefit itself. Much later in the brochure, however, there is a paragraph titled "Benefits to You and Your Organization," which has two weaknesses: One, it dilutes any effect it might have had by listing no fewer than 10 alleged benefits, and two, several of those alleged benefits are simple iterations and reiterations of the message already furnished by the title/headline. The proof of validity is a list of former companies who sent employees to attend earlier sessions of the seminar and a brief bio of the instructor, along with program details. After a bit of searching in the small print you will discover that this is a three-day session for which the producer wishes you to pay $795.

In general, most of the brochures do a fairly satisfactory job of furnishing both details of the presentation and evidence of the presenter's competence in the subject, while most also fall down rather badly in leading off with a motivating promise in the title/headline. Few of the latter are especially motivating for either the prospective attendee or the employer who is asked to pay for the registration, because few explain or even hint at major benefits to either the individual or the organization. For example, the title of the first seminar listed here offers no clue as to *why* one should want to become a more assertive manager. What is the benefit to the individual or the organization?

That same is true for most of the others. Even such titles as **"Writing Effective Advertising"** and **"Analyzing and Improving Direct Mail"** only hint at the major benefit, instead of plainly stating it. Quite obviously most of the writers of these brochures believe that the seminar title must be as specific as possible about what it will teach, and they appear to believe also that the seminar title must be the headline of the brochure. Many brochures also allot generous space on the front cover to the name of the seminar producer and, in some cases, to the name of the instructor. Whether this is pure vanity or whether the producer really believes that these names add validity and appeal is unclear, inasmuch as the fame or celebrity status of these names is extremely limited in most cases. Whatever the facts, the space could be put to far better use to expanding and reinforcing the main appeals.

First of all the notion that the seminar title ought to describe the seminar content is not an unreasonable one, but neither is it obligatory that the title be a lengthy narrative, as many are. One peculiar characteristic of many inexperienced writers, especially those who are highly specialized technical experts, is an apparent compulsion to explain everything in detail in the first sentence, and that strange compulsion apparently also occurs among some who title seminars. The seminar title **"Training & Computer Seminar: How to Teach People to Use Computers"** appears to fall into that category, for example. Would not "Teaching Computer Usage" say the same thing with far greater impact and with much more clarity of intent?

On the other hand there is absolutely no necessity for defining the entire seminar content in the title. The title can be used to identify the major objective of the seminar in such a manner that it suggests the content, identifying it indirectly or in general. The explanation can come in follow-up text or subtitles. This is far more effective because the title is an opening statement, and an opening statement ought always to be simple and direct, containing a single idea. Certainly the opening statement should not cause the reader to pause immediately to ponder and digest its meaning!

Solution to the Problem

There are two ways to overcome the problem of creating a headline that presents an appealing and attention-getting promise while still identifying the subject and content of the seminar. One is to compose a seminar title that makes or at least incorporates the promise with reasonable clarity. It is easily possible to do this and also identify the objective and content of the seminar accurately. The other way is to create a suitable headline without regard to the seminar title. There is absolutely no necessity to use the seminar title as an advertising headline nor is there any special benefit in doing so. Quite the contrary, imposing such a mandate on yourself creates an obstacle in the development of effective sales literature. It creates an unnecessary restriction that tends to handicap your marketing effort and complicate your problems.

Of the two alternatives I favor the first one, although what I am about to say on the subject may appear paradoxical. But bear with me, and I will ultimately explain the apparent paradox.

First of all, I see no logical connection between how I name my seminar and how I explain why the reader ought to attend; they are entirely separate matters. Few products or services explain themselves by their names or try to use their names as sales arguments. One kind of product that sometimes does, however, is the book. Sales of a book titled *Five Acres* languished until direct-mail expert Maxwell Sackheim suggested changing its title to *Five Acres and Independence*, which resulted in greatly increased sales. And there is little doubt that the dual motivation of the hope for gain and the fear of the future clearly expressed in *How to Prosper in the Coming Bad Years* made a substantial contribution to the great success of that best seller. Titles *are* headlines when they make statements, and if they are designed to make those statements as persuasive sales arguments they serve as effective advertising of the product at each and every mention, verbally or in print.

For Instance...

To illustrate this, let's experiment with two of the titles we have looked at here, **"How to Be an Assertive Manager"** and **"How to Buy Printing and Related Services"**. Here are alternative titles that include a specific (rather than vaguely implied) promised benefit to the individual and/or the employer:

"Assertiveness Will Make You an Outstanding Manager"
"Assertiveness, the Key to Managerial Excellence"
"Become a True Expert in Buying Printing and Related Services"
"How to Cut Printing Costs by One-Half"

The idea is to set the theme with the title and follow up immediately with arguments and discussions expanding on that theme and offering inducements (motivators) to both the individual prospective attendee and the employer. (I am assuming here that most seminars will be on professional and business subjects that will induce employers to register employees for attendance.) It is, of course, necessary to motivate both employer and the individual who is the prospective attendee.

The follow-up copy may include subtitles or blurbs before going on to the body copy (main text), and that type of transition is usually more effective than an abrupt shift to the body copy. A blurb is a brief statement often found between a headline or title and the main text, usually set in a distinctive typeface and indented to set it apart and indicate clearly that it is not the beginning of the main text. Following, to illustrate this, are examples of title and subtitle and then title and blurb:

ASSERTIVENESS WILL MAKE YOU AN OUTSTANDING MANAGER
How to Gain Recognition in Your Company

ASSERTIVENESS, THE KEY TO MANAGERIAL EXCELLENCE
Here is how to gain recognition in your company
as a results-oriented and result-getting manager

It is easy enough to turn to the obvious alternative of running a thematically compatible headline over the seminar title, as illustrated here:

BE RECOGNIZED AS AN OUTSTANDING MANAGER
Learn how to command the attention and respect of everyone
in your organization through the outstanding methods taught
in our dynamic new seminar:
"Assertiveness, the Key to Managerial Excellence"
A results-oriented, result-getting approach to management

The Paradox and an Explanation Thereof

After I declared my preference for creating seminar titles that are also good advertising headlines I argued enthusiastically for the development and use of independent headlines to which seminar titles would be subordinated. I did so with full knowledge that it appeared, at the least, to be ambivalent, and I promised to clarify my position in this, which I shall now do.

The chief reason that I chose to argue so vehemently for constructing good advertising headlines, along with subheads, blurbs, and other ancillary material needed to support the marketing effort, is simply that I believe it to be the number-one consideration. I consider it so important that I believe you should permit nothing to interfere with or distract you from creating the best (i.e., most persuasive) marketing materials possible. I think it is necessary to think in terms of what will be needed to *sell* your seminar—i.e., persuade people to attend— before all other considerations, at least in the initial stages of developing the whole program. Time enough later to worry about a seminar title. I chose, therefore, to devote the major discussions to only that which applied directly to getting attention and arousing interest in the seminar—to selling it.

In fact, if it is necessary to choose between a good seminar title and a good headline, I would unhesitatingly opt for the good headline. And in some cases it may be necessary. I happen to believe that it is usually possible to devise a seminar title that serves as both a good title and a good advertising headline, but should you encounter an exception I sincerely believe that you should choose the headline.

To that end, I urge you to choose any rough "working title" for your seminar while in early stages of planning, with the clear intention of settling on a final title *after developing your marketing materials*. (I do exactly this in developing my books: My "working title" helps me sell the idea to my publisher; my final title, often developed cooperatively with my editor, helps sell the book to the ultimate reader.) Then, and only then, should you choose a seminar title. Usually you should be able either to make it a variant of your main advertising headline or to use the headline itself. You may even want to make a slight change in the headline to make it serve in the dual function. But until then I would not worry about the seminar title. It is the headline, with its subhead and/or blurb, that will sell the seminar, not the title.

MARKETING IN-HOUSE SEMINARS

In the next chapter we will discuss the elements of the direct-mail package, along with principles and procedures for creating the package and each element of it. But we have not quite finished our discussion of marketing yet. We have been discussing marketing seminars to individuals and their employers on an open-registration basis, but for the remainder of this chapter we will focus on, the market for custom, in-house seminars. And we will also necessarily discuss what those terms, especially *custom*, really mean.

The Idea of an In-House, Custom Seminar

Most seminar brochures include an offer of on-site or in-house presentations on some special basis, even offering to customize the presentation if desired. Some suggest that this is a practicable option for anyone with a group of 10 or more to be trained, while others suggest even five attendees as a large enough number to warrant a special presentation. Again, there are no guidelines in this; you must be guided by your own judgment and experience, but to a large degree the decision should be linked closely to the fee basis. That is, those for whom seminars are the main activity have a somewhat different basis for judgment than do those for whom seminars are an ancillary activity. The next few paragraphs will clarify that.

It has been my personal experience that organizations retaining me to present a seminar in-house generally produce from 25 to 50 attendees. That may or may not be of great importance, depending on how you opt to quote for your services—that is, whether you ask for a flat fee or quote a fee based on the number of attendees.

The Fee Basis for In-House Seminars

There is no standard or universally accepted method of charging for custom, in-house seminar presentations. Not too surprisingly, the practices in charging for such services tend to reflect the other, usual practices for charging clients. That is, those whose principal business is presenting seminars on an open-to-the-public, individual-registration basis tend to charge for in-house presentations on the basis of the number of attendees. Those whose sole or main business is seminar production and presentation tend to duplicate their regular seminars with discounted rates for multiple registrations. But those who are consultants or other technical/professional specialists and who normally charge fees based on time expended usually charge a flat daily rate for presenting a seminar in-house.

An Ancillary Consideration

Making in-house seminar arrangements always raises the question of handout materials, which are normally a *sine qua non* of seminars. In my own case, as I explained earlier, I choose to furnish the client a copy of my proprietary seminar manual with permission to duplicate as many copies as are required for the session. However, many others choose to have their seminar manuals and/or other handout materials printed and bound in quantity and make a per-copy charge for them. Some even consider that to be an important element of their custom-seminar income. I have no quarrel with them or with that practice, of course; it is a perfectly legitimate approach and a matter of personal choice. The handout materials are proprietary, and the owners certainly have both the moral and the legal right to sell copies. (My own choice is based strictly on convenience: I simply do not wish to be bothered with all the details of printing, shipping, invoicing, and so on. But that is certainly not offered as a model for or recommendation to others. My laziness in this matter probably costs me substantial number of dollars every year!

More important is the matter of customizing your seminars for clients. Just what does that mean?

THE CUSTOMIZED SEMINAR: WHAT DOES "CUSTOMIZED" REALLY MEAN?

In its classical sense *customized* means designed specifically to the client's requirements or specifications. In its strictest sense, as concerns the subject at hand here, that means redesigning your seminar each time to the exclusive or specific needs of the client. Of course, each client has a different set of needs, and in practice you will find customizing to be a considerable job. The labor alone will probably represent between 20 and 30 percent of the original design burden. That means a substantial, although not prohibitive, cost to the client. It might mean, in the case of a typical one-day seminar, one or two days of your time, and should not mean more than that if the client's needs are reasonably close to those addressed by your original seminar program. But you are likely to find that even that cost becomes a problem and that it is only on rare occasions that you can close a contract to truly customize your program for a given client.

In short, as you will almost surely learn, it is an impracticable approach in most cases because few clients are willing to pay for truly customized programs. They do not usually have any idea of the cost involved, and they tend to recoil in horror when you quote a realistic price for such an effort. That is not to say that there are no exceptions; I have, indeed, been awarded contracts to develop truly customized seminar programs, but only occasionally. I have been amazed, time and time again, at the naivete of some executives regarding costs in the real world. There are an amazing number of executives in large corporations who still think of $500 or $1,000 as a great deal of money to pay for custom services, and you must therefore learn to cope successfully with such modern myopia. It is possible to do so.

In the beginning, when I naively assumed that large corporations wanted the truly customized programs they inquired about, I expended the time and effort necessary to calculate what was needed to develop such programs. I was not asking for huge sums of money, so it was not the price per se that scotched all of those deals immediately. I am sure now, in retrospect, that it was simply the notion that they were to pay me for my time, effort, and knowledge in developing a special program that killed each of those prospective sales. The prospective clients simply objected to investing money in custom work that did not result in a physical product they could show their superiors! For whatever reason, I lost 100 percent of those first few inquiries about customized seminars from large corporations. I tried to be as reasonable as possible in my quotations, and documented them fully with cost analyses and explanations of what I proposed to do, but to no avail: I was unable to sustain their interest after I had submitted my quotation.

I soon learned that unlike the government agencies, who usually demand a fully detailed analysis of all costs, most firms in the private sector are most receptive to a single "for the job" price, at least for those purchases of relatively small magnitude. The "why" of this is not important; suffice it to say that when I proposed a customized presentation and quoted a single figure (plus reimbursement of travel and subsistence expenses, of course), I had no further difficulty in negotiating contracts and purchase orders for virtually all of these prospective seminars. And I have continued to do so, although I have raised the rates over the years as costs have risen.

I find it necessary to use the term *customize* rather flexibly, as the account of my experiences should suggest. In practice I simply request as much literature as is available about the client organization and customize my presentation spontaneously, primarily by slanting it to the client organization's interests. For example, if the organization is an electronics engineering and development firm, I cite examples relevant to that industry; if a training developer, I find examples relevant to that; etc.

This approach satisfies both the clients and me, and it is not as difficult as it may sound. I rather enjoy doing this, but it is not absolutely necessary to do even this if it is impractical for you. Many seminar programs really do not need to be customized in the sense of changing any of the content. In most cases the "customize" requirement is satisfied by simply taking the time to learn a little of the client organization and what they do so that you can react intelligently to questions and observations from your audience. But you should do that. Ask the client to supply whatever brochures and other descriptive literature they can well in advance of the presentation and study them enough to become reasonably familiar with the organization. Displaying some knowledge of the organization and its needs proves highly gratifying to the client and is usually accepted as customization.

WHO ARE THE CLIENTS?

The tendency of many is to assume automatically that all the clients for custom or in-house seminars are profit-making companies in the private sector. The fact is quite different: The clients for custom seminars are generally the same as those who send employees to open-registration seminars, but there are client organizations who do not fit this description and who would not be your customers or clients under any arrangement other than that of the in-house seminar!

My own client organizations have included both for-profit and non-profit corporations, associations and trade groups, community groups, colleges, and government agencies, among others. Here are a few examples:

Private-Sector For-Profit Organizations

The size of the organization is no determinant; clients for in-house seminars have included small, medium-sized, and large companies—even several of the so-called supercorporations—in electronics, training and education, graphic arts, management services, financial information services, computer manufacturing, computer software development, furniture manufacturing, and several other fields. Large corporations who utilize the service have sometimes organized corporate-wide efforts to which several divisions were invited to send participants, or have arranged for divisions to hold their own seminars independently. In some cases companies with large sales staffs may arrange a seminar as a key activity for an annual or semiannual sales meeting, and large organizations have sometimes had me return several times to present the seminar for different groups or departments. Too, multi-office organizations have sometimes had me present a seminar at each office, which was probably less costly than transporting large numbers of attendees to a central location.

Private-Sector Nonprofit Organizations

Colleges supporting adult-education programs—often junior colleges and especially community colleges—are excellent prospects, as are associations of various kinds (usually in connection with conferences and conventions), and self-help groups often utilize seminars presented by specialists. Groups organized especially to help members succeed in business are often interested in having private seminars, for example. National associations are especially good prospects for this. However, anyone who organizes or sponsors annual conventions and conferences, is likely to be interested in including seminars in their programs. It is only fair to note, however, that the college programs do not pay very much, but many consultants find the exposure helps materially in marketing themselves generally.

The Public Sector

Government agencies at all levels—federal, state, and local—are often interested in sponsoring seminars for such constituents as small businesses and minority enterprises. In my own case I have been called on by the Office of Minority Business Enterprise (now the Minority Business Development Agency) of the Department of Commerce, the Michigan Employment Training Institute, and sundry other government agencies to support their small- and minority-business development programs. (Sometimes these are run in conjunction with programs in state colleges.) My clients have also included a special organiization of Congress, the Northeast-Midwest Congressional Alliance, organized to aid businesses and the economies in general of those geographical areas.

PHYSICAL FACILITIES AND ARRANGEMENTS

In many cases clients ask you to present your seminar on their premises in a meeting room of some sort, but I have found it a more common practice of clients to rent a meeting room at a local hotel. This is not necessarily because the clients do not have suitable meeting rooms of their own, but is more often because they believe it helpful to have the seminar away from the daily business environment. Sometimes the client will ask for your recommendations concerning the location. My own preference is for a site remote from the organization's own premises because too often there are distracting influences when the seminar is in a conference room at the plant or offices of the client. Secretaries sidle in quietly, clutching slips of paper with messages on them, and whisper urgently to individuals, officers of the company enter and stand quietly in the back for a few minutes, telephones can be heard ringing outside, and often there are even loud voices heard beyond the walls and doors of the room.

With the high cost of money today, the relative slowness of many organizations to process the payment of invoices, and the resultant cash flow problems that result, laying out many hundreds of dollars for expenses on the basis of dollar-for-dollar reimbursement can work a burden on you. (I have had to wait as long as 90 days for payment from major corporations, although that is a rather extreme case.) There are two options for relieving the cash flow problem: Add a charge, over and above the direct cost of the expenses, or ask the client to handle as many of the expenses as possible.

My own choice had always been to charge the client my actual out-of-pocket expenses for travel and subsistence, and I did not want to change that policy. Therefore, as economic changes began to create cash flow problems, I began the practice of asking the client to take care of making my hotel and airline reservations and to have both billed to the client organization. I thus have to bill the client for only incidental travel and meals.

I have rarely had great difficulty in arranging this. Clients understand the problem and certainly welcome the practice of being billed only the actual out-of-pocket costs in return for handling the two major expense items. Even in the case of large and bureaucratic corporations, where slow-moving paperwork is necessary to move the ponderous machinery, it has often (although not always) proved a practicable approach. Certainly you can make the request, explaining why you ask and pointing out that there is a benefit to the client, as well as to you.

FINDING CLIENTS

Finding clients for in-house seminars is very much like finding clients for consulting services. Conventional direct advertising does not work as well as indirect advertising does. It is almost as if you must somehow induce clients to find you and solicit your services. In almost every case where I was retained to present a custom, in-house seminar the client sought me out and initiated the request or, at least, gave some indication of interest. A few brief case histories will illustrate this:

I once engineered my appearance in a major newspaper by sending a letter to a reporter that induced him to ask his editor for an okay to interview me for a possible story in the business pages. (I told him in my letter that I was in the then-rather-novel profession of helping clients write proposals for government contracts and thought it might be a good story for his readers.) As a result of the story that followed, another writer interviewed me and did a piece in a magazine owned by Control Data Corporation. After that latter article appeared, Control Data Corporation retained me to go to their Minneapolis headquarters to present a seminar for them.

Some years ago (at least 10) I spoke—without compensation—to a small group of mail-order dealers convened in Harrisburg, Pennsylvania. (I have made and still make many presentations without compensation as a kind of *noblesse oblige*, and have never regretted doing so. It often proves to be bread on the waters.) Last year one of those who had been in the audience had me come to Jacksonville, Florida to make a seminar presentation to his organization (a prominent, international charity) at my full rate.

Two years ago I appeared (again without compensation) as a guest speaker at a workshop sponsored by a small-business "opportunity" magazine. Within days I was retained by an entrepreneur in attendance to do a paid seminar at a local hotel.

A company who had been on my mailing list for years without once responding in any way suddenly found themselves in need of the kind of training I deliver in my proposal-writing seminars and retained me to present my seminar at three separate locations.

The training director of one of our largest international corporations was asked to develop a proposal-writing training seminar for one of the corporation's divisions. He went in quest of a suitable expert, asking one of the leading associations of training specialists for suggestions. The response from the association was not helpful, but the training director was inspired to visit a bookstore, barely more than a few steps from his own New York office. There he found a book on the subject which I had written, and on that basis he invited me to submit my own proposal for the contract. I did so and was rewarded with the assignment, a sizable and profitable one.

As you can see, in every case there was preliminary groundwork. It is most unlikely that you will be chosen at random to present a custom, in-house seminar. Most such assignments will result from other work you have done that has impressed someone with your qualifications for the job. Your general reputation is most helpful, of course, but most often someone will retain you or recommend your retention after having actually seen and heard you making a presentation. To that end, I recommend the following actions to you in a descending order of priority:

1. Run your own "regular" (open-registration) seminars as often as possible and make sure that everyone in the audience knows that you are available for custom, in-house seminars. Be sure that everyone has your card, understands *all* the subjects you lecture on, and and knows how and where to get in touch with you.

2. Speak as often as possible, preferably on the same subject(s) as that of your seminars, even if you have to make many brief presentations without compensation for them.

3. Miss no opportunity to get publicity, appearing on radio or TV talk shows, writing articles for and even letters to the editor of appropriate and relevant publications, and getting yourself written about whenever possible.

4. Be a joiner. Belong to associations, professional societies, community groups, and other relevant organizations and be active:

Attend meetings, speak up, participate, and be sure that everyone knows who you are and what you do.

5. Make it apparent in all your literature—brochures, business cards, and other materials—that you are available for custom seminars.

SOME SPECIAL MARKETS FOR SEMINARS

Your own open-registration sessions and custom, in-house presentations represent the two main markets for seminars. But there are other, rather special markets. Or perhaps it is more accurate to say that there are some other, rather specialized ways of marketing your services as a seminar presenter, and you should know about them.

Seminar Sponsors

One class of seminar producer is that which I refer to as a "seminar sponsor." That is, you do the seminar under their sponsorship.

Although I had appeared at others' seminars as a guest speaker, sometimes without compensation of any kind and other times for honoraria or even for substantial fees, it had so far never occurred to me that there was a third way to present my seminars profitably. My education in this came about almost by accident:

There is an organization that presents seminars in the Washington area on a variety of subjects, hiring various specialists to make the presentations. An acquaintance who happened to be a contracting official with the Treasury Department had been presenting seminars in contracting for this organization. Suddenly, circumstances prevented his appearance at the next session, for which he had been already scheduled. He suggested my name to the organization and they called me to ask if I could fill in for the other man. I agreed, after we settled on a fee, and I presented the session.

I rather liked doing this. I had reduced the frequency of my seminars as I became busier with other matters because each day of seminar presentation meant many days of work in preparation. I could easily spare the one day to make the presentation, but I could not spare many days for preparatory work.

I have since presented many seminars for organizations who handle all the production and marketing work. There are more than a few of these whose business is seminar production and presentation, and who retain specialists to make the presentations.

Brokers and Agents

It has happened that more than a few people have acted as brokers in arranging for me (and other consultants) to present custom, in-house seminars for their own clients. On occasion it has been a seminar sponsor who does this. But other people have sometimes encountered opportunities to sell a seminar session or found that one of their clients required a training service and acted as my broker, thereby earning a commission.

Many who function as professional speakers get at least some of their engagements via lecture bureaus. These engagements are sometimes for seminars, as well as for briefer lectures. The usual arrangement is for a lecture bureau to bill the client and pay the speaker, after subtracting some percentage (which varies quite widely, from 20 percent upward) as their fee or commission.

In other cases, as when an editorial-services firm has retained me to deliver a seminar for them, we have a fee arranged between us, and they bill their client for whatever they have quoted.

There is no special rule about fees or commissions for these special arrangements. In my own case I generally work for a set fee for the day. But there are at least some sponsors of seminars who offer the presenter a modest guaranteed fee and an "override" or percentage of the total revenues resulting from registrations.

7 | DESIGNING THE MARKETING PACKAGE

The effective marketing package is a carefully designed, integrated implementation of a grand marketing strategy, although many do appear to be random collections of vaguely related items.

CONVENTIONAL SEMINAR MARKETING

If we cling to what is quite clearly conventional wisdom in marketing seminars this will be a very thin chapter indeed, for it will then be confined to the development of a brochure and a press release. That is how most seminar producers market their product. Even the two most prominent exceptions I know of do not deviate greatly from this practice. They each utilize a bound booklet that is somewhat more extensive in its content than are the typical seminar brochures, but is even plainer and less dramatic physically, being composed entirely by typewriter or computer printer on sulphite paper and also mailed flat as a self-mailer under bulk-mail rates.

The strength of this approach lies solely in quantity: the mailings are done—*must be done*—in many, many thousands. They must be done in such quantities because brochures mailed flat are instantly recognizable as advertising literature, which some people refer to as "junk mail," and many will be discarded immediately without a second glance. That is the weakness of this approach to marketing; only some unpredictable small portion of the mailed literature will get a reading, much less serious consideration. The waste is quite enormous, and that alone gives me pause in using this method. However, there are other considerations stemming from this primary characteristic of being obvious advertising matter.

The investment is relatively heavy for a mailing of this type, at least $225 per 1,000 pieces, and since it is usually necessary to mail at least 10-15,000 pieces, you are facing at least a $2,000–$4,000 investment. (You could cut the per-1,000-piece rate a little with a much larger mailing, but the investment, and thus the risk, is even greater then.)

I favor the alternative, the method I have usually used myself, of a conventional direct-mail package. That consists of at least the following obligatory minimum mailed in an envelope:

1. A sales letter.
2. A brochure.
3. A "response device" (order form).

Beyond these there is a universe of possibilities, some relevant to seminars, many not. Of course, we will confine ourselves to that which is relevant. But first let's take a broad look at this different approach to direct-mail marketing of seminars.

Even in this approach there are often practices used that mark the package as advertising literature. The fact that the envelope is thick, obviously stuffed with literature, is one indication. The use of bulk-mail postage is another, while the use of an envelope that is of an odd size or shape is yet another. And the practice of using the outside of the envelope as a billboard on which to post more advertising is still another.

This leads to two opposing schools of thought on the use of a business-type envelope for mailings. At one extreme is the strategy of making the package appear to be serious business correspondence, which will ensure that the recipient will at least open it and read the contents. (I do so, for example, even when the use of a preprinted label and/or bulk-mail postage tells me that the envelope almost certainly contains advertising matter.) Of course, there is no guarantee that the recipient will not deposit the material directly and immediately in the "round file" as soon as he or she realizes that the contents of the envelope are advertising literature. This realization should take only a few seconds, of course. That is the argument against making the envelope appear to be business correspondence of some sort, an argument with some validity.

At the other extreme are those who are reluctant to "waste" the clean white space of the outer envelope and thus tend to use "envelope copy"—advertising copy on the outside of the envelope—making no effort to disguise the package as other than what it is: advertising matter. Quite the contrary, they use the outside of the envelope to write messages exhorting the recipient to open the envelope and see what is inside. Some of the messages are along the following lines, often in red ink and quite bold:

Urgent information inside!!
This is the information you requested.
A limited time offer.
The chance of a lifetime!

Other messages deal a bit more directly with the content:

Information inside: How to be your own boss.
The latest and best moneymaking deal ever!

Still others identify the specific offer that is contained in the envelope, in the belief that this is the effective way to use envelope copy. Nor is all envelope "teaser copy" confined to a single phrase or two: Many mailers all but cover the exterior of the envelope with messages, often in several colors, sometimes with illustrations.

I am personally somewhat reluctant to use envelope copy, except on a highly dignified scale. I might, for example, use a line similar to one of the following:

> *An invitation to a graduate seminar on proposalmanship.*
> *Some strategies for winning contracts.*
> *Inside: The key to winning more contracts.*

I believe that commercial huckstering works against your interests as a professional. My experience has been that as a professional specialist you must maintain a certain dignity at all times and in all matters, and that you must do your marketing in general and advertising in particular quite discreetly. Obviously we must advertise our services in some manner, but we cannot do so successfully if we do not maintain a dignified, professional image, one that commands respect.

This does not mean hiding your light under a bushel; you need not be a shrinking violet by any means. Quite the contrary, you must be exceedingly self-assured in representing *what you can do* for the client (which is far more important than what you *are* or claim you are). Bear that idea in mind as we begin to examine the specific materials needed and their development.

THE SEMINAR BROCHURE

The sales letter contained in any direct-mail package is usually considered to be the central or main element. In the case at hand, however, it is probably more realistic to make the brochure the central element. This is not to diminish the usefulness of the letter or of other elements; far from it, the letter can be of extreme importance, as you will see presently. But it is in the brochure that you will offer the most important information dealing directly with the seminar, and readers will expect to find it there. In any case, let us consider the brochure and its contents first.

What You Are Versus What You Do

There is a pronounced tendency for independent consultants to think of themselves as individuals, rather than as instruments for accomplishing something. With a great many beginning consultants seeking clients this manifests itself in the form of a brochure that is really little more than a personal resume. Even when established consultants are preparing literature to sell attendance at their seminars, there is a strong tendency to devote far too much space to their personal qualifications at the expense of other, probably more important, coverage.

This is a matter of priorities. It is necessary, of course, to provide information about the source of the expert information and guidance that is to be provided—your personal qualifications, that is. But the prospect's first concern is for what you propose to *do* for him or her—what benefit, that is, will come from attending your seminar. Only when and if your promise of benefits is attractive enough to generate active interest does the reader look to your personal qualifications (assuming, of course, that it is you who will present the seminar). Your personal qualifications are the evidence or *proof*, to use the term introduced earlier, that you can deliver on the promise. But since it is the promise and not the proof that attracts the respondent, who and what you are is not the main theme.

The Main Theme

Theme can be an elusive idea. The word itself has many synonyms and several definitions, but as used here it refers to your promise of what your seminar will do for the participant. And that is where so many brochures fall down, in my opinion: they fail to establish a clear theme immediately, and many never establish the theme at all. Let's look at the titles of several seminars and see how well each establishes its theme:

"How to Work with Customers." This is an appeal that should attract the interest of employers, since (it is quite clear from the content of the brochure, if not from the title) the main theme is that of how to keep customers happy, while a secondary theme is that of selling effectively. It seems rather clear, from study, that the producer has retail businesses in mind as the primary targets. The title does not get that message across nearly as effectively as the later copy does, however: Just what does "work with" mean? Why not *state* the main theme, *how to please and keep customers*, instead of avoiding it? Probably because the author of the title was so intent on absolute accuracy. Or perhaps because of the peculiar reluctance of many people to make a firm commitment. In any case, the result is a resort to a broad and sweeping term, such as "work with," which is necessarily vague.

Even so, the theme "pleasing customers" is not the right one because the art of pleasing customers is part of the means to the end, not the end itself. The end itself is improving the business or business growth; that is what the respondent wants to accomplish, and it is that promise that will prove attractive. So the theme is, properly, helping business to grow through better handling of customers.

You may now observe, "But surely the respondent recognizes that keeping customers happy is one key to business growth. Why must we drag the message in by the ears and throw it at the prospect?"

The short answer is that experience proves it is necessary. The reason is simply that in today's world you must compete for the prospect's attention, and you have only seconds to gain that attention. Don't ask the prospect to do any part of the selling for you—not even the logical transition of reasoning from the means to the end. *You* must do that.

"Desktop Publishing: A practical tutorial featuring product comparisons" is even less clear in establishing its theme, and the body copy is a formidable array of small print in forbiddingly solid blocks of text. However, the caption for the first paragraph begins to clarify the matter. It says "Harness the Power" and presents the main argument for attending the seminar: learning how to use desktop publishing to produce documents in your organization. For some reason that eludes me the sales argument continues in the following paragraph, which is captioned "Topics." It is thus not easy to guess at what the main theme was intended to be, learning how to use desktop publishing or learning how to select the right hardware and software—or both. The producer of this seminar is trying to cover all the bases, obviously, hoping to maximize the appeal by offering something for everybody. But trying to please—or reach—everybody rarely works; you must select your target and work with it. In this case the seminar is intended to be desktop publishing from a to z, and one suitable theme might be something along the lines of "Your in-house desktop publishing capability; getting it right the first time!" (The significance of that idea will become clearer in subsequent discussions of positive and negative motivations.)

"Analyzing and Improving Direct Mail" is much closer to the mark, although it too can be improved greatly. "Analyzing and improving" are part of the means; the end is greater sales, and the should theme address that directly, delivering the promise that the seminar will train participants in creating and running successful direct-mail marketing campaigns.

Figure 7-1, United Business Institute's brochure, based on copy ideas supplied by me, illustrates this concept. First of all, it focuses on a single theme, that of success in winning consulting contracts with government agencies. Once that theme (and objective) is established clearly in the headline/title, the copy settles down to the means of achieving the promised success by revealing the main topics to be presented and discussed.

Inside, that theme is expanded steadily and is validated with a list of previous participants from well-known organizations and with the presenter's credentials as an authority on the subject. Included are paragraphs titled "Who should attend" and "Materials," the latter explaining what kinds of handout materials will be supplied to participants. (In this case it will be a special seminar manual on proposal writing.)

The third page offers a complete and well-detailed outline listing 15 major topics with three to six subtopics under each. Included beneath that outline is a form that the reader is invited to use to register for the seminar. (More than one participant may register on that form.)

Finally, on the back page of this four-page brochure are administrative details on registration, with directions for reaching the seminar site, and an address block with bulk-mail indicia which permits the brochure to be mailed without an envelope.

Despite the fact that I think the copy of this brochure quite acceptable and quite right for the purpose, I dislike the idea of the self-mailer brochure for seminar marketing. It is, to me, far too "naked" as direct mail. (I can't quite bring myself to refer to a single brochure, mailed without even an envelope to cover its nakedness, as a direct-mail "package.") There is something quite cold about it, and even with my special clinical interests I often cast these self-mailed brochures straight out of my postoffice box into the large circular file.

Later we will examine the type of brochure that I find more suitable and more effective. It is not because it is a smaller brochure physically, nor even simply because it goes out in an envelope that I think it much more suitable and effective, although I think that that alone helps it materially; it is that it is an element in an integrated package, doing its job but not expected to carry the burden all alone. So we will return to the matter of the brochure presently, after we take up some other matters that will help lay the groundwork for further discussion.

presents a *marketing seminar*

Secrets of Success in Winning Consulting Contracts with Federal, State, and Local Government Agencies

- **How government agencies buy**
- **How to sell to government agencies**
- **Finding the contract opportunities**
- **Writing winning proposals**
- **Beating the competition (under the new Competition in Contracting Law**
- **Benefiting from government budget cutbacks**
- **And many, many more insider tips and secrets**

Personally conducted by Herman Holtz.
  author of the best-selling book:
  "How to Succeed as an Independent Consultant"

Washington, D.C.   **May 7, 1986**

Figure 7-1. Front panel of a seminar announcement brochure. Copyright © by Herman Holtz.

THE SALESLETTER

Whether you regard the brochure or the salesletter as the central piece of your direct-mail package there is no doubt that the salesletter is a most important element. Where, by its very nature, the formally typeset brochure comes across as a highly impersonal piece of literature that is quite easy to discard, the salesletter can and should be an informal and warm personal message from you to the prospect, worth at least a minute or two to read. The salesletter is in fact one of the chief distinguishing features of the classic direct-mail package, and the lack of such a letter is one of the chief weaknesses of many direct-mail seminar promotions: The practice of mailing only a glossy brochure, sans envelope and letter (and often arriving in the rumpled and ragged state that appears to characterize the Postal Service mode of handling our mail today) makes the process a cold one indeed. If you are one of the many whose mail includes a bundle of self-mailer brochures every morning, you may already have developed the habit of speeding up your morning routine by systematically discarding such items immediately. (Or perhaps you have instructed your secretary or the mail room clerk to do so.)

Even in the allegedly heartless and impersonal arena of the business world the personal touch can make a difference; no one is truly proof against the friendly note. But that friendly note will never come across in a printed brochure as it will in a letter that has been—or appears to have been—composed by typewriter.

The difference is not a subtle one, nor is it mere nuance; it is most basic, resulting from the differences in tone, style, and physical appearance between the two. Consider, for example, the difference in tone and general impact between the following copy, taken from a formal brochure, and the copy that follows it, taken from a salesletter:

1. *From a brochure:*
    "Herman Holtz can point to specifics—about $360 million worth—of success in marketing through his own direct efforts as a proposal specialist, director of marketing, and general manager of various organizations, and as a consultant to many companies. He has been employed by such major corporations as RCA, GE, and Philco-Ford, and has served many others—IBM, Control Data Corporation, and Dun & Bradstreet, for example—as a consultant. As an independent consultant he also lectures and

conducts seminars on marketing, proposal writing, and a number of other subjects about which he has written extensively as the author of a number of books."

2. *From a salesletter:*
"Please forgive me if I appear to be bragging a bit here, but you are entitled to know my credentials—why I believe that I can help you and why I believe that it is worth your time to listen to what I have to say. These are the simple facts: I am the author of four books on government marketing and proposal writing, and I am under contract to write several more. I have been a technical writer, proposal writer, marketing director, and general manager for large prime contractors, including RCA, Philco, Vitro Laboratories, and U. S. Industries. I am now or have been a consultant to such organizations as Dun & Bradstreet, Chrysler Corporation, World Wide Wilcox, GE, Sperry-Rand, IBM, the Northeast-Midwest Congressional Coalition, OMBE, and lesser-known organizations. My proposals have won over $300 million in contracts from the U.S. Labor Department, U.S. Forest Service, U.S. Army, U.S. Navy, OEO, FAA, GSA, Postal Service, Civil Service Commission, EPA, NASA, and the governments of Jordan, Greece, India, and the Sudan."

The letter is, first of all, a message directly from you to the respondent and should therefore be in the first person, unlike the third person of the brochure, and conversational in tone. It uses the word *you*, that most important word in our language, as it says "*You* are entitled to know my credentials." (Who does not wish to have his or her personal rights and interests recognized and considered?)

Make that letter as warm and personal as you can if you want it to work for you, and remember at all times that the recipient does not care much about what you want; he or she is concerned with only his or her own needs and desires. Recognize and respond to those directly and you will never have any difficulty in getting and holding the prospect's attention.

Letter Format and Style

You may have been indoctrinated with the false notion that everything but a personal letter must be in the third person. If so, forget it immediately; that notion is hopelessly out of date. You may write all but the most formal material in the first person, using the pronouns *I* and *you* quite freely. As Samuel Clemens (Mark Twain) was reported to have remarked, "Only royalty, editors, and people with tapeworm ought to say 'we' when they mean 'I.'"

The letter presenting an appeal to attend a formal seminar should not be a typical high-pressure sales letter. Those letters are usually of several pages, printed in black ink with many words in red ink and with handwritten interjections, notes, underlines, and comments printed in blue ink. They all but boil with enthusiasm, superlatives, and eager urgings, backed by carefully worded guarantees. (Most of those guarantees found in the typical high-pressure presentation are only promises to do what federal law says the vendor must do and what the Federal Trade Commission is charged with enforcing.)

That kind of overheated hype is all wrong for seminar appeals. The right tone is one of friendly informality—subdued, respectful, and sincere. High-pressure hype is almost sure to fetch your salesletter a resting place in an overflowing trash basket.

One problem that concerns many mailers is that of addressing letters sent out in direct-mail packages. Perhaps you have received some of those letters addressed "Dear friend" or "Dear neighbor. " The fact that it is a form letter is painfully obvious, and that declaration that I am the writer's friend or neighbor always comes across as somewhat presumptuous and therefore slightly offensive to me.

On the other hand, modern computers, using a "mail merge" kind of processing, can individually type and address each copy of a form letter to an individual by name. But even then there is a hazard because computers are not really very bright. For example, I still get form letters that salute me as "Dear Mr. Publications," because years ago I once used the name "Herman Holtz Publications" for a business venture. And sometimes the computer even abbreviates that to "Dear Mr. Publica" (and sometimes even to "Dear Mr. and Mrs. Publica") because some systems limit the number of characters and require the program to cut off any above the maximum. That is even more offensive than being appointed the writer's friend gratuitously, despite its mildly amusing side. The most tolerant human is usually a bit sensitive about misuses of his or her name. Even a mistake in an individual's middle initial is likely to be annoying.

If you are going to use some sort of computer program to address letters and envelopes to individuals by name, you will do well to scan each name on your list for such obvious errors. Only personal checking can clean up the absurdities a computer cannot even detect, let alone refrain from committing.

For these reasons I long ago decided not to use any salutation, and I recommend that approach today. I have been gratified to discover recently that I am not alone in that reasoning; others, who are experienced direct-mail experts, agree that the salutation in the letter is not obligatory and the campaign does not lose anything by omitting it. My own experience supports that belief; I have been unable to detect any ill effects resulting from this practice.

The fact is that not only is there no noticeable downside to this practice of eliminating the salutation, but it leads to an advantage: Without a salutation it becomes possible to lead off the letter with a headline. But don't confuse this with brochure practices. This headline is not in any special type fonts, but is in the same typewriter-style font as the rest of the letter. All that is done to mark the line as a headline is that it stands alone on a line, usually centered, and is either all capitals, underlined, or both. Some marketers print the headline in a different color ink, such as red, but I oppose this idea, just as I oppose all those notes, exclamation marks, underlines, and other devices scrawled bold with a marker pen. Such things make the letter far too "busy," and mark it as a huckstering circular or flyer, not a letter.

These are devices used to get attention generally and to point to certain items especially. But they are devices used by those who are not truly effective writers or effective marketers. They are in themselves, by their very use, a confession of weakness, of inability. The authors of such salesletters lack the imagination to get attention and arouse interest without all that garish apparatus of the huckster. Figure 7-2, the first page of a salesletter, is an example of how to get attention by appealing to the reader's self-interests, rather than by artificial devices that try to compel attention.

Note that the headline appeals directly to a specific interest (benefit)—the desire for more government business—and follows immediately with the promise of helping the reader achieve that. It then goes on in that same vein, addressing the subject of the seminar quite clearly and giving a bit of useful information away.

Giving some useful information away is important. The salesletter is itself worth reading for the tips it contains whether or not the reader intends to attend the seminar or send someone to it. It is, in fact, a good sample of what will be revealed at the seminar. For some readers who are not familiar with marketing to government agencies, much of the information in the salesletter alone will be an eye-opening revelation. But even for those who are old hands at government mar-

Seminar Associates, Inc.
17 Hopeful Lane
Bookends, MA 02345

PROPOSALMANSHIP
IS THE WAY TO INCREASE YOUR SHARE OF THE GOVERNMENT MARKET
and we can teach the art to your entire staff
at our exclusive seminar

It is no secret that government contracts are awarded to the best proposal writers, who may or may not be the best qualified contractors or the best performers. That's the nature of the system because the law requires the proposal competition for all but the competitive-bid procurements, and the law requires on objective evaluation in selecting the wining proposal.

But what is a winning proposal? What does it take to write one? Writing excellence? Technical knowledge? Inside information? Marketing skills?

In fact it takes all of these, to some degree, but most of all it requires marketing skill, for the winning proposal is always the winning *sales presentation*. Without effective marketing skills, the most masterful writing, technical knowledge, and even inside information are rarely enough.

But even that needs some qualification, for the key marketing ingredient that results in success is *strategy*. And that requires a profound knowledge of how the system works, what motivates individuals, and marketing intelligence — getting inside information when you are not an insider.

It is not writing per se that we teach in our proposal-writing seminar; we teach winning, with many exclusive strategies and tactics we have developed over the years and which we distinguish with the name *proposalmanship*. Here are just a few of the topics your people need to know about and which they will learn at this unusual presentation:

* Worry items: What are they, what do they do for you, how do you find them, and how do you use them to win?
* Cost strategies: What are they? How to *appear* to be a low bidder, even when you are not. Examples.
* Technical strategies: What are they? How do you find or develop them? Some classic examples of successful technical strategies.
* Presentation strategies: Getting extra impact with your proposal. Some unusual ideas that have worked in the past.
* Overcoming common problems: Different kinds of problems and solutions that have been successful for others.
* Marketing intelligence: How to gather it, do's and don'ts, using the Freedom of Information Act effectively. Examples.

Figure 7-2. First page of salesletter.

keting and quite expert in proposal writing and therefore find no new information here, the revelations are useful because they are valid and so reveal that the author of the lettter is, indeed, thoroughly competent in the subject. That gives comfort to the reader who wishes to have a staff trained because it is evidence that here is a qualified trainer.

The items enumerated at the bottom of the page are especially important. They should certainly whet the reader's appetite for more. Who would not like to know how to appear to be the low bidder when he or she actually is not? Who would not like to have suggested solutions for the common problems? And who would not like to learn another's suggested strategies for winning?

This is only a first page. It makes the basic promise and begins to provide the necessary evidence that the seminar can and will deliver on that promise, while it also begins to list teaser items—special inducements, such as hints of very special insider know-how. A second page (Figure 7-3) continues that trend, invoking the brochure, and makes the close—urges the reader to act promptly in registering for the seminar.

Many salesletters in direct-mail packages are a single page, but many others are several pages long. You can make your letter as long as you wish. Make it as long as you believe is necessary to do the job, to incorporate all the right ingredients; that is the right length.

Necessary Ingredients

There are consultants who appear to live in fear that they will give away some of the information and counsel that they expect to sell. In fact, some of those who write and lecture on the subject of how to be a successful consultant make a major point of how to avoid giving away information. They even headline this in advertising their lectures and publications, first arousing and then exploiting this fear.

I am personally dismayed and astonished by the susceptibility of so many to this apprehension. We live in a highly competitive society and in a highly competitive age. Many companies today offer special inducements to attract new buyers, including cents-off coupons, rebates, trial sizes, and free samples. The fear of doing this—of giving away a few samples—implies some fear on the part of the seller that the product or service is not truly worthy. You cannot blame your prospects if they infer that. But the fact is that trial sizes or samples should be used to convince the prospect of the quality and worthiness

* Managing the effort: Assembling the proposal team, organizing the effort, coordinating the work, and "bird-dogging."
* Using desktop computers: Computerizing your swipe files and other labor- and time-saving applications.

Not the least reward to each person who attends this session is a copy of our own exclusive proposal-writer's manual. This is a 75-page reference guide, based on the experience of success in winning dozens of contracts whose value has totaled over $360 million, written by our seminar leader, Joshua Ringgold, a well-known expert in this field. This copyrighted manual is available only at this seminar, and distributed to registered participants only. In it, Mr. Ringgold reveals any of his own "tricks of the trade" and other tips that will serve your staff in developing winning proposals in the future.

For more details see the enclosed brochure, where you will find a complete outline of the session, an account of Mr. Ringgold's credentials, and other information, including a registration form.

I must caution you that seating is limited, since we deliberately list the size of seminar groups, as we must of this type of instruction. I therefore urge you in all sincerity to act promptly in registering and thus ensure yourself of as many seats as you require for your staff.

I look forward to seeing you and/or your staff at our next presentation and plan to be on hand to welcome you.

With best wishes for your continued success,

Harmon T. Whistlebottom
Director of Marketing

P.S. Many organizations make multiple registrations, sending several people to attend our seminars. If you have as many as 10 individuals for whom you want this training you will probably find it more practicable to have this seminar presented in-house for your staff. Please feel free to call me personally to discuss this.

Figure 7-3. Second page of salesletter.

of the product or service, should offer further assurances by demonstrating that the vendor has faith in the quality of the offering, and should whet the appetite of the prospect for more. That is the reason that the salesletter illustrated here included some of the useful information that some consultants might be reluctant to "give away."

Try to bear in mind that you are asking your prospects to spend more than a dollar or two—frequently the investment is many hundreds of dollars—and that some risk factor is therefore involved. The prospect needs some kind of assurance that the investment is a good one that will probably produce a worthwhile return. Even more important than this, however, is the whetting of the prospect's appetite for more. There are certain key characteristics of offerings that have that effect, that most prospects find particularly attractive and appealing, that is. Following are brief discussions of several of those characteristics, along with some guidance in how to use them and some ideas for each:

Tips and Insider Information

It always helps to label appropriate items as "tips" and "inside" information. Everyone is eager to get in on little-known information, especially when that kind of information is likely to produce such direct benefits as money or added business. However, it is dangerous to mislabel what is common knowledge, common sense, or trivia in this manner; you are almost sure to be exposed and seriously harmed by it if you do. Have respect for your prospect's intelligence. If you insult it you do so at your own risk. Be assured of this. Don't promise what you cannot deliver, but do make a prominent feature of tips and/or inside information if you can deliver it, and do give away a tidbit or two in your letter as proof. There are also kindred items that are appealing because they are tools that attendees can use, and they suggest a kind of shortcut to achieving skills and finding success. You can always come up with some of these attractive items to feature in your letter, and perhaps even in your brochure. Here are a few of the kinds of things to promise. You can always manage to develop one or two of these tools in any how-to seminar program. (Probably you can think of many more.)

- Inside tips.
- Checklists.

- Do's and don'ts.
- Procedural guides.

New

The word *new* is itself an attention-getter. Most of us are interested in anything new in any matter that affects us. Again, be honest about this. Use that word only if you can use it honestly. That does not mean that you must find new information, however; even if you do not have truly new information you can always use *new* in one of the following ways and yet use it honestly:

- A new seminar.
- A new approach.
- New tools for your use.
- A new concept.

Free

The word *free* never loses its appeal apparently, despite the tendency of many sophisticates to sneer at it. But, again, use it honestly and in some manner that makes it clear that it is honest—in a credible manner. Of course the seminar is not free, but you may wish to offer something free, such as one of the following. (Oddly enough, the offer of a free gift is motivating far beyond the intrinsic value of the gift.)

- A free manual included.
- A free initial consultation.
- A free tape cassette (or other physical item).

Latest

We all want the latest of whatever we are interested in. In a dynamic and rapidly changing society only the latest has full value. Again, try to find or create a "latest" claim that is honest and does not represent an effort to trick the prospect. Here are a few suggestions:

- The latest information on the subject.
- The latest instruction techniques.
- The latest materials available.

Shortcuts

Shortcuts are in a category with tips, checklists, and other such items, but it helps to actually call them shortcuts to success to give them the most appealing characterization for the reader. Here is one way to list such items as examples of the special kinds of information and help to be revealed in your seminar:

Shortcuts to success:
  Insider tips.
  Checklists.
  Do's and don'ts.

Exclusive

Exclusivity is also in a class with insider tips, is another characterization that has great appeal. If you have an exclusive handout of some kind, such as a seminar manual that is available to only attendees of your seminar, that is a valid opportunity to use that word; by all means point out that this is an exclusive feature of your seminar. If you have a speaker who has unusual credentials, his or her appearance may very well also justify the use of that term *exclusive*. With a little effort, you can almost surely find or create some opportunity to use the word legitimately and justifiably, possibly along the following lines:

Exclusive features:
  - Complete seminar manual. Not available elsewhere.
  - Insider tips from expert Howard Hollaway.
  - Original strategies.

A Word of Caution

Many marketers make claims of such characteristics, simply including them in lists, such as the following:

  NEW! First time ever!
  The Latest Findings.
  Inside tips.
  Shortcuts.
  Exclusive.

That isn't enough. Such broad claims of being new, the latest, the best, and so forth are only promises without proof. They are mere hype and will be recognized as such unless and until you prove otherwise. Don't get confused about this; you must distinguish between promise and proof, for many readers certainly will. It is fine to promise these things *if you can produce the proof*, but not otherwise. If you claim inside tips, explain why/how you can deliver these, but even better, list a couple of the items as proof positive that you are not bluffing. Apply this reasoning to the entire process. It is far more effective to make modest claims that you can support with evidence than to make extravagant claims that you cannot support. The word *exclusive* can be applied to content and coverage, as well as to features, using items such as the following to illustrate and prove your claims:

Exclusive coverage:
- Worry items: What they are, how to find them, how to use them to win.
- Cost strategies: How to *appear* to be low bidder when you are not.
- Using Freedom of Information to gain valuable marketing information.
- Brainstorming to devise capture strategies.

Asking for Action: Closing

Experience in direct mail shows clearly the need to urge respondents to act, and to act promptly. Procrastination is a far more common ailment than you might imagine. Even those who read your letter and brochure, and who decide to register, are prone to putting it off. Unfortunately, in the case of a seminar or workshop, there is a deadline: If the respondent does not act in time the intention to register is of no avail. Thus arises the common exhortation to act without hesitation, and often the rationale for doing so. In the case of a seminar the usual rationale is that seating is limited; therefore the urgent need to act immediately.

That is a close—asking for the order. But that is by no means all that can be included in the letter. There are other profitable uses that can be made of your letter, including at least one additional close that I found most successful. I added a postscript to my letters along the following lines:

It is understandable that you may be unable to register for any of the listed seminar sessions for any of many possible reasons. We invite you to indicate below any special preferences you have for seminar dates and places, and we will try to accommodate you if possible. In any case, we will place your name on a special mailing list for notices of future events.

Preferred date(s) _____

Preferred locations _____

Name _____

Title and company _____

Address _____

City, State, and Zip _____

One benefit of such an additional close is that you do, indeed, develop an additional and especially valuable mailing list of those who have expressed interest in attending your seminar, although unable to take advantage of your current offer. When you have collected enough responses you have a basis for judging which dates and locations are most likely to produce good results. And because this is a list of those who actually responded to your appeal it is a premium list of prospects for whatever you may wish to offer subsequently, including your regular consulting services.

A More Effective Brochure

When you use that large-format brochure as the entire direct-mail "package," it must carry the entire weight of the campaign. But when you have and use a properly developed salesletter you relieve much of that burden and no longer need that oversize (8-1/2- × 11-inch) brochure. You can now make your brochure a size that will fit into a conventional (number 10) business envelope, along with the letter and whatever else you choose to send. You thus gain in more than one way:

- Your mailing is almost sure to be opened and at least scanned briefly because it is in a standard business envelope.
- Because the discard-without-reading figure falls dramatically when you mail material in a business envelope, rather than as obvious advertising, the total mailing can be much smaller and thus less costly and easier to handle.
- Even more important than either of these, however, is the greater effectiveness of the multi-element direct-mail package.

The Total Direct-Mail Package

That latter fact that the direct-mail package must include an assortment of elements to be maximally effective has been established by many mailers in many campaigns, including my own. Selling in general, and selling by mail especially, requires repetition. It always helps to make the sales arguments several times, especially if different motivators can be used each time. The salesletter, which, you hope, will be read first, lays the groundwork, introduces and summarizes the sales arguments, and makes the close. The brochure makes the sales arguments again, but in greater detail, beginning with a suitable headline on the front panel and ending in what direct-mail specialists sometimes refer to as a "response device." That is a euphemism for the order form, and I've no idea why the euphemism is used, other than to add mystique to direct mail, perhaps. These four items—letter, brochure, order form, and return envelope—are considered obligatory and the minimum configuration of a proper direct-mail package. In fact, many packages include flyers, circulars, broadsides (very large foldout circulars), and novelties such as plastic membership cards that resemble credit cards, stickers that must be affixed to the order form, and other "involvement" devices. (The theory—unproved, as far as I can determine—is that if the reader can be persuaded to get involved in the process his or her interest is more likely to become aroused and a sale is thus a more likely consequence.)

You can prepare and include a separate order form. However, I have found it practicable to use one of the panels of the small brochure, perforated by the printer for easy separation, as the registration form (Figure 7-4). This brochure is 4×9 inches, and is created by printing on a 9- $\times$ 12-inch sheet and folding. The folded brochure fits comfortably into a number 10 envelope. However, it is also feasible to print this on an 8-1/2- $\times$ 11-inch sheet and fold to get a slightly smaller brochure, and many small brochures are created in exactly that manner.

A postage-paid return envelope is a good idea when mailing to individuals in their homes. They tend to respond more promptly and more certainly when they do not have to search out a stamp and envelope. However, mailing to business offices is another matter. There, mailing facilities are conveniently at hand, and I found in my early direct-mail adventures that few registrants were using my return envelopes; almost without exception they sent in their registrations and checks in their own business envelopes. So I soon stopped wasting money on return envelopes.

SEMINAR OUTLINE

I. Introduction

A. What Is a Consultant Today? Which Type of Consultant Are You?
The Essential Elements of Consulting Services.
B. Marketing as the Key to Consulting Success.
Are Technical Skills Enough?
Mastering Sales and Marketing Skills.

II. Understanding the Marketing Process

A. The Three Elements of Marketing Successfully.
B. The Elements of Selling: Promise and Proof.

III. Marketing Your Consulting Services Generally

A. The Basic Need to Instill Confidence.
B. How to Gain Prestige and Build a Professional Image.
C. Developing the All-Important Leads.
D. Following Up Leads Correctly.

IV. Marketing To The Public Sector

A. Understanding Public Sector Markets.
B. The Skill of Proposal Writing.

V. Broadening The Base of Your Consulting Practice.

A. Expand Your Profit Centers.
B. Writing: How To Write and Sell Successfully.
C. Publishing: Including newsletters, reports, books, tapes.
D. Public Speaking For Profit.

VI. Open Discussion.

If you have the technical skills and even sales ability — it isn't enough to become a successful consultant. This one day seminar focuses on the marketing of your skills and developing other Profit Centers to keep your business growing.

Learn how to not only market your consulting services generally, but how to tap into the public sector markets on the federal, state and local levels. Learn first-hand how to create proposals, successful bids and contracts. Let Mr. Holtz show you how to expand your business into the profitable areas of WRITING, PUBLISHING, PUBLIC SPEAKING and other FREELANCE PROJECTS.

For the man or woman who's considering consulting professionally, or who's starting a practice and wants to develop it, HOW TO SUCCEED AS AN INDEPENDENT CONSULTANT is an A-Z seminar that will guide you to success.

Each participant in the seminar will receive a copy of Mr. Holtz's book: HOW TO SUCCEED AS AN INDEPENDENT CONSULTANT.

Instructor

HERMAN HOLTZ

- Consultant
- Lecturer
- Author
- Engineer
- Seminar Leader
- Winner of over $125 million in government contracts

Herman Holtz is an independent consultant in Washington, D.C. and the author of several books including:

- HOW TO SUCCEED AS AN INDEPENDENT CONSULTANT
- PROFIT FROM YOUR MONEY-MAKING IDEAS: How to build a new business or expand an existing one.
- DIRECTORY OF FEDERAL PURCHASING OFFICES: Where, What, How to Sell to the U.S. Government.
- GOVERNMENT CONTRACTS: Proposalmanship and Winning Strategies.
- THE WINNING PROPOSAL: How To Write It.

Mr. Holtz has been Director of Marketing at Volt Information Sciences, Inc. and Applied Science Associates, and has worked in various capacities as Editorial Director of the Educational Science Division, U.S. Industries. He has been a successful seminar leader in the marketing field in Washington, D.C.

Figure 7-4. Inside panels of small brochure with order form. Copyright © by Herman Holtz.

172

Credentials

The letter should probably have made at least some brief reference to the credentials of the presenter(s) (some brochures refer to the presenters as the "faculty"), but the details normally appear in the brochure. However, that does not mean a full resume; there is neither room nor necessity for that much detail. What should be here are the most impressive credentials, such as graduate degrees, unusual honors, remarkable achievements, significant and relevant past positions, or books published, and a quite-brief summary of relevant background. Do try to find something noteworthy to feature, however. This is a case where just being adequate is not nearly enough; you should try to find something few competitors could claim. Do not waste time and space on trivia here; that does harm by making it appear that the presenter has no real credentials. If you truly cannot find anything noteworthy to say about your presenter(s), you are probably far better off to be silent on the subject or to supply name(s) only.

Testimonials

You will not have testimonials for your first seminar, of course, unless you have conducted seminars for others—a past employer or client, perhaps—or spoken at others' seminars and have gotten some on-the-record remarks concerning your presentations. That is one reason for asking participants to fill out evaluation forms. From those forms I was able to glean and use such comments as these:

- Everything was presented at three levels, meaty for both beginners and experts.
- Excellent case histories; well done.
- I picked up 12 pointers, including how to appear to be the low bidder and how to get their attention with your proposals.

An indirect testimonial used quite commonly is a list of former participants, usually listing attendees by their companies and focusing on the well-known companies. In my own case, for example, I often listed Western Union, Bethelehem Steel, Sikorsky Aircraft, and similarly well-known companies as having sent employees to attend my seminars and workshops on government marketing and proposal writing.

"Who Should Attend"

A paragraph titled "Who should attend" appears commonly in seminar brochures. The intent is to make clear who can gain benefits from attending, in the event the reader is unsure about this. It should help the reader reason out which employees in the organization ought to attend the seminar.

For example, a brochure for a seminar on desktop publishing says under that caption, "This seminar will be of value to anyone producing newsletters, instruction manuals, or other materials distributed to customers, prospects, members, or employees." (It goes on in that vein for several more sentences.)

Other Elements

There are other items you can include with this mailing, but since that is a more fitting subject for the next chapter, we will discuss those later. One thing more that should be discussed here before going on, however, is marketing the in-house, custom seminar. Obviously, that is a somewhat different marketing challenge, although you can make use of some of the materials already discussed here.

MARKETING THE CUSTOM, IN-HOUSE SEMINAR

The prospects you address in selling in-house presentations of your seminar are the same prospects as you address in seeking the registration of employees. The main difference is in the appeal and in what is offered, but there is also a difference in prospect: The smallest employer, even the self-employed entrepreneur, is a prospect for the open-registration seminar, but only the employer with a number of employees to have trained—usually, I would estimate, at least 10— is a prospect for the in-house presentation. That, however, is not the only category of prospect; I have also encountered these:

- The membership organization interested in presenting one or more seminars as special events or as part of the program at an annual convention or conference.
- The membership organization interested in staging a seminar as a fund-raising promotion.

- The manufacturing organization staging a seminar for their major customers, especially OEMs (original equipment manufacturers who buy the major system components from the manufacturer).
- Groups organizing an annual convention that includes seminars to which admission is charged.
- The organization—a government agency, for example—with a comprehensive training program to which they may be persuaded to add your seminar.
- The seminar producer or other large training organization who may be amenable to adding you and your seminar to their resources and promotions.

The term "membership organization" includes a wide variety of associations, including at least professional societies, trade associations, community groups, and clubs. Among those I have encountered and presented seminars to and for have been the Automotive Parts and Accessories Association, the Land Improvement Contractors Association, and the Northeast-Midwest Congressional Coalition, but there are literally thousands of associations in the United States, many of them large enough to become suitable prospects for in-house seminars. In fact, the United States has developed something of a reputation internationally for organizing associations of all kinds, and there are several rather thick directories listing them.

Approaching Potential Clients

There are several possible routes for marketing in-house seminars to organizations. Some of the general methods and approaches, especially those that are also commonly used to market consulting services generally, were mentioned and discussed briefly in the preceding chapter. But there are other possible approaches that ought to be mentioned before discussing the materials you need to market custom seminars.

The direct route, when dealing with a typical corporation, usually means making your offer to one of several executives. In some large corporations, a manager of training programs would be a good entry point for your direct-marketing effort and may even be delegated to find a program such as the one you wish to offer. (I was once favored with a $17,000 contract to develop a custom program as a result of such a training manager being directed to find someone qualified for such an assignment.) However, your best bet in many cases is the executive heading up the department most relevant to the subject matter of your seminar—the marketing director, comptroller, purchasing agent, publications manager, or other executive who is most likely to derive benefits from the presentation.

In the case of associations you usually deal with the individual functioning as program manager, whether or not that is the title used. You may use that as a generic title for mailings or, when otherwise making a direct approach to the association, for seeking the right individual to talk to.

There are also many indirect ways of approaching associations and corporations. Many organizations of both types turn to lecture bureaus for aid in finding speakers, and they are often open to suggestions for full seminar presentations. Moreover, when it comes to conferences and conventions many organizations turn to convention managers (these are usually companies, not individuals) and/or special meeting and convention consultants for help in putting a program together and making all necessary arrangements.

The Direct-Mail Package

Obviously there are a few differences in the approach and materials necessary to market your seminar on a custom basis. You do not need to abandon all the materials you use for marketing your seminar to the public at large, however, if you have done so and thus have the relevant brochures and letters. You can make good use of these, but you also need to develop a new salesletter, whether you do or do not use the old salesletter.

You need only prepare a salesletter that explains briefly who you are and what you propose and that refers to the enclosed brochure. You may also enclose a copy of the salesletter you use for your other direct mail, but that means incurring the potential hazard of confusing the reader with two salesletters; it is probably more practical and more effective to alter the original salesletter and adapt it to the new purpose. That should not be especially difficult. In fact, when I receive an inquiry from a potential new client for a custom seminar, my response always includes a copy of one or more of the open-registration brochures I have used in the past, and I write a letter based on the letters I have used to solicit seminar registrations. (This is easy to do if you keep appropriate "swipe files" in your computer system.)

Your brochure includes prices for individual registrations, which are irrelevant in this case, of course. You may block these registration fees out if you wish, but it is unnecessary because you will discuss or at least make reference to your fee in the letter.

Lecture Bureaus and Fees

It is necessary to understand that lecture bureaus, convention managers, meeting consultants, and others who may act as brokers in arranging for you to present your seminar on a custom basis are the agents of the client organization, and they represent the clients, not you. The clients may have asked the broker to try to get some specific speaker or they may have asked for recommendations. Any agreements you reach with a broker for an engagement is probably tentative and depends on getting client approval, so it is unwise to make any firm plans or expend time and money on the project until you get a confirmation. (Personally, if I am dealing with an unknown organization or individual, I like to have a confirmation of some kind in written form.) Until I get that confirmation I do not list the engagement on my calendar or make any plans for it.

Auditions

Even after you have presented seminars for years, have something of a reputation, and can produce many testimonials and other bona fides, you occasionally encounter prospective clients who insist upon auditioning you before making a firm commitment. Presumably they want to review and confirm the acceptability of both your qualities as a speaker and the content of your presentation. You may be able to satisfy them with an audition tape (more on this subject shortly), but you may run into a demand for an actual presentation.

I have encountered this demand for auditioning me personally only twice, fortunately. The first time I neglected to follow up and arrange for the prospect's attendance at my next seminar, and so let the matter drop entirely. The second time has been a recent event. Although I sent this prospective client an envelope containing my credentials and an audition tape, he asked to sit in on one of my seminars. Fortunately, I was able to arrange for his invitation to an upcoming seminar with the assumption that he will be satisfied and retain me to present a seminar at his organization's convention.

Audition Tapes

An audition tape is always useful, but it is especially so when you are still rather new and unknown. However, it must be a good tape, for a poor one is worse than none.

Many seminar presenters make arrangements to tape their seminars, select the best recording, and have the tapes duplicated and packaged for sale as cassette seminars. Unfortunately, these come across as what they are: amateur efforts. The recordings are uneven in level (sound volume), and full of echoes, throat clearing, inaudible remarks, and other such flaws.

To attempt to use a portion of such a recording as an audition tape is a fatal error. Such tapes are hardly good advertisements for you. To get a good audition tape you must get professional help.

There are two ways to go about this. The ideal way, from one viewpoint, is to do all the recording in a sound studio. That assures you of good tape quality. However, it lacks the real dynamics of an energy-charged live seminar. From another viewpoint, therefore, the truly ideal way is to have an expert come to your seminar with professional recording equipment and handle the whole job, which includes the editing for the final cassette.

That latter method can be quite expensive. But there is a compromise method: Tape several of your seminar presentations and entrust a professional sound studio with making a final set of tapes from those recordings. That will require extensive editing and patching together of the best portions of the various recordings, and your help will be needed to ensure proper continuity and to make a few bridging remarks in the studio, which the editor will splice in appropriately.

All of that is appropriate to the making of a tape version of your complete seminar, and there is a market for such tapes. However, to make an audition tape—and it need not be more than 15 minutes long—you can prepare a special script and record it in the studio. That makes a proper tape which presents you at your best as a speaker.

The Salesletter

Like all salesletters this one should make its main point immediately—that you are offering a custom seminar (or a choice of several, if that is the case) on a fee basis. It can open with a headline that makes the main point and an introductory paragraph that may vary according to what services you wish to offer and to whom you wish to offer them. You can mention all your services in a single letter or you can prepare several different letters. A desktop computer and word processing program enable you to do this easily, and in fact I keep a number of files as "boilerplate" for such purposes. Here is a partial list of some of these files, describing what each contains, to illustrate the utility of maintaining such material ready at hand:

Program Descriptions

I keep a number of these because I offer several different programs. These files include schedules, outlines, and narrative descriptions of each program and of the handout materials for each program. In fact, there are also complete manuscript files of various brochures and salesletters included here. With the small cost of floppy disks today it is entirely practicable to keep archive copies of even old and obsolete files, for they often become unexpectedly useful later.

Credentials

There are several versions of my biography, each written to support a different purpose or different type of program. There are also lists of my books, articles, and testimonials, lists of clients, and other supporting evidence of credentials for making the presentations.

Seminar Handouts

There are files for all kinds of handouts, including complete manuscript copies of outlines, manuals, exercises, and other such items.

Introduction

In most cases someone who is a stranger will introduce you to the audience. It is a good idea to have an introduction on paper prepared in advance and handed over to whomever will introduce you. In this way, the introducer, who does not know you or know much about you, will not stumble and flounder about. In fact, you may find it expedient, as I do, to have several such introductions, each for a different kind of occasion.

Miscellaneous

I find it useful to maintain a number of files for miscellaneous purposes. One is a file of all dates of significance, including appointments. Another is for notes. Another is for diaries or logs.

Letters

I have certain more or less standard form letters I use for different purposes. However, because the desktop computer makes it so easy, I use these as basic models only, and modify them as each occasion demands. It's quite easy to do so, I find, with all the boilerplate files listed here readily available.

I add to these files frequently. When I prepare custom materials or revise or update a file, I often keep a separate copy of the original file. I even keep a copy of each letter at least temporarily, reviewing later to decide what can be safely discarded, what ought to be kept in current active files, and what ought to be stored in archives for possible future need. That has frequently proved itself a sensible practice.

There are a number of possible options open to you. Here are six you may wish to consider in connection with doing custom, in-house seminars:

1. A single standardized seminar, offered wherever it fits.
2. Two or more standardized seminars, offered where they fit.
3. A basic seminar that you customize on a limited scale for each client.
4. Two or more basic seminars that you customize on a limited scale.
5. Totally customized seminars based on your own basic seminars or seminar materials.
6. Custom development of new seminars from the ground up.
7. All of the above.

You may wish to undertake only one of these, several of these, or all of these. If you choose all or, at least, more than one of these approaches, you should create a different letter for each option. Figure 7-5 presents some basic ideas for a headline and paragraphs for a salesletter offering such custom, in-house seminar services as those listed here. Of course, you may select suitable materials from these or develop new ones.

CUSTOM SEMINAR PRESENTATIONS FOR ANY OCCASION

Our exclusive seminar, [title], is available in its original form on short notice and at highly competitive rates. This seminar has been presented open to the public many times to representatives from such organizations as [names of prominent companies and/or other well-known organizations] and as an in-house, custom presentation to [names].

A brief description of the seminar and several of its outstanding features follows, but there is also enclosed other literature, including a descriptive brochure used for open-registration announcements of this seminar, providing more complete details.

We offer a variety of standard seminars, all of which have been well received by audiences in many earlier presentations, and all of which are available as custom presentations for in-house training, part of convention or conference programs, as special events, or for other occasions and uses. The enclosed literature describes these programs in detail.

We offer these presentations on a modest fixed-fee basis, to be negotiated. We can customize our presentations to individual needs on a limited basis without penalty or we can carry out more extensive customization at slight additional costs. If you wish to propose some basis other than that of a flat, fixed fee, we are open to discussion and negotiation regarding this.

We offer also to provide full services for the development of completely new seminar programs to your specifications or to conduct initial analysis to help develop the specifications as a first step.

Figure 7-5. Suggested headline and paragraphs.

8

MINIMIZING COSTS AND MAXIMIZING INCOME

The line between profit and loss in seminars can be quite a thin one, but a little well-placed parsimony and piggyback marketing can broaden the margin of safety.

STARTING OFF ON THE WRONG FOOT

A great many of us tend to go overboard a bit in spending when we begin a new venture, especially when we accept gratuitous advice. For example, an acquaintance who learned that I was organizing and presenting my own seminars and who had had some experience in doing just that volunteered many well-meant suggestions. One was the suggestion that I make a double mailing to my list, since conventional direct-mail wisdom holds that repeat mailings often produce even better results than the original mailing does. Too, my friend was a firm believer in "envelope copy"—teasers printed on the outside of the envelope that will potentially help capture interest, persuade the recipient to study the content, and reward you with an order. He also believed in doing things in a big way generally, and encouraged me to think on a somewhat grander scale than my normally penny-pinching nature would permit.

I have no quarrel with the ideas of repeat mailings and envelope copy in principle. In fact, I believe that they are very sound ideas, when used appropriately. My continuing experience with seminar marketing, however, cast doubt on the applicability of these to my own needs. I found the extra cost did not produce proportionately greater results and so soon abandoned these practices.

I had much the same experience with some other ideas. My first seminar included a luncheon, for example, and although the seminar was a great success in many ways—it brought out 54 participants, despite a most modest marketing effort, and the participants obviously enjoyed both the luncheon and the luncheon speaker—the luncheon was quite expensive and I could not justify the extra cost in either added appeal or a greater registration fee. It ate heavily into the profits, as did some other "big" ideas. To this day I am unable to justify included luncheons as beneficial to the marketing effort, and they may even be a negative factor, since their inclusion suggests to some that the seminar registration may be far more costly than it ought to be.

LITTLE MARGIN FOR ERROR

There is a definite risk factor in producing seminars to which you invite the public on an individual basis. One of my sponsors who has in the past run many highly successful seminars recently planned three that had to be canceled because his mailings drew too few registrations. That cost him his initial investment in the mailing—printing, postage, mailing lists, and labor.

His major problem is that he is unable or unwilling to make his own seminar presentations or even personally manage each presentation. Since he must therefore pay a presenter-manager a substantial fee for this service, he cannot afford to run a seminar that does not draw a reasonably large number of registrations. But a consultant handling his own seminar presentations and management can turn a profit on approximately one-half the number the first individual requires for profitable operation.

The margin between profit and loss—between a "go" and "no go" for a projected seminar—can be quite thin. I have observed more than one consultant launch a seminar venture and ultimately abandon it because the economics of the operation demand an unrealistically large number of attendees. One of my professional acquaintances produced a seminar to which he invited a prominent consultant/speaker as his main attraction. That individual did quite well; my acquaintance barely recovered his costs plus a most modest profit after paying the consultant speaker. The speaker did well because of his "back-of-the-room sales," about which more will be said later, although he complained that he did not do as well as usual.

BROADENING THE MARGIN FOR ERROR

One way—probably the ideal way—to overcome this economic problem is to handle everything yourself, as I have trained myself to do. (I started out relying on others, but soon learned to do it all myself.) Once I got my act together, I became quite independent. My own seminars open to the public drew, typically, 20–50 participants, and were quite profitable for me at 20 attendees. However, since I ultimately learned to do it all myself and could have a worthwhile day with as few as 10 participants, while breaking even on fewer, I was never forced to cancel an announced seminar session.

Alternatives to Doing It All Yourself

Many individuals are willing to appear as guest speakers without charge or for modest honoraria. Unfortunately, many of these are worth no more than they cost you. It is not a good idea to use such speakers, except in exceptional circumstances. The exceptional circumstances that occur to me are when the individual has some unusually important information or is an unusually important or prominent individual, and is going to speak quite briefly. I know, for example, of one individual who is most highly regarded as an expert in his field—he has, in fact, an international reputation—but who is, most unfortunately, a truly dreadful speaker; I would never want him to address an audience of mine for more than five or ten minutes! I think his name and reputation might carry him that far but not farther!

This does not mean that it is not possible to get excellent speakers at little or no cost. Do not make that common mistake of judging quality by the cost; it's a false standard. You will recall, I hope, that earlier I pointed you toward organizations in your area who would be likely to furnish speakers free of charge. Government agencies are especially good resources for this. The Small Business Administration, the Department of Commerce, the National Science Foundation, the Internal Revenue Service, and many other government agencies, including those of state and local governments, are usually quite cooperative in this. If you need assistance in finding speakers from government agencies try calling your local representative in Congress. Representatives get involved in many such projects, and will probably furnish direct help.

You should "audition" potential speakers, even those whose services cost you nothing, to make sure that their delivery and information is appropriate and acceptable for your needs. You can do this by taking the time to attend free sessions, of which there are many. Read the business pages of your local newspapers and be sure to check the bulletin boards and other places where notices of free lectures and seminars appear.

There are many other possible resources. Try also local business groups, including the Lions Club, the Rotary, the Better Business Bureau, and the Chamber of Commerce. Ask to be placed on their distribution lists for press releases and other releases of public information. Visit your local public libraries and see what special events they have listed on their bulletin boards. Use the telephone directory to find companies in related businesses, who are often delighted to furnish literature, information, and speakers, and send them notices of your interests or call them for specific requests. Look up related newsletters and other periodicals and read them. These also have other values for you: The publishers are often delighted to furnish sample copies for your participants and even come and address your group.

It is not only those who are new and struggling to get started who are willing to help by donating their time and energies. Many who are successful and well established are eager to help. Why? Is it because we are all natural hams who can't wait to get on the platform—*any* platform? Is it a sense of obligation to others who are struggling to get started and need any help they can get (even as we once did)? Is it a sympathy for the underdog? Is it because we have retired or become semi-retired and are uneasy to be out of harness? It may be any or all of these, but whatever it is, it exists and you can take advantage of it. Here is an example:

The Washington editor of a business magazine organized a small-business seminar to be presented at our local community college. She persuaded a number of experienced professionals to make personal presentations. I was one, with a half-hour presentation on marketing generally, and there was a retired advertising executive who spoke on the subject of advertising, another who lectured on how to encourage customers to complain as a method for improving whatever you do, and a number of others, each of whom spoke on his or her own subject. My reward—an unexpected one, I admit—was a subsequent paid seminar presentation for one of the attendees, but the greater reward was the satisfaction I derived from taking part. Strangely, there is a great deal of satisfaction in these activities when you no longer *need* to do them. And with a rapidly expanding population of retired experts in a broad variety of fields, there is a vast pool of such support readily available.

ATTACKING THE HIGH COST OF ADVERTISING AND PROMOTION

By far the major cost in seminar ventures is that of sales promotion—advertising, principally, whether in periodicals or by direct mail. All other expenses are usually almost incidental. And so if you are going to try to reduce your costs, it is in this area that you must make the major effort.

The Press Release

One way to do this is to take advantage of every opportunity to win publicity, which is free advertising, in effect. Write a press release (Figure 8-1) and send it to appropriate newsletters and other periodicals.

Seminar Associates, Inc.
17 Hopeful Lane
Bookends, MA 02345

NEWS RELEASE

March 23, 1999

                           Contact Jeremiah Marsh
                              999/999-9999

        SECRETS OF WINNING GOVERNMENT MILLIONS REVEALED

    On May 7, 1999, marketing consultant Peter Peters, of Seminar Associates,

Inc., will reveal to attendees of his seminar the methods by which he has

managed to win over $425 million in contracts with the federal, state, local,

and foreign governments over the past 20 years.

    "Whether you are or are not the best engineer or best contractor is not

the issue," says Peters. "What counts is whether you are the best proposal

writer, for it is the best proposal writer who wins the contract. And so that

is what our seminar is all about: how to write the best proposal."

    Peters says he has been presenting this seminar all across the United

States for the past 10 years and has trained thousands in his methods. This

year, he says, the training is more critical than ever because the Pentagon is

trying to compress the budget and there is great emphasis on keeping costs

down without sacrificing quality.

    For a brochure and complete details, says the sponsor, Seminar

Associates, Inc., call 999 999-9999 or write Seminar Associates, Inc. at 17

Hopeful Lane, Bookends, MA 02345.

                     ###

Figure 8-1. Example of news release.

The chief problem with this is time. Most monthly magazines, and even some monthly tabloids, require two or more months lead time to publish anything of note. Weekly publications and most newsletters, however, operate in something closer to "real time" and so are appropriate targets for releases. And most newsletters whose coverage and readership are appropriate to your seminar will run the notices you send them, helping you get the announcement out in time to be of some help.

The news release is not an advertisement and will rarely be reproduced exactly as you wrote it. Instead, the editor who uses it will extract the essential information and present it as he or she sees fit.

So it does little good to write an inflated account of your seminar. It is usually better to be concise and to let the editor know where readers can learn the details, as in the news release illustrated in the figure.

Writing the Press Release

In practice, try to treat news releases as though they were print advertising or brochures by finding a headline and lead that will capture the editor's attention and arouse interest. Remember that the editor is always looking for items that will be of interest to the readers and judges your release on that basis primarily. The editor knows, of course, that your motive is free advertising, in the form of publicity, and is willing to trade that for information that is "newsworthy"— likely to be of interest, although not *news* in the technical sense.

Mailing Lists for Press Releases

The main consideration in selecting publications for your releases, other than the time factor already discussed, is whether the publication is addressed to and read by individuals who are the right prospects for you. (This is as much a concern of the editor as it is your concern.) If your seminar concerns computer technology, you want to seek out newsletters and tabloids for computer technologists, for example. But some general publications are also frequently appropriate. A local newspaper, for example, may carry a regular column on local events of all kinds, business or otherwise, and you should address that column especially, not the newspaper generally.

Even in the case of small and specialized publications, such as a newsletter for coin collectors, there may be "departments" or special columns, and you must address these especially if you want to maximize the probability that your information will be published. Busy editors are not always willing to take the time to figure out where your release would best fit; it is a wise move for you to do this yourself, as much as possible, when sending your releases.

This means that you must do some research to develop a proper mailing list for your releases. Read as many relevant publications as possible. Either buy one of the several directories that list periodicals or visit a nearby public library and ask the librarian for help.

Recognize in this research that you have both vertical and horizontal markets, depending primarily on the nature and appeal of your seminar. If your seminar deals with the technology of computer design, for example, it is likely to be of interest to electronic engineers and possibly to some computer programmers, but to few others. That makes it a vertical—narrowly specialized—market. But if it deals with the business applications and office uses of desktop computers, it is of potential interest to almost everyone who owns or uses a computer, and that makes it a horizontal—broad and almost universal—market. (Presumably you took that into consideration when drawing up your original plans, so you need only remind yourself of those plans now.)

Ways to Broaden the Distribution

Be sure to include relevant associations on your list. Most associations have some kind of newsletter or similar periodical. In addition, many associations, especially large ones, maintain offices and facilities, such as internal libraries, reading rooms, meeting rooms, and lounges for members. In such cases your releases may get posted on bulletin boards. Notices that are designed especially for posting on bulletin boards—signs, with large type and succinct messages, that is—can be of even greater help, indicating by their very appearance to what use they should be put, as well as being more effective in that use than a memorandum or release would be. Send them to places where they are likely to be posted. (You can make up a master list and make a few copies or you can use the facilities of a computer and printer to print out as many copies as you need.)

You can post such notices and copies of your releases yourself in many places, such as in public libraries, in public community buildings, and perhaps even in supermarkets that have bulletin boards. Don't overlook nearby federal, state, and local government offices, for many government employees may be interested and apply to their employers for authorization to attend at public expense. Never overlook that public sector in promoting and publicizing your seminar, or you are overlooking an important market segment. And that means hand carrying your releases into many of these offices and personally posting them on bulletin boards.

There is still another way to widen the distribution of these releases and get them into the hands of those who might not be reached via a newsletter or a mailing list. That is by including a routing box or "buck slip," as some have called it, with your releases and letters. This is a simple device, probably already familiar to you, as it is to most people who have worked in busy offices (see Figure 8-2). It is used to circulate a memo, letter, or other document within the organization.

This is a very useful device that enables you to get inside help in circulating your appeals to those within the organization. In fact, this device can be used on any literature you send out, including salesletters, newsletters, brochures, releases, memoranda, and others. You can include this as a box imprinted on the document itself in the upper right or left corner or as a slip attached to the document. (The first alternative is usually the most desirable for several reasons.)

The box may be blank, with merely the word "routing" or "circulation," to suggest the use, or it may have the first line or two addressed by you to someone in a particular position. This is an excellent device to use when you are unsure of names within the organization or of which individual is the best prospect, but is also put to good use merely to broaden the circulation of your literature within the organization. The small box at the right is for the individual to check off, after inscribing the name of the next individual to whom the item is to be circulated.

Routing:	

Marketing Manager	

Figure 8-2. Routing box.

These forms need not be very long; three or four lines are usually adequate. Now that circulation of the item has been suggested by use of that box, if more lines are needed, someone will probably attach an internal routing slip, such as many organizations use.

Starting Names for Routing Boxes

The nature of your seminar itself should suggest the most logical functional title for the first line of the routing form—or, for that matter, for someone to address on the envelope. In my case the most logical person is the director of marketing. However, some of the organizations I have worked with have had proposal managers, some have made proposals the responsibility of their publications department, and some have assigned the responsibility to the engineering chief or other line executive. Moreover, some make an individual permanently responsible for proposals, while others select a different manager for each proposal. Too, some organizations have both a marketing director and a sales manager, while others have one, but not the other.

Among the types of functionaries to be found in business organizations, regardless of their actual titles, and depending on the nature of the organization, are these:

Chief executive officer (CEO)/president/chairman.
Executive vice president.
General manager.
Comptroller/accounting manager.
Administrator.
Director of marketing.
Sales manager.
Advertising manager.
Data systems manager.
Purchasing agent/buyer.
Personnel manager.
Production manager.
Librarian.

In short, there are no universal practices, and unless you can ascertain who is the best addressee for you in each organization, you must trust to general devices, such as broadly functional titles and routing forms.

If you look back at some of the seminar titles cited earlier, you find that in at least some cases the title of the seminar suggests the kind of functional title to be used. Here are some of those seminar titles repeated:

1. "How to be an Assertive Manager"
2. "How to Buy Printing and Related Services"
3. "Training & Computers Seminar: How to Teach People to Use Computers"
4. "How to Work with Customers"
5. "Proposals & Competition: How to Develop Winning Proposals"
6. "How to Supervise People"
7. "How to Get Things Done"
8. "How to Write and Design Sales Literature"
9. "Developing Applications with dBase III Plus"
10. "Networking IBM Personal Computers"
11. "Writing Effective Advertising"
12. "Designing & Preparing Camera-Ready Artwork"
13. "Basic Supervision Seminar"
14. "Advanced Supervision Skills"
15. "Strategic Planning for Data Base"

Seminar number 1 on the list is for all managers, and literature is thus probably best addressed to the CEO, executive vice president, or general manager, executives to whom all the other managers normally report. You would expect one of these to decide whether to send some of the managers to the seminar.

The second seminar on the list is obviously intended primarily for the purchasing agent, but may be of equal interest to anyone responsible for buying printing—publications managers, advertising managers, and even sales or marketing directors. (The purchase of printing is not necessarily centralized in an organization, but may be done independently in and by each department.)

The third seminar might be addressed to the manager of training, but since relatively few of any but the large corporations have a training manager, the responsibility for training may fall on anyone, especially the executive in charge of computer operations and/or data systems, if the organization has such an individual. The same reasoning may be applied to the other seminars listed. There is no standard practice for assigning responsibilities for the functions that are the subjects of the seminars.

In any case, much depends on the kind of organizations you decide are right for you, those you wish to address, but think carefully about this: You may get an occasional surprise. In this case, the first seminar addresses a truly horizontal market: The appeal can be equally great for all kinds of organizations. The second seminar is almost as broad, since virtually all organizations must buy at least some printing, and almost anyone in the organization may be assigned the responsibility for doing so (although only someone who buys a great deal of printing would normally be motivated to attend this seminar). The third seminar is a somewhat different story. In organizations that do not have a training department, the publications department may be responsible for writing and administering training. However, consider this: Is this a seminar whose appeal is to only those with a need to use the training internally—to train their own employees or members (in the case of an association)? Or is there another possible prospect in the many companies whose own business is the development, sale, and administration of training programs?

The fact is that many such companies would be good prospects for this kind of seminar because most of them have only limited subject-matter expertise in-house. Their expertise lies principally in training design and development, and in training methodology generally; they need such expert technical advice as that offered by this seminar to help them in developing their own programs. Ergo, it would not necessarily be only general managers, training managers, or even publications managers in user organizations who would find this a seminar of interest, but marketing chiefs and others in training-development companies might also be customers. (You will often discover, if you are objective enough and introspective enough in your analyses, that even competitors do not always have adverse interests.)

Of course, these seminars are also of potential interest to members of relevant associations, to nonprofit corporations, and to government agencies of all kinds, and few organizations are more interested in training employees than are government agencies. They are almost always excellent prospects for seminars and all other training projects, including the development of special custom training programs.

One way you should consider distributing literature is by making it available in help-yourself stacks at appropriate locations, such as meetings, conferences, and conventions. In many cases you can get a free pass to enter the exhibit hall, but in any case you can always get to the registration desk where you can often find places for your literature.

ANOTHER PR/PROMOTION IDEA

If you publish a newsletter of your own, you will of course use it to help attract registrants for your seminar. However, in the likely event that you do not publish one as yet, you may wish to utilize the idea as a convenient and effective way to promote your seminars. It is quite easy to do and not very expensive.

The promotion newsletter—and I am suggesting here that you create a small and inexpensive newsletter that you will distribute free of charge—need not be very expensive. It can be a single sheet—two pages—or a folded sheet—four pages—and it can be published on an infrequent basis when you see fit.

Its chief function is to publicize and promote your seminars, but it must have something more than advertising in it if you expect recipients to read it and value it. Therefore, do include some useful information about your special field—even mention prominently the consulting services you provide—but also give the readers a reason to read the newsletter and pass it around to others.

Be sure to put a routing box in the upper right or left corner. (I favor the upper right corner as the more prominent position.) And be sure to list a subscription price on it, despite the fact that it is free. It's also a good idea to 3-hole punch it as a suggestion to readers to save it.

You can make this a formally typeset piece, if you wish, but that is not really necessary; typewriter or computer-printer composition is perfectly adequate. However, the nameplate—that box at the top with the title and relevant data about the publisher and editor—ought to be set in type of suitable sizes and character.

Because it is a newsletter, it is especially suitable for help-yourself supplies at meetings and conventions or other such places.

You can often make deals with others running seminars to make each other's promotional material available on literature tables. And if you are willing to make brief presentations at others' seminars as a guest speaker, you can widen the distribution of your literature and have your own seminars announced from the dais by your host. You can also exchange complimentary subscriptions with other newsletter publishers and help each other publicize seminars and/or other events.

For some applications the newsletter is even more suitable than is the news release, but you should use both.

ADDING PROFIT CENTERS

Professional public speakers are often also consultants and/or writers, both of which appear to be natural adjuncts to public speaking. Moreover, a great many of these consultant/writer/speakers publish their own books and tape cassettes and sell them directly as "back-of-the-room sales" (sometimes literally that) during or after (usually after) their lectures and seminars.

In fact, these individuals report that the "BR" (back-of-the-room) sales should and do at least equal their speaking fees or the revenue gained via registrations. They state that they *expect* this volume of revenue from the BR sales. This revenue not only increases the profitability of the seminars, but it can make an otherwise marginal or even money-losing seminar into a profitable operation. So profitable is this part of the operation for some speakers that one of my acquaintances complained rather bitterly that he had spent the whole day delivering a seminar in which his BR sales were "only" about $6,200! (Calculate conservatively at least 50-percent gross profit.)

This individual sells several books and tape programs, some of which he publishes himself and some of which are published by commercial book publishers. Since he generally sells his own packages of books and tapes at prices of $250 and above, it does not take a great many sales to add up to a substantial day's income.

He keeps his products on daylong display near his rostrum and refers to them periodically, but does not offer them for sale until the closing moments of his presentation, by which time he has prepared his participants to make the purchase. (Not too surprisingly, he is a master salesman and lectures on that subject.)

There is an interesting variant of this idea that I experimented with successfully. At the time I was publishing a newsletter of my own, a series of manuals, and a number of special reports, as well as producing occasional seminars open to the public, and was promoting all of these principally by direct mail. Then one day I began to wonder why I was spending so many dollars on postage and printing to mail separate offers to the same target prospects.

As a result of that sudden insight into what should have been obvious much earlier, I began to include sales literature in the package

I was mailing out to solicit seminar registrations. In a short time I discovered that the responses to these mailings were at least large enough to defray all the seminar costs. Suddenly, I couldn't lose on seminars. I had taken most of the risk out of both ventures by making them share the costs of labor, mailing and some printing, and I did so at no sacrifice of any kind.

One other reason I especially like this idea is that I prefer to use first-class mail instead of bulk and permit mail, despite the difference in cost. Since first-class rates are based on a one-ounce weight, you can mail up to five 8-1/2-× 11-inch sheets in a number 10 envelope with a first-class stamp. Frankly, at today's high cost of postage it bothered me to mail fewer than the five sheets my first-class stamp entitled me to. I welcomed the opportunity to get a fuller value for my postal dollars.

Five sheets equal 10 pages, which can total 5,000 or more words of information and sales arguments. And if you choose to use a lighter weight paper you can add another sheet. In any case, that means that you can send out a fair amount of literature under that first-class postage. If that enables you to combine two separate direct-mail campaigns, as it did me, you have effectively halved the cost of the postage while keeping the benefits of first-class mail, a sensible and desirable economy.

Of course, this is a useful idea only if you have some other products to sell. Even if you are not yet ready to publish printed material or tape cassettes of your own, you can include literature promoting your consulting services, especially if you can come up with some kind of special offer, such as a half-price initial appraisal. (It is possible to do things such as this without losing dignity, if you handle it well.) Whether you consider resulting sales additional income or reduced promotion costs, the result is the same: You have reduced the costs and risks and you have increased the net profits, certainly a worthy achievement.

9 DOING IT YOURSELF

We live in a do-it-yourself era for a number of reasons, but it is the benefit of being in control that is the most important consequence of this revolution.

A MODERN ANOMALY

That we live in an increasingly do-it-yourself era is strangely anomalous when you consider that it is also an era of increasing specialization. It is technology that is largely responsible, as it has built into modern equipment and methods the specialized skills formerly necessary for many processes. Today, as soon as you learn the basics necessary to operate a desktop computer you can carry out many kinds of fairly intricate editorial processes with little more skill than is required to operate a common typewriter. The revolution that made offset printing the successor to letterpress printing also made unnecessary and obsolete the traditional lengthy apprenticeship necessary to become a qualified printer. However, the xerographic office copier made even that revolutionary development nearly obsolescent for much of today's short run printing. Anyone can learn to operate an office copier in minutes.

It is thus possible today for you personally to produce, promote, market, and present your seminars, and in this chapter we will discuss a few of the processes you can use to do most things for yourself.

The computer is a key item in this, and it alone enables you to handle many chores you would once have had to call on vendor specialists to do for you.

THE DESKTOP COMPUTER

It is not known who decided that the new microcomputer was a "personal" computer and should be so named. In any case, the name *desktop computer* is far more appropriate, for many of today's desktop models can do far more than the behemoth *mainframe* computers of only a few years ago. The model I own and operate is itself probably quite typical at the moment (although at the rate changes occur in computers it may be a doddering old relic of times long gone by the time you read these words!) It is an XT "clone," also called a "compatible," which means that it is patterned after the IBM XT™ model and is nearly identical in all respects. It has a 640K RAM (memory), two 360K floppy disk drives, a 20M hard disk drive, a high resolution amber monitor, runs Leading Edge MS DOS 3.1 operating-system software, and is supported by a dot-matrix printer, a Hayes 1200 modem, and a 64K buffer. I am currently using the latest WordStar Professional™ word processor, 4.0, for my writing. All of this is quite conventional today, although an increasing number of people have been buying AT type machines, which are somewhat further advanced, but not radically so. There are probably several million computers similar to this in use, the chief differences among them probably the size of the RAM memory (640K is tops for an XT, but there are many with 256K and some with 512K RAMs), and the configurations of disk drives. Those differences are relatively superficial, functionally. For example, I have yet to use more than about one-half the memory capacity of this machine, and I have so far used only about one-third of my hard-disk storage capacity.

What that means is that the typical modern desktop computer, such as this one, is entirely adequate to most of the tasks you will require of it, and owning such a system makes you almost self-sufficient in developing and conducting your seminar ventures. With a good printer and proper software the system will help you greatly in doing at least the following tasks for yourself:

- Creating and producing manuscripts and, in many cases, reproducible master copy for your marketing materials: salesletters, news releases, memoranda, posters, newsletters, and brochures.
- Developing and producing manuscripts and master copy for seminar handouts: manuals, exercise sheets, other paper.
- Developing and producing transparencies for projection.
- Tracking marketing operations to analyze results, rates of response, rates of return, and other relevant monitoring and recording.
- Building, maintaining, and managing your house mailing lists.
- Administering the project, including setting up and maintaining records, acknowledging and confirming registrations, and keeping records of income and expenses.

The objective and benefit of doing these things for yourself is not only saving money and thus reducing costs and risks; it is also having and keeping as much control as possible. As you proceed and begin to vend out even the simplest tasks, such as printing, illustrating, or typesetting, you will discover for yourself the frustrations of being at the mercy of suppliers who may or may not deliver what they promise when they promise at the price they promise. Somehow, their estimates—and many insist that they are providing "only" estimates—tend to fall short of reality and always in their favor, not yours. A few such experiences and you begin to perceive the value of becoming as independent of such suppliers as possible and maximizing your personal control of all necessary resources.

PRODUCING MARKETING MATERIALS

The major computer tool for producing your marketing materials is the word processor. A word processor is not a piece of hardware (with the exception of a few early "dedicated" word processors, which were computers designed especially for word processing alone); it is a software program.

There are many word processors and they have been undergoing steady change and improvement, as has the hardware. The pioneer, long-time best-selling word processor was WordStar. Recently another, WordPerfect,™ became the best-selling word processor. Now there is a new, greatly improved WordStar 4.0, which obviously represents manufacturer MicroPro's bid to regain first place in the word-processor-sales sweepstakes. Whether they succeed in this or not, I have found the new WordStar a pleasant and convenient program to use, and it still has my vote.

Despite my own bias, there are many other prominent word processors, and most of the leading ones will do everything WordStar 4.0 will do. I will use WordStar 4.0 as an example simply because I know it best (and because as the pioneer word processor it influenced most of the other word processors and supplemental programs, an effect still visible). In any case, the following paragraphs list and describe first what the older WordStar and many other word processors offered, then programs that supplement and support word processing by providing additional editorial functions, and finally what the new WordStar offers, which are the typical features of most of the latest word processors.

Older Word Processor Main Features

Earlier word processors had two main functional areas: an editor and a formatter. The keys on the keyboard were in a "qwerty" arrangement matching that of the conventional typewriter, but there were a number of additional keys to permit you to do things that you cannot do with a typewriter, principally the following:

Make changes and corrections before printing.

Do extensive revisions before printing by moving whole paragraphs and even pages about in an electronic version of cut-and-paste editing.

Make additional copies of paragraphs, pages, even entire manuscripts in seconds.

Have the computer search for words or phrases.

Have the computer make automatic changes throughout an entire manuscript—for example, seek out every use of "ebony" and change it to "black".

Justify copy—make lines end at same place, for an even right margin, as in formally typeset and printed materials.

Format copy into two or more columns, with either ragged right or justified right margins, at your option.

Supplemental Editorial Programs

Spelling checkers were and remain popular supplements to word processors. I happen to be especially fond of Webster's New World Spelling Checker,™ but there are many excellent checkers offered in the marketplace. The most basic of these review and check a completed manuscript—a computer file—by comparing each word with the dictionary that is the main element of the program. It stops at each unknown word and you then decide whether to change the word, alter its spelling, accept it as it stands, or ask the program to display the correct spelling. But as spelling checkers have become more sophisticated (and their dictionaries larger) they offer more help, such as suggesting the correct spelling without being asked to do so and including in the suggestions alternative words that appear or sound similar.

Thought processors came along to help you think out and outline a project. Their principal features include a great deal of flexibility in shuffling words and phrases about, shifting levels of subordination in displays, adding descriptive paragraphs wherever needed, and otherwise encouraging and aiding logical analysis and development of ideas in outline form to as great a degree of detail as you wish. Probably the oldest of these were KAMAS and its spawn, OutThink, although others were soon developed and have become popular, especially with those for whom writing does not come easily.

There have also been a few grammar-checking programs offered, although these have not been very popular because they are necessarily quite limited in the help they can provide; the function is difficult to automate effectively.

Other programs, rather simple and mono-functional, include sorting programs, which are used to organize or reorganize lists; indexing programs, which gather up the key words you mark and prepare an index; footnoters, which post the footnotes where they belong; and even programs to prepare a table of contents. And whereas the internal search programs of word processors normally search for a word, phrase, or page number within a single file, there have been some that can do this across a complete disk or across entire sets of files, even if they are on more than one disk.

One other quite popular and widely used type of supplemental program, although not designed for word processing exclusively, is the key redefiner or "macro" program, of which the best known is probably SmartKey.™ This is a program that permits you to set up and store a new definition or "macro" command for any key on your keyboard. For example, one of the commands I sometimes use is "toascii <c:\ch.6 >c:\ch.asc," which thus requires more than 30 keystrokes (counting strokes of the shift key). Using SmartKey I can reduce this to one or two keystrokes. You can also store entire paragraphs or even longer texts that can be summoned instantaneously with a keystroke or two. I have, for example, keystrokes (macros) for my letterhead, for summoning up certain files I use frequently, and for other multikey commands and text structures.

A most important program, one that probably is used most often to support marketing, is the mail-merge program. This program enables you to merge one file, containing a form letter, with a mailing list in another file so that you can have the printer print out and address a copy of the letter for each name on the list. And, subsequently, you can use that list to address envelopes.

Today's Word Processors

Today's WordStar, edition 4.0, and many other word processors have incorporated many of these supplemental programs into the word processor itself. Because these are internally integrated the features work more smoothly and more rapidly than when they must be summoned up from another program. Here are the chief integral features of WordStar 4.0 (in addition to the usual word processor features), most of which may also be found in the latest models of other leading word processors:

Spelling checker.

Thesaurus.

Built-in one- or two-key macros for many functions.

Key redefiner.

Indexer.

Mail merge.

On-screen calculator.

Limited graphics feature (boxes and lines).

Undelete (recall accidentally erased word or line).

The useful feature of having all these integral functions is that not only do you not have to leave the word processor to invoke these other programs, but usually you do not even have to leave the edit mode or the file on which you are working. That is, you just "step out for a moment" while you do some calculations, draw a box, rule a table, or look up a word, and then you return to your file and resume work as though you had never left.

You can see why word processing is by far the most widely used application of the desktop computer and why it is the most common reason people give for buying a computer; it is easily the most useful kind of computer program and alone justifies computer ownership, whether you do or do not use it for other things. But we will discuss a few other uses later.

WRITING WITH A WORD PROCESSOR

In the early desktop computers the keyboard contained only a few "extra" keys. One reason was simply that the memories—RAM (random access memory) chips—of those computers were quite small by today's standards. They grew gradually, from 4K to 16K, to 32K, and finally to 64K. Programs and keyboards for computers with small memories had to be relatively simple. The consequence of that, however, was that the user had to learn many various key combinations in order to instruct the computer and the printer to do what the operator wished. Many people thought WordStar far too complex and difficult to learn, and the software developers began to develop programs that did not require as much memorization. They called this feature of software "user friendliness." This meant that the program was arranged so that the commands were simpler, and the user was aided by the program itself through such devices as "menus," which listed the commands on the screen, and built-in macros. As RAM chips grew larger and provided larger memories—128, 256, 512, and 640K—the keyboards and on-screen help grew steadily. So today you need not learn any but the simplest basic commands for many hardware and software systems; the programs provide extensive guidance. In fact, this is now so commonly taken for granted that the term "user friendliness" has all but vanished. (It is widely believed that it was the failure of Micro-Pro™ to follow the trend and make WordStar more user friendly that cost the company and its leading program to lose its first-place status to WordPerfect.)

In any case, if you use any of the leading word processors, you will get most of the features listed and described here, along with a great deal of help in learning to use the systems. It has become very easy. (Many modern programs actually include tutorial subprograms, and even the manuals have improved in many cases.)

The beauty of word processing as an aid to the writing process is that, used properly, word processing improves the quality of the writing. That is so primarily because it makes self-editing, revision, rewriting, and polishing of your manuscript incalculably easier. Quality of prose is almost invariably linked closely to the amount of rewriting done.

Probably the chief difference between the typical professional writer and the typical nonprofessional writer is that the nonprofessional tends to believe that a first draft is satisfactory, whereas the professional knows that the first draft is never the best work possible and needs at least one rewrite.

Rewriting is the most onerous and distasteful chore to some professionals (although some few appear to relish the process). Over the years that I labored over a typewriter all day I devised as many schemes as I could to minimize the retyping I had to do. Philosophically, I accepted the need to rewrite, but in practice I tried to salvage as much original typing as possible. I bought white-out fluid by the carton of 12 bottles (some of my editors were sure that I bought it by the gallon!), I had several pairs of scissors, many sharp razor blades, and numerous paste pots, and I spent a small fortune making copies of draft pages to cut and paste up and then making copies of the completed paste-ups.

The word processor has put an end to all that. I rarely use white-out fluid for anything today, I own one pair of scissors, and a paste-pot that lasts for a year or more. I do almost all of my editing, rewriting, and polishing on-screen, before printing copy out. Now I review, edit, rewrite, and polish most of my copy at least three to six times before printing it, where before it was only two to three times. I no longer ponder whether a contemplated small change is worth the trouble because there is now so little trouble attached to it.

This, beyond a doubt, is by far the greatest single benefit of word processing. There is simply no reason to fail to edit and rewrite your copy today *if you work at the computer as you write*. Too many have not changed their habits. They still scrawl in longhand and turn it over to someone else to keyboard and enter. They have exchanged their typewriters for keyboards and computer screens, but since they have not changed their working habits, they have not gained the true benefits and advantages of the system.

Some Practical Considerations

A few years ago, when desktop computers and accessory systems were still relatively crude, the only printer worth considering for correspondence and final copy was a so-called letter-quality printer. This was usually a daisy wheel type, using a disk-shaped printing element, from which it derived its name. The machine resembled a typewriter without a keyboard and produced copy virtually identical with that of a typewriter but had most of the same limitations. The type was limited to a selection of perhaps three sizes, and to change type sizes or fonts it was necessary to stop and change the daisy wheel. The only things that could be done without changing the element were to produce boldface, underlines, justified copy, and, in some cases, proportionally spaced copy. The other type of printer was the dot matrix printer, which could create alphanumeric characters within a 5×7 or 7×9 matrix or pattern. A series of dots portrayed each character, resulting in a rather sketchy product.

That has changed. Dot matrix printing has improved rapidly, and today produces a "near letter quality" (nlq) output. More recently laser printers and 24-pin dot matrix printers have appeared and produce output called LQ for letter quality. All dot matrix printers, even the current 9-pin models, offer many advantages over daisy wheel printers in their flexibility. Most offer a variety of fonts, including those with foreign alphabets, a variety of type sizes, and graphics, all printed and intermixed spontaneously, as ordered by the software programs driving them. With a good-quality 24-pin printer, or even a good 9-pin printer, you have a substantial in-house capability for producing master copy for printing letters, flyers, posters, manuals, and other such materials.

It is possible to produce brochures by this method also, but unless you have some rather costly equipment, primarily a laser printer, you can't achieve the quality of formal type, and you will probably do well to have the brochure typeset.

Newsletters are another matter. Here again, you may wish to use formal typesetting services to create the top of the first page, which is referred to as the nameplate, and which presents the name and other basic data in large type font. However, you can do the rest of the newsletter via word processing, especially if you have one of the graphics program designed for the purpose. These programs are designed especially for such work, and offer clip art, a variety of fonts, and tools for layout and makeup so that you do not have to be an expert to achieve a professional result. They are, in fact, better suited to the production of manuals, letters, and other such things, but are relatively slow. The on-screen representations are of excellent quality, but it does require a rather costly printer to transfer that same quality to paper.

Transparencies, those 8- × 10-inch plastic (acetate) sheets that you can use with an overhead projector to cast the image on a large screen, can be made in any good office copier, using the acetate instead of paper and copying the image on it in the usual manner. (You run a few copies on paper first to ensure that all is in order.) You can make up the original copy in your printer, at whatever type sizes you wish. Of course, if you wish to include paper copies of your acetate as handouts, that is easy enough to do also.

MONITORING AND TRACKING

Testing is obligatory in direct mail if you wish to run your campaigns efficiently. Most people run a preliminary test mailing or two of a few thousand pieces each and then roll out the total mailing as soon as they are assured that everything is working satisfactorily. From my viewpoint there are at least two things wrong with that:

1. My entire mailing is likely to be about 5,000–10,000 pieces, so if I were to test in the manner described the preliminaries would have to consist of only a few hundred pieces each.

2. It is impractical to do this kind of testing with seminar mailings, regardless of the sizes of the mailings, because of the time element. The tests would have to be for a seminar several months away, and that would cloud the results.

As a consequence, the only practical test is the actual mailing and its results, with the improvements, if any, made in the next mailing. And I am convinced—based on my experience—that the results of a previous seminar campaign are not a reliable indicator of probable results of the current or the next campaign. Conditions change continuously, and any totally unexpected and unpredictable influence may occur and change the result. So I make it a practice, when I conduct such mailings, to monitor and track results continuously throughout all the mailings.

Figure 9-1 is a simple form for recording results, but it is so simple as to be almost useless. Whether you track and record results on paper or in your computer you need something a little more sophisticated than that to know what you are doing.

Figure 9-2 is a step in that direction. It is designed to record the number of registrations received for up to six seminar sessions, dates, and locations announced in the mailout. The head data tell you when you made the mailing, how many pieces were mailed, and what it cost

Day & Date _____

Key	No. orders	Sales $
Totals:		

Figure 9-1. Simple form for recording daily orders.

Date of mailing: _____ No. pieces: _____ Cost: $ _____

Date	Registrations						Sales						Notes
	1	2	3	4	5	6	1	2	3	4	5	6	
Total													

Figure 9-2. A more sophisticated accounting.

you made the mailing, how many pieces were mailed, and what it cost in dollars. By making this a daily or at least weekly accounting you can soon discover the *patterns* of response—at what points registrations tend to speed up and when they decline. In fact, you can even plot this as a curve for each session, as in Figure 9-3, which is based on the premise that the seminar date is approximately eight weeks after the mailing.

In fact, response to seminar appeals does tend to peak about as shown, although there is no guarantee that this will always be the case. The peak tends to occur at about 75–85 percent of the way to the date of the seminar, and then drops off sharply. After plotting the curve for each session, you may detect a more or less consistent pattern, which will of course be a great help in future planning.

You may wish to calculate the response percentage, as many do, to help yourself grasp the pattern mathematically, although the percentage response really has no great significance. The formula for calculating it is, however, simple enough: It is the total number of registrations (sales) divided by the total number of pieces mailed out, and multiplied by 100. For example, if you mailed 10,000 pieces and got back 150 registrations for all the sessions scheduled the rate is $150/10,000 = 0.015 \times 100 = 1.5$ percent.

If that figure is of interest, inscribe it as a note in the bottom right-hand box of the form of Figure 9-2. However, the ROI—return on investment—is of far greater significance and should be of far greater interest to you. That is the profit on your investment. If you calculate

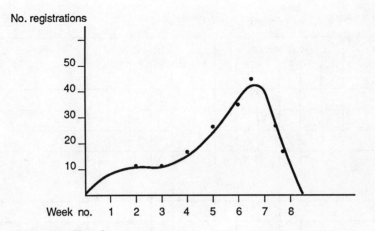

Figure 9-3. Plot of a response curve.

that your investment totals $17,500 for all expenses, including the fees you pay yourself for presenting the seminars, and you received a gross income of $22,500 on the seminars, your ROI can be calculated as follows:

$$\$5,000/22,500 = 0.222222222222 \times 100 = 22.22 \text{ percent}$$

That is quite an excellent return on investment today, especially since at least some of the investment—the costs of marketing the current schedule of seminar sessions—is recent and short-term. You may wish to add a provision to the form of Figure 9-2 to accommodate those figures, as I have done in Figure 9-4, which provides also a block for recording the rate of response and reminders of how to calculate each.

The ROI is by far the more important figure. It tells you what the risk factor is, enabling you to judge whether you are getting a fair return on your investment, both short- and long-term, and whether you should be satisfied or disturbed over the rate of return. If you fail to calculate the ROI you may miss the point because you are functioning in a dual role, as both the presenter and as the investor. Thus you may earn generous fees as the presenter, and yet overlook your other interest, as the investor. You may concentrate on the large presentation fees and therefore fail to determine whether your investment is earning a reasonable profit and justifying the risk. If you allow your-

Date of mailing: _____ No. pieces: _____ Cost: $ _____

Date	Registrations						Sales						Notes
	1	2	3	4	5	6	1	2	3	4	5	6	
Total													

Rate of response: (Total registrations / Total no. pieces mailed x 100	%
ROI (Total profit / Total investment)	%

Figure 9-4. Adding provision for response rate and ROI.

self to be so lured, you will have masked the true ROI by incorporating some part of it into your fees. Try, therefore, to set your fees realistically, charging the venture only what you would expect a sponsor to pay.

Thus the ROI has some absolute value or significance, while the response rate does not. However, the rate of response does have some utility for you if you monitor and track all your seminar promotions because it ultimately furnishes you a reference by which you can measure seminar-marketing campaigns. It gives you a window on your ventures in the seminar business, and you ought to be able to make at least a rough correlation of the rate of response with the ROI, if your marketing costs are fairly consistent.

If you are selling tapes or printed information of some sort, either in the original mailout or in the back of the room, you will have to set up records to account for this too, and the proceeds from these sales should enter into your calculations, of course. Your records ought to include an accounting of what has been sold in this manner to guide you in what prospects find most acceptable and thus what you should continue to offer.

Key: Mailout Ident _____ MO Sales [ ]   BR Sales [ ]   Date _____

Date	Item	Item	Sales $	Notes
Totals				

Figure 9-5. Recording other sales.

Figure 9-5 suggests a form for this. The head data key the form to tie it to the seminar mailing, if the sales are "MO" (mail order) sales received as the result of a solicitation accompanying the direct-mail package, or to the individual seminar session if the sales were in the back of the room. The totals should then be added to the main monitoring form to calculate the final response rates and ROI, both of which are affected if the sales were mail order. However, only the ROI is affected if the sales were in the back of the room. The form shown provides for only two items, but it can be expanded to make columns for more than two items, of course.

LIST MANAGEMENT AND MAINTENANCE

One of the greatest boons of owning a desktop computer is the contribution it makes to the management and maintenance of your house mailing lists. With the right software programs, which are not difficult to find today, you can manage and maintain your own mailing lists as easily as the professional managers do with their large, mainframe computers.

First of all, you should segregate your lists into two broad categories, clients and prospective clients. This is not only for your own use—the client list is usually far more productive than is the prospect list—but because the lists have definite value. The client list is the more valuable of the two if you maintain it separately and can certify that everyone on the list has bought something—a seminar registration and/or other items, in this case—from you. You will probably find it useful to segregate lists further by various classifications—size of contracts or purchases, types of businesses or professions, locations, and other factors. The more detailed the identification of (that means the more detailed the information about) the names on the list, the more valuable the list is.

Although, I believe, you ought to keep client lists and prospect lists absolutely separate—in physically separate files—the other divisions may be made by coding the names in some manner so that the computer can sort them accordingly. In the case of some of my own files, for example, I can sort them alphabetically, by date, by size, or by any of several other codes.

List maintenance is important, and if you do not keep up with it, your list is soon full of "nixies," undeliverable names and addresses. Since one of the measures of list quality is the percentage of nixies in it, it is important to remove a name and address as soon as you learn that it has become a nixie.

Another consideration is that of duplicates. You must be alert for names that appear more than once on the same list. If you have ever yourself been the recipient of several copies of the same mailing, you can get an idea of how common and how wasteful this fault is. This should also dramatize the need to clean lists. Sometimes brokers are suspected of being slow to clean their lists, especially of duplicates, because it reduces the number of names they have available for rental, but whether that suspicion is justified or not, it senseless not to clean your house lists for it is sheer waste of postage and other resources.

Maintenance consists also of adding new names to a list, and new names come from various sources. When anyone becomes a new client, that name goes on the list, even if the name came from a rented list originally. (You are entitled to add those names to your house lists.) If the name is already on your prospect lists, you transfer it to the client list; it has become a more important and more valuable name by virtue of becoming that of a buyer. If someone calls or writes with an inquiry, add that name to the prospect list. And if you acquire a new list by trading or other means, you must integrate it with your own lists, although you may have to first recode the names. You must be particularly alert for names on the new lists that are duplicates of those on your own lists, for it is almost certain that you will encounter a certain degree of such duplication.

ADMINISTRATION

The management of your mailing lists is probably as much a part of your general administration as it is part of marketing. Certainly it is part of asset management, and your accountant may suggest calculating the value of the growing mailing lists and counting that as income or, at least, adding it to the net worth of your enterprise. If the idea does not occur to your accountant, it may be worth bringing the matter up with him, and asking for his counsel in this. (A good accountant is a consultant too, of course.) There are also several other administrative matters for which you can use your computer effectively.

Inventory

If you do establish and sell information products—books, manuals, tapes, reports, and others—an inventory can grow rather rapidly and require some record-keeping to manage. (At one point, before I owned a desktop computer, I was carrying approximately 40 such products in my own inventory, and was often unable to determine, without a physical search, whether I could fill any given order immediately.) Inventory records in disk storage can be summoned up in a flash for inspection or updating. (Inventory records, like mailing lists, must be managed and maintained through regular updating.)

Appointments and Schedules

It is not likely that you will forget the dates on which you are to deliver seminars. Still, most individuals find it necessary to keep a reminder list of appointments and other commitments to have as a ready reference when discussing possible dates for future events.

In my own case I find it much easier both to record the appointments and to refer to them by keeping them in my computer (literally "in" the computer, on a hard disk, in this case). I am not a "clean desk" worker, possibly because of my pack-rat nature, but more likely because clutter is an occupational disease of writers generally and certainly of this one. So even when I kept a special, bound book for recording appointments and schedules, I could never find the book when I needed it! In any case, I do not have that problem with the computer. It sits on my desk grinning at me all day long, and two or three swift key presses persuades it to present me with my appointments and schedules immediately, even while I am on the telephone. (Actually, I use a speaker telephone so my hands are completely free.) It also enables me to make new entries while I am speaking to someone, another time saver, but, much more importantly in my case, a loss preventer: I never mislay those important notes now; they are all in one easily and swiftly accessible place.

Miscellaneous Items

All the foregoing argument applies equally to many other items that I once scrawled on scraps of paper and promptly lost or mislaid—telephone numbers, ideas, memos, special dates, and other such things that make the paper business the big business it is. I now keep a number of logs, diaries, reminder files, reader files, and the like on my hard disk, each with a SmartKey or other macro code that summons it up with the press of a key or two. It has made me personally efficient beyond my wildest dreams! I heartily recommend it to others, even to those who do not suffer clutteritis, as I do.

10 A FEW REFERENCES

The essence of education—and perhaps of wisdom too—is knowing how and where to get the information you need.

A FEW (NEARLY) FINAL WORDS

Planning and managing a campaign of seminar production and presentation is a complex undertaking, requiring a great many different
kinds of skills and resources. It is obviously impractical to present
within the pages of a single book all the specialized knowledge you
need for this. Instead, I have tried to pass on what I do know as a
result of my own studies and experience, to put your feet on the road.
But equally important with what I have thus far written here, and
probably of even greater importance in many ways, is the knowledge
of a great many other people expressed in many forms and places. I
therefore devote this final chapter to directing your attention to some
of these sources but with the notation that these are only a few, and
there are many others.

PERIODICALS OF DIRECT INTEREST

Here, in no particular order, are some of the periodicals that may
be of interest and value to you. Some of these are "controlled circulation" publications, which means that subscriptions are free to qualified
applicants.

Meeting News, Gralla Publications, 1515 Broadway, New York, NY
10036, a trade paper of hoteliers and others with an interest in
business meetings and relevant conclaves of all types.

Corporate Meetings & Incentives, also for hotel operators and meeting planners, Harcourt Brace Jovanovich Publications, 1 East First
Street, Duluth, MN 55802.

Meetings & Conventions, a monthly slick-paper trade journal, Ziff-
Davis, One Park Avenue, New York, NY 10016.

Sharing Ideas!, Dottie Walters, P.O. Box 1120, Glendora, CA
91740. This is bimonthly, generally runs on the order of 30 pages,
and is the bible of the public-speaking industry for many readers.

DM News, a monthly tabloid read by members of the industry. 19
West 21st Street, New York, NY 10010.

Target Marketing, monthly slick-paper trade magazine for marketers, 401 N. Broad Street, Philadelphia, PA 19108.

Personal Selling Power, a monthly tabloid published by Ger___ Gschwandtner at 1127 International Pkwy., Suite 102, POB 5467, Fredericksburg, VA 22405, for marketers.

The Direct Response Specialist (formerly *Mail Order Connection*), a monthly newsletter of direct-marketing ideas and guidance by direct-mail consultant Galen Stilson, P.O. Box 1075, Tarpon Springs, Fl 34286-1075.

Writer's Digest, a monthly magazine, in existence for many years, the bible for many professional writers. (I have been reading it since 1937.) You can find it on your newsstand, but you may want to write to the magazine at 9933 Alliance Road, Cincinnati, OH 45242.

The Writer's Yearbook, an annual of the *Writer's Digest*, published every spring, worth reading. Full of useful articles, guides, directories.

The Writer's Market, published by the book publishing division of the *Writer's Digest* magazine, an annually revised and updated guide to markets for writers.

BOOKS

There is an enormous variety of books relevant to many of the subjects of concern here. A few are listed below:

Communicate Like a Pro, by Nido Qubein, published by Prentice-Hall, Inc., 1986, words of wisdom on public speaking, offered by a leading light of the industry, past president of NSA, highly regarded by the professionals of the industry, and a respected figure in his chosen profession. Information is given in this book that you will find nowhere else and, best of all, is based on the author's personal experience and personal successes. Available from Nido directly. Write him at address given in list on page 221.

Money Talks, by Dr. Jeffrey Lant, JLA Publications, 50 Follen Street, Suite 507, Cambridge, MA 02138, 1985. Still another of Jeffrey Lant's books for consultants and other professionals. Over 300 big pages (this is an 8-1/2- x 11-inch book) of detailed information as promised by the subtitle, "The Complete Guide to Creating a Profitable Workshop or Seminar in any Field."

The Business of Public Speaking, by Herman Holtz, loaded with details on many of the subjects discussed in this book, John Wiley & Sons, Inc., 1985.

The Direct Marketer's Workbook, by Herman Holtz, details on direct marketing, John Wiley & Sons, Inc., 1986.

How to Succeed as an Independent Consultant, by Herman Holtz, John Wiley & Sons, Inc., 1983.

The Computer Phone Book, by Mike Cane, a Plume Book published by New American Library, 1983. This is a directory to online databases, electronic bulletin boards, and similar facilities and resources.

How to Hold Your Audience with Humor, by noted comedy writer Gene Perrett, published by Writer's Digest Books, 1981. (Foreword by Bob Hope, for whom Perrett has written.)

SOURCES FOR AUDIOVISUAL MATERIALS

Many public libraries have stock films and slides that can be rented for small fees or borrowed free of charge. Moreover, this is not the only source: Many government agencies also have films and other aids available for loan or rental. Check with the nearest Federal Information Center or the nearest Government Printing Office bookstore for a government publication listing these.

Collect as many publisher's catalogs as possible, too. (Most publishers will send you a copy on request.) These will help you locate useful books when you are researching something. Also ask the Government Printing Office to put your name on their list for their "Selected Publications" mailer. All of these will help you in your presentations, especially seminars and training programs, and they will also contain information useful for backing up your proposed program with specific detail when you are writing a proposal or making a sales presentation. (On one occasion, these resources were most helpful in writing a proposal that won an $8.7 million government contract for training programs.)

Here are a few other sources to try for audiovisuals and printed materials that can be helpful in your presentation and your marketing:

Marilyn Van Derbur
Motivational Institute
1616 Champa Street
Denver, CO 80202

Dartnell
4660 Ravenswood Avenue
Chicago, IL 60640

Motivation Media
1245 Milwaukee Avenue
Glenview, IL 60025

BNA Communications, Inc.
9417 Decoverly Hall Road
Rockville, MD 20850

Robert J. Brady Co.
Routes 197 & 450
Bowie, MD 20715

American Management
Associations (AMA)
135 West 50th Street
New York, NY 10020

Meeting Makers, Inc.
5 Lexington Avenue
New York, NY 10016

National Park Service
Division of AV Arts
Harpers Ferry Center
Harpers Ferry, WV 25425

PEOPLE AND ORGANIZATIONS WHO CAN HELP

Many successful speakers are also lecture agents, consultants, publishers, and trainers of speakers. Some conduct seminars for experienced speakers, where even these veterans of the platform can get guidance to help them increase their success. The following are among the many who offer products and/or services of one sort or another:

Dottie Walters
18825 Hicrest Road
Glendora, CA 91740
(818) 335-8069

Lou Hampton
Hampton Communication
   Strategies
4200 Wisconsin Avenue
Washington, DC 20016
(202) 363-4941/363-5575

Mike Frank
Speakers Unlimited
POB 27225
Columbus, OH 43227
(614) 864-3703

Ed Larkin
Speakers Guild
93 Old Kings Highway
Sandwich, MA 02563

Bob Montgomery
12313 Michelle Circle
Burnsville, MN 55337
(612) 894-1348

Nido Qubein, CPAE
Creative Services, Inc.
POB 6008
High Point, NC 27262
(919) 889-3010

ASSOCIATIONS

There are a number of speakers associations. Here are several you should know about:

National Speakers Association
 (NSA)
5201 N. 7th Street, Suite 200
Phoenix, AZ 85014

Toastmasters International, Inc.
POB 10400
Santa Ana, CA 92711
(714) 542-6793

International Platform
 Association (IPA)
2564 Berkshire Road
Cleveland Heights, OH 44106
(216) 932-0505

CONVENTION PLANNERS AND MANAGERS

There are a great many convention plannners, managers, consultants, and others who support such events. A small sampling is offered here:

Program Support Specialists
POB 15464
Phoenix, AZ 85060

California Assn. of Meeting
 Planners
888 Airport Blvd.
Burlingame, CA 94010

California Leisure Consultants, Inc.
2760 E. El Presidio Street
Long Beach, CA 90810
& 3714 Fourth Street,
San Diego, CA 92103

Gann Carter Convention Services
261 E. Tahquitz
McCallum Way
Palm Springs, CA 92262

Convention Services International
139 S. Beverly Drive
Beverly Hills, CA 90212

Meeting Masters, Inc.
4000 MacArthur Blvd.
Newport Beach, CA 92660

Professional Speakers Bureau
POB 2007
Buellton, CA 93427

Show Marketers, Inc.
4508 Third Street, Suite 20
La Mesa, CA 92041

CCR, Inc. Convention Service
1130 E. Missouri, Suite 210
Phoenix, AZ 85014
& 2625 East Third Avenue
Denver, CO 80206

Conference Management Corp.
17 Washington Street
Norwalk, CT 06854

Meetings Unlimited
POB 5052
Westport, CT 06881

Round Hill-IVC, Inc.
89 Erickson Drive
Stamford, CT 06903

Details
1750 Pennsylvania Avenue, NW,
Suite 1208
Washington, DC 20006

The Meeting Market
2025 Eye Street, NW, Suite 507
Washington, DC 20006

CMC Management Services
5224 Riverhills Drive
Tampa, FL 33617

Conference Consultants
International
700 Diplomat Pkwy.
Hallandale, FL 33009

Adelle Cox Convention Services
& Consultants
POB 69-4770
Miami, FL 33169

Gelco Convention Services
924 Sligh Blvd.
Orlando, FL 32806

Professional Meeting Organizers,
Inc.
POB 141423
Coral Gables, FL 33114

Donna Ray Associates
3050 Biscayne Blvd., Suite 100
Miami, FL 33139

Success Leaders Speakers Service
Lenox Square, Box 18737
Atlanta, GA 30326

Bostrom Management Corp.
435 N. Michigan Avenue
Tribune Tower, Suite 1717
Chicago, IL 60611

CMR/Ltd
801 Knightsbridge Lane
Schaumburg, IL 60195

Communications Connection, Inc.
1723 W. Devon
POB 60276
Chicago, IL 60660

Convention & Conference
Consultants
644 Timber Lane
Lake Forest, IL 60045

The Eventors, Inc.
213 W. Institute Place
Chicago, IL 60610

Events Alive, Inc.
222 W. Adams, Suite 1200
Chicago, IL 60606

McRand, Inc.
210 E. Westminster
Lake Forest, IL 60045

Arthur Meriwether, Inc.
1529 Brook Drive
Downers Grove, IL 60515

The Program People
POB 1426
Oak Brook, IL 60521

Conference Resources, Inc.
1821 E. Fairmount Avenue
Baltimore, MD 21231

Prince & Company
White Flint Mall
Kensington, MD 20895

DeAnne Rosenberg, Inc.
28 Fifer Avenue
Lexington, MA 02173

Meeting Concepts, Inc.
511 11th Avenue, S, Suite 261
Minneapolis, MN 55415

Experience Conferences, Inc.
835 Glen Elm Drive
St. Louis, MO 63122

St. Louis Scene, Inc.
8600 Delmar
St. Louis, MO 63124

A&B Businessworks, Inc.
529 Bay Avenue
Point Pleasant Beach, NJ 08742

ACA Atlantic Conventions
POB 891
Cherry Hill, NJ 08003

Sol Abrams Associates
331 Webster Drive
New Milford, NJ 07646

Atlantic Convention Associates
POB 2285
Ventnor, NJ 08406

A.V.P.S. Corp.
225 E. 45th Street
New York, NY 10022

Atlantic Exhibit Services
62 W. 45th Street
New York, NY 10036

Audrey Hoffman Enterprises
12 Prospect Terrace
Albany, NY 12208

Ray Bloch Productions, Inc.
230 Peachtree Street, NW
Atlanta, GA 30303
& 1500 Broadway
New York, NY 10036

City Welcome Corp
100 Jericho Quandrangle,
Suite 212
Jericho, NY 11753

Harrison-Berkall Productions,
Inc.
527 Madison Avenue
New York, NY 10022

ISAACS Enterprises, Inc.
Old Route 17
Harris, NY 12742

Laddin & Company, Inc.
2 Park Avenue
New York, NY 10016

Passkey Associates, Inc.
425 Park Avenue
New York, NY 10022

Red Carpet Associates, Inc.
19 E. 57th Street
New York, NY 10022

Promotions for Industry, Inc.
6545 Carnegie Avenue
Cleveland, OH 44103

Promotional Planning, Inc.
502 Hulmeville Avenue
Langhorne Manor, PA 19047

Dr. Art Garner & Associates
2519 Lovitt Drive
Memphis, TN 38138

Meeting Services
& Conventions Consultants
95 Whiteridge Road, Suite 401
Nashville, TN 37205

Reception Ontario
200 Ronson Drive, Suite 606
Rexdale, Ontario
M9W 5Z9 Canada

LECTURE BUREAUS

There are a great many lecture bureaus—thousands—since many professional public speakers also act as bureaus. Only a small representative sampling is given here.

National Speakers Association
5201 N. 7th Street, Suite 200
Phoenix, AZ 85014

Plaza Three Talent Agency
4343 N. 16th Street
Phoenix, AZ 85016

Summit Enterprises
3928 E. Corrine Drive
Phoenix, AZ 85032

Sun Safari Tours, Inc.
7500 E. McCormick Pkwy., #33
Scottsdale, AZ 85258

David Belenzon Management
Box 15428
San Diego, CA 92115

Della Clark
D.L. Clark & Associates
2295 N. Tustin, #4
Orange, CA 92665

George Colouris Productions
1782 West Lincoln, Suite J
Anaheim, CA 92801

Ray Considine
25 West Walnut Street
Pasadena, CA 91103

Bobbie Gee
Orange County Speakers Bureau
31781 National Park Drive
Laguna Niguel, CA 92677

Verne Bennom Grimsley
International Broadcaster, WBN
Box 347
Berkeley, CA 94701

Donna Hoffner
Market Consultant
Continuing Education Corp.
17291 Irvine Blvd., Suite 262
Tustin, CA 92680

Dean Howard Success
  Seminars
1539 Monrovia Avenue, Suite 14
Newport Beach, CA 92663

Masters of Ceremonies
POB 390
Monrovia, CA 91016

Meeting Masters, Inc.
4000 MacArthur Blvd.,
  Suite 3000
Newport Beach, CA 92660

Mr. Put Ons
Put Ons Productions
415 Alan Road, Dept M
Santa Barbara, CA 93109

Darlene Oram
J.E.O. Marketing
Box 60719
Sacramento, CA 95819

A. Byron Perkins & Associates,
  Inc.
1201 W. Huntington Drive,
Suite 102
Arcadia, CA 91006

The Podium
(Women speakers only)
Sandra Shrift & Jill Henderson
3940 Hancock Street, Suite 207
San Diego, CA 92110

The Program Exchange
Sue Clark
1245 E. Walnut Street, Suite 104
Pasadena, CA 91106

SRI International
333 Ravenswood Avenue
Menlo Park, CA 94025

San Jacobi Star Productions
4000 Mission Blvd., Suite 3
San Diego, CA 92109

Staff Development, Inc.
1411 W. Olympic Blvd.
Los Angeles, CA 90015

Paula Sullivan
542 5th Avenue
San Diego, CA 92101

Temple Berdan II
National Real Estate Sales
  Seminar
Professional Speakers Bureau
Box 2007
Buellton, CA 93427

Virginia M. Thomas
West Coast Speakers Bureau
3500 S. Figueroa, Suite 108
Los Angeles, CA 90007

Dorothy M. Walters
18825 Hicrest Road
Glendora, CA 91740

Samuel Westerman
4062 Camintito Dehesa
San Diego, CA 92107

Denver Executive Club
409–410 Republic Bldg.
Denver, CO 80202

John Heckman Enterprises
Box 15577
Lakewood, CO 80215

High Flight Foundation
202 East Cheyenne Mountain
Blvd., Suite 1
POB 1387
Colorado Springs, Co 80901

International Speakers Bureau
100 Everett Street
Lakewood, CO 80226

McBride Speakers Bureau
870 Quail Lake Circle, Suite 101
Colorado Springs, CO 80901

Conference Management Corp
17 Washington Street
Norwalk, CT 06854

Connecticut Speakers Bureau
91 Reservoir Road
Newington, CT 06111

Master Talent
993 Farmington Avenue
West Hartford, CT 06107

American Society of Association
   Executives
1101 16th Street, NW
Washington, DC 20036

Conference Speakers International, Inc.
1055 Thomas Jefferson Street
Suite 300
Washington, DC 20007

Freeds Speakers Bureau
927 15th Street, NW
Washington, DC 20005

International Association of
   Professional Bureaucrats
1032 National Press Bldg.
Washington, DC 20045

The Lobbyist Federation
National Press Bldg.
Washington, DC 20045

Potomac Speakers, Inc.
3001 Veazey Terrace, NW, #1625
Washington, DC 20008

Stull Lecture Bureau
National Press Bldg.
Washington, DC 20045

James Arch & Associates
POB 37
Maitland, FL 32751

Bureau for Speakers & Seminars
POB 37
Maitland, Fl 32751

Al Heydrick Associates
2830 NE 29th Avenue
Lighthouse Point, FL 33064

Jerry Marshall Musical
   Enterprises, Inc.
1110 NE 16 Ord Street, Suite 219
North Miami Beach, FL 33162

McCollum Management &
   Meetings
POB 10523
Tallahassee, FL 32302

Peg McCollum
The Program People
I I A of Greater Tampa
POB 270334
Tampa, FL 33688

Ida McGinniss Speakers Bureau
2500 East Hallandale Beach
   Blvd.
Hallandale, FL 33160

Gerry & Roland Tausch
3530 Pine Valley Drive
Sarasota, FL 33579

Ralph Andres, VP
International Assn. of Speakers
   & Sales Trainers
Box 3309
Augusta, GA 30904

Ray Bloch Productions, Inc.
230 Peachtree Street, NW,
Suite 1417
Atlanta, GA 30303

Steve Brown
4675 N. Shallowford Road,
Suite 200
Atlanta, GA 30338

Convention Consultants of
  Savannah Delta, Inc.
117 W. Perry
Savannah, GA 31401

Jordan Enterprises
Success Leaders Speakers Service
Lenox Square Box 18737
Atlanta, GA 30326

Speakeasy, Inc.
400 Colony Square, Suite 1130
Atlanta, GA 30361

Bradley Barraks
Speakers Corner
2018 29th Street
Rock Island, IL 61201

Burns Sports Celebrity Service
230 N. Michigan Avenue
Chicago, IL 60601

CMR, Ltd
524 Chatham Road
Roselle, IL 60712

Carleton Rogers, Jr.
Expo Management, Inc.
The Apparel Center, Suite 1
Chicago, IL 60654

The Contemporary Forum
2528A W. Jerome Street
Chicago, IL 60645

Convention & Conference
  Consultants
Box 313
Deerfield, IL 60015

Convention Entertainment
  Productions
1645 River Road, Suite 12
Des Plaines, IL 60018

Davis Marketing Group, Inc.
1550 N. Northwest Hwy.
Suite 40
Park Ridge, IL 60068

Impact International
John Hancock Center
Chicago, IL 60611

International Language &
  Communications Center
33 N. Dearborn, Suite 1300
Chicago, IL 60602

Jane Marks
The Program People
Box 1426
Oak Brook, IL 60521

Midwest Meeting Services, Inc.
Box 9412
Schaumberg, IL 60194

National Assn. of Bank
  Women
111 East Wacker Drive
Chicago, IL 60601

National Speakers Bureau, Inc.
222 Wisconsin Avenue, Suite 309
Lake Forest, IL 60045

Programs Unlimited
515 N. Main Street
Glen Ellyn, IL 60136

The Sanford Organization, Inc.
4300-L Lincoln Avenue
Rolling Meadows, IL 60008

VIP Productions, Inc.
750 West Algonquin Road
Arlington Heights, Il 60005

Fred J. Young
516 Provident Avenue
Winnetka, IL 60093

Bill Carson
Home Builders Assn. of Indiana
143 W. Market, Suite 204
Indianapolis, IN 46204

Renee Nipper
Midwest Program Service
Bane-Clene Corporation
4533 Millersville Road
Indianapolis, IN 46205

Program Dynamics
2229 Forest Glade
Fort Wayne, IN 46825

The Associated Clubs
One Townsite Plaza
Topeka, KS 66603

National Assn. of Sales
  Education
POB 12222
Overland Park, KS 66212

Custom Conventions
1739 Julia Street
New Orleans, LA 70113

Helen R. Dietrich, Inc.
333 St. Charles Avenue,
Suite 1221
New Orleans, LA 70130

Talbot, Talbot & Berlin, Inc.
9441 Common Street, Suite C
Baton Rouge, LA 70809

R. Joseph Advertising, Inc.
8201 Corporate Drive
Landover, MD 20785

Wedgewood Productions, Inc.
Box 440
Crownsville, MD 21032

American Program Bureau
850 Boylston Street
Chestnut Hill, MA 02167

The Forum Corporation
84 State Street
Boston, MA 02109

Frothingham Management
Helsey Frothingham
384 Washington Street
Wesley, MA 02181

The Handley Management
51 Church Street
Boston, MA 02116

K & S Associates
308 Brookline Street
Cambridge, MA 02139

Lordly & Dame, Inc.
51 Church Street
Boston, MA 02116

Speakers Guild
93 Old Kings Hwy.
Sandwich, MA 02563

Universal Speakers Agency, Inc.
235 Bear Hill Road, Suite 203
Waltham, MA 02154

Robert P. Walker Enterprises,
  Inc.
63 Atlantic Avenue
Boston, MA 02110

Convention Services
International
494 Lake Shore Lane
Grosse Pointe, MI 48236

Mark Greenburg Bureau, Inc.
Box 358
East Detroit, MI 48021

Growth Unlimited
31 E. Avenue S.
Battle Creek, MI 49017

Cheri Veakey
1326 McKay Tower
Grand Rapids, MI 49503

J. Warren Burke
Midwest Program Service
5309 Vernon Avenue
Edina, MN 55436

Leopold Hauser, III
Personal Dynamics Institute
5186 West 76th Street
Minneapolis, MN 55436

Liemandt's Tour & Convention
Service
1010 Second Avenue
Minneapolis, MN 55403

Meeting Concepts, Inc.
511 11th Avenue S, Suite 261
Minneaplis, MN 55415

Midwest Speakers Bureau
6440 Flying Cloud Drive
Suite 205
Minneapolis, MN 55344

R.L. Montgomery Associates, Inc.
12313 Michelle Circle
Burnsville, MN 55337

Judy Hornsey
Synergetic Systems
3214 Halliday
St. Louis, MO 63118

Richard Stull
Speakers Bureau International
POB 19442
Las Vegas, NV 89119

Universal Models & Convention
Service
953 East Sahara Avenue
Bldg. 28-B, Suite 207
Las Vegas, NV 89104

How to Create Incredible Edibles
21 Almroth Drive
Wayne, NJ 07470

JR Associates
263 New Street
Belleville, NJ 07109

Leigh Bureau
49–51 State Road
Princeton, NJ 08540

The Lyons Co., Inc.
309 South Street
Murray Hill, NJ 07974

Sussex Business Communica-
tions, Inc.
Box 585
Summit, NJ 07901

Training Services, Inc.
130 Orient Way
Box 388
Rutherford, NJ 07070

Unconventional Conventions
8 Park Road
Paterson, NJ 07514

The Bookers—Specialists in
Tel/Radio Press Interviews
200 West 51st Street
New York, NY 10019

Build Power, Inc.
2090 7th Avenue
New York, NY 10037

CMR, Ltd.
524 Latham Road
Mineola, NY 11501

Royce Carlton, Inc.
866 United Nations Plaza
New York, NY 10017

Alan Cimberg
83 Tilrose Avenue
Malverne, NY 11565

The Conference Board
845 Third Avenue
New York, NY 10022

R.E. Delaney Associates
1270 Avenue of the Americas
New York, NY 10020

EGR Travel International, Inc.
290 Madison Avenue
New York, NY 10017

Easter Eagles Association
305 East 24th Street
New York, NY 10010

Executive Enterprises, Inc.
10 Columbus Circle
New York, NY 10019

Lois Fenton
721 Shore Cares Drive
Mamaroneck, NY 10543

Russell Flagg, Inc.
103 East 84th Street
New York, NY 10028

Group Consultant International, Ltd.
70 Glen Cove Road
Roslyn Heights, NY 11577

Will Jordan
435 West 57th Street, Apt. 10F
New York, NY 10019

Rich Keegan Associates
524 Latham Road
Mineola, NY 11501

Leigh Bureau
1185 Avenue of the Americas
New York, NY 10036

Nina Little Productions, Inc.
527 Madison Avenue, Suite 1406
New York, NY 10022

Penton Learning Systems
420 Lexington Avenue
Suite 2846
New York, NY 10017

Program Corp. of America
595 West Hartsdale Avenue
White Plains, NY 10607

Rainbow Lectures
31 Nottingham Terrace
Buffalo, NY 14216

Blanche Ross Ross Associates
515 Madison Avenue, Suite 1225
New York, NY 10022

Charles R. Rothschild
Productions
330 East 48th Street
New York, NY 10022

A. Sheen Management
2703 Batchelder
Brooklyn, NY 11235

Fran Slotkin
Programs & Promotions for
Business & Industry
POB 327
Mineola, NY 11501

Thalheim Expositions, Inc.
98 Cutter Mill Road
Great Neck, NY 11021

Harry Walker Agency
Empire State Bldg., Suite 3616
350 5th Avenue
New York, NY 10018

Bannister & Associates
50 West Broad Street
Suite 1331
Columbus, OH 43215

Bestconventions, Inc.
401 Euclid Avenue, The Arcade
Cleveland, OH 44114

Bonnie Marshall, RN
Holistic Communications
 Consultants
4162A Indian Run Drive
Dayton, OH 45415

Tourcrafters, Inc.
3 East 4th Street
Cincinnati, OH 45202

Weber & Associates, Inc.
3200 Valleyview Drive
Columbus, OH 43204

Seymour Davis
Box 75171
Oklahoma City, OK 73107

Greater Life Rallies
Gainey Archard & Paul Boston
2907 E. 51st Street S., Suite G
Tulsa, OK 74135

Rob Fussell
People Potential Speakers
 Bureau
3560 Lancaster Drive, NE
Salem, OR 97303

Donald J. Moine
3040 Harris Street, Nob Hill
Eugene, OR 97405

Eastern U.S. Show Productions
121 Chestnut Street
Philadelphia, PA 19106

Dr. Bern rd B. Goldner
4026 MacNiff Drive, POB 279
Lafayette Hill, PA 19444

LB Associates
231 Hay Avenue
Johnstown, PA 15902

Dr. Art Garner & Associates
2519 Lovitt Drive
Memphis, TN 38138

Meeting Services & Con-
 vention Consultants
4515 Harding Road, Suite 110
Nashville, TN 37205

Shea Management, Inc.
John R. Handick
Personal Development
Enterprises, Inc.
2114 Seton Place
Germantown, TN 38138

Ed Bernet
7027 Twin Hills Avenue
Dallas, TX 75231

Ray Bloch Productions, Inc.
6060 North Central Expressway
Dallas, TX 75206

Contemporary Programs, Inc.
3136 Lafayette
Box 25101
Houston, TX 77005

Garuth Management Consul-
 tants, Inc.
2715 Peachtree
Carrollton, TX 75006

Billy Jack Ludwig
8330 Meadow Road, #130
Dallas, TX 75231

Billy Jack Ludwig
4537 Fremont Lane
Plano, TX 75075

Parker Chiropractic Research
   Foundation
Dr. William D. Brown
Box 40444
Fort Worth, TX 67140

Richard Russell
4342 Sexton Lane
Dallas, TX 75229

Dr. Charles Edward Smith
Women in Communications, Inc.
National Headquarters
Box 9561
Austin, TX 78766

John Wolfe Institute, Inc.
12335 Boheme
Houston, TX 77024

Ralph Andres
POB 1093
Tappahannock, VA 22560

Alan L. Freed & Associates, Inc.
Box 304
McLean, VA 22101

Hampton, Bates, & Associates,
   Inc.
1121 Arlington Blvd.
Arlington, VA 22209

Washington Speakers Bureau,
   Inc.
201 N. Fairfax Street, #11
Alexandria, VA 22314

George Carlson & Associates
Western Lecture/Entertainment
   Bureau
113 Battery Street
Seattle, WA 98121

MAILING LIST BROKERS

Here are a few—and only a few—of the many list brokers offering
their wares to the public:

The List House
130 Lyons Plain Road
Weston, CT 06883
(203) 227-6027

List Services Corp.
890 Ethan Allen Hwy.
POB 2014
Ridgefield, CT 06877
(203) 438-0327

R.L. Polk & Co.
3030 Holcomb Bridge Road
Suite F
Norcross, GA 30071
(Send for catalog; Polk has
   has offices throughout U.S.)

Names & Addresses, Inc.
3605 Woodhead Drive
Northbrook, IL 60062
(312) 272-7933

Potentials in Marketing
  Magazine
731 Hennepin Avenue
Minneapolis, MN 55403
(800) 328-4329

American List Counsel, Inc.
88 Orchard Road
Princeton, NJ 08540
(800) 526-3973

Hayden Direct Marketing
  Services
10 Mulholland Drive
Hasbrouck Heights, NJ 07604
(201) 393-6384

Ed Burnett Consultants, Inc.
2 Park Avenue
New York, NY 10016
(212) 679-0630

The Kleid Company, Inc.
200 Park Avenue
New York, NY 10166
(212) 599-4140

NCRI List Management
30 East 42nd Street
New York, NY 10017
(212) 687-3876

Qualified Lists Corp.
135 Bedford Road
Armonk, NY 10504
(212) 324-8900
(914) 273-3353

Chilton Direct Marketing
  & List Management Company
1 Chilton Way
Radnor PA 19089
(800) 345-1214
(215) 964-4365

Texas Direct
5100 Rondo Drive
Fort Worth, TX 76106
(817) 625-4221/429-4120
(800) 433-7750

Seminars
525 N. Lake Street
Madison, WI 53703

TIPS ON DIRECT-MAIL COPY

Here are a few reminders, as a checklist to refer to when preparing direct-mail copy:

- Always make things as easy as possible for the customer. For example:
  a. Make it easy to understand what you are saying. Use short words, short sentences, short paragraphs. One thought in a sentence, one subject and one main point in a paragraph. (Be sure first that you yourself fully understand the main point.)

b. Make it easy for the customer to order, ask for more information, or otherwise reveal interest by providing a return card, telephone number, or other convenient means for responding.

c. Make it easy for the customer to understand what you want him or her to do by *telling* the customer what to do. A great many sales are lost by advertisers who fail to tell the customers what they want them to do.

- A direct-mail cliche (which is nonetheless a truism) is "The more you tell the more you sell." Don't stint on copy. Be sure to include a letter, a brochure or flyer of some sort, and a response device (envelope and/or order form) as an absolute minimum, and there is no harm in enclosing even more. The experts claim that three-quarters of the response results from the letter, and that a good circular or brochure can increase response by as much as one-third. My own experience bears this out quite emphatically.

- Don't tell it all in the letter. Split the copy up among the various enclosures, or at least provide additional details in the various enclosures. Make it clear that additional information/details are to be found elsewhere in the enclosures. Give the reader good reason to read everything, if you want maximum impact.

- Geography makes a difference. Prospects who are nearby tend to resond better than those at a distance. Know nearby zip codes, and use these. But do test, for there are always exceptions. Example: When it comes to consulting and speaking services, there is some appeal, even a kind of mystique, to the expert from a distant place. If you are mailing from a major industrial or business center, such as New York, Chicago, or Washington, take advantage of it by giving it prominence in your copy.

- If you use envelope copy—advertising and sales messages on the outside of the envelope—do two things:

a. Use both sides of the envelope. If you are going to make a bulletin board of the envelope, you might as well get full use of it; copy on both sides pulls better than copy on one side only—if the copy is powerful.

b. Now that you've served notice that the envelope contains advertising matter, why pay first-class postage? You might as well save money by using bulk mail or, at least, something less expensive than first class.

INDEX